D1188478

Duquesne Studies

LANGUAGE AND LITERATURE SERIES

VOLUME SIXTEEN

LITERARY MILTON

Literary Milton

❦❦❦

Text, Pretext, Context

❦❦❦

edited by
Diana Treviño Benet
& Michael Lieb

DUQUESNE UNIVERSITY PRESS
Pittsburgh, Pennsylvania

Published in the United States of America by

DUQUESNE UNIVERSITY PRESS
600 Forbes Avenue
Pittsburgh, Pennsylvania 15282–0101

Library of Congress Cataloging-in-Publication Data

Literary Milton : text, pretext, context / edited by Diana Treviño
  Benet and Michael Lieb.
      p.   cm. — (Duquesne studies. Language and literature series
  ; v. 16)
    Includes bibliographical references and index.
    ISBN 0–8207–0259–5
    1. Milton, John, 1608–1674—Criticism and interpretation.
  I. Benet, Diana. II. Lieb, Michael, 1940– . III. Series.
  PR3588.L58   1994
  821'.4—dc20   94–11292
                                                         CIP

#303195560

For
John T. Shawcross

🍎🍎🍎

Contents

Introduction
Diana Treviño Benet & Michael Lieb   xi

1 • The Toad at Eve's Ear:
From Identity to Identification
                          Regina M. Schwartz   1

2 • That Old Man Eloquent
                          Annabel Patterson   22

3 • Forced Allusions:
Avatars of King David in the
Seventeenth Century
                     Mary Ann Radzinowicz   45

4 • "The Copious Matter of My Song"
                          Diane McColley   67

5 • Hell, Satan, and the New Politician
                     Diana Treviño Benet   91

6 • "Two of Far Nobler Shape":
Reading the Paradisal Text
                          Michael Lieb 114

7 • "Inspir'd with Contradiction":
Mapping Gender Discourses in *Paradise Lost*
                     Joseph Wittreich 133

8 • Intention and Its Limits in *Paradise Lost*:
The Case of Bellerophon
Stephen M. Fallon 161

9 • The Law in Adam's Soliloquy
Jason P. Rosenblatt 180

10 • Milton and the Hartlib Circle:
Educational Projects and Epic *Paideia*
Barbara K. Lewalski 202

Notes 221

Publications of John T. Shawcross on
John Milton 257

About the Contributors 265

Index 269

Introduction

Michael Lieb & Diana Treviño Benet

I n his recent book, *Intentionality and the New Traditionalism: Some Liminal Means to Literary Revisionism,* John T. Shawcross reasserts the legitimacy of the relationship between author and text. "While some current modish literary criticism still offers *the author dead/ the reader born* as a first given," Shawcross declares, "I eclectically maintain that what the author does and what the author intends to do are important issues for anyone interested in the creative process, as well as for a means to understanding a literary work, and that what the reader elicits from a literary work is a major factor in determining what the author does or does not do."[1] Emphasizing the significance of intentionality ("the writer writing") in the creation of texts, Shawcross bestows upon the author as literary craftsperson a renewed sense of the authorial role in the act of making.

In the fulfillment of that role, the author establishes thresholds or "limina" that define the work and that bestow upon it that form and that identity through which the author's work is to be understood. In this respect, genre, for example, "becomes a limen into the work, a threshold to aid the reader in entering the world which is that work" (23).

Whatever form these limina assume, they are all part of the network of contexts that establish the essential interchange between author and text, on the one hand, and between text and reader, on the other. A sympathetic reading of the work that the author creates implies a full awareness of the contexts through which the work is delineated. These contexts, Shawcross asserts, "may range from associations with other literary works—as in a sequence or collection, as well as alongside a literary work of similar subject or type—to political, historical, biographical, ideological, and other worlds" (198–99). At the forefront of Shawcross's approach stand the author and the author's created work. In his assessment of both, Shawcross is determined to reclaim the author's act of creation as a specifically *literary* endeavor and the resulting creation as a *work of literature*.

Essentially traditional in focus, such an approach assumes that the act of interpretation ("the reader reading") is ancillary to the author and the text being interpreted, that both author and text "exist," and that the creation of the text is a deliberate and self-conscious act. It also assumes that whatever the limina that define the text, a literary work is imbued with its own values and its own meanings and that those values and meanings can (indeed, must) be ascertained in order to give the work in question its due. It is here that "the reader reading" comes into play. Fulfilling this crucial role in the critical paradigm, "the reader reading" reflects the reader's own great importance as one whose act of interpretation implies a recognition of what "the writer writing" has accomplished.

In this respect, the limina through which a work of literature is delineated and understood require us to attend not only to the text in question but to its "pretexts," on the one hand, and to its "contexts," on the other. As delineated here, the term "pretext" implies authorial intention (*inventio*) made evident by "the writer writing." Pretext suggests that which occurs before the text comes into being. As such, the term is to be construed as "pre-text." Because of the difficulties attendant upon the discovery of intentionality, "pretext" also carries with it that sense of possible subterfuge implicit in something that is put forward to conceal a true purpose. As a result of this concealment, the act of discovery is problematized, "inspir'd with contradiction" (to borrow the title of one of the essays collected here). Complementing "pretext" is "context." This term encompasses all those determinants (psychological, biographical, social, political, theological, historical and the like) that constitute the *milieu* in which a text exists and by means of which the "the reader reading" is able to gain a sense of its intertextual circumstances. So conceived, pretext and context become essential constituents in the establishment and interpretation of meaning.

From the perspective of such a theoretical approach, the essays that follow have been assembled both to explore Milton, his works and his milieu and to reflect upon the thought of John T. Shawcross, supreme Miltonist and major force in the field of English literary criticism and scholarship of the seventeenth century. These essays provide a wide-ranging view of what it means to reassess the uniquely "literary" dimensions of the Miltonic corpus. As they focus upon various aspects of that corpus, the essays take into account such matters as authorial identity, the relationship between author and text and text and reader, the theme of self-portrayal in the works and the bearing of this theme on matters of chronology, the recourse to allusion in the establishment of meaning, the significance of historical and political contexts to an understanding of literary nuance, the issue of language and resonance in the appreciation of style, the delineation of gender and its bearing upon epic discourse, the formulation of dispensational matrices in the development of narrative, and the function of pedagogy in the determination of an author's point of view.

As might be expected, *Paradise Lost* represents the primary focus of the volume. The centerpiece of Milton's poetic *oeuvre*, this work, more than any other, provides the occasion by which the scholars whose essays constitute this volume are able to address the issue of what is implied by the epithet "literary Milton." At the same time, the diffuse epic is not the only text under consideration here. One finds astute analyses of works ranging from the sonnets and the brief epic to such prose works as *Of Education*, the divorce tracts, the antimonarchical tracts, the defenses and *Christian Doctrine*. A consideration of these works becomes the means of assessing Milton's conduct as a writer, the strategies that his writings reflect, the presuppositions they embody, the contexts they embrace and the accomplishments they achieve. In keeping with the literary focus of the volume as a whole, each essay attests in its own way to the "real presence" of the author.

The urgency of that presence is precisely what underlies Regina Schwartz's exploration of the power of Milton as author to create a sense of "identification" between himself and his readers that extends beyond a momentary bonding that occurs at any given point in the act of reading. Exploring what she calls "the permutations of identification, imitation and identity," Schwartz distinguishes between categories of epistemology and ontology in order to generate a theory to accommodate the idea of the transference that results in the reader's encounter with Milton as author and implicitly as literary presence. Her primary text for the discovery of the dynamics of transference is *Paradise Lost*, and the discipline to which she has recourse in order to elaborate her theory is that of psychoanalysis. As Schwartz demonstrates, the transactions between author and reader that Milton creates in his texts result, in effect, in the creation of a new identity. Analyzing the implications of that creation, Schwartz offers a new and cogent reading of what the idea of a "literary Milton" implies.

Moving from the psychoanalytic domain to the political sphere, Annabel Patterson demonstrates, in turn, the way in which Milton's literary presence is inextricably tied to the historical circumstances of his time. Focusing upon the sonnets as a means of portraying what is signified by literary enactment, Patterson reveals the profound difficulties of coming to terms with the autobiographical and chronological implications of the sonnets viewed as a "sequence." Milton's behavior in the sonnets constitutes a "poetics of sequentiality" that is immensely important to an understanding of the author's presencing of self in his works. Elaborating upon this poetics in depth, Patterson argues that, in constructing his sequence, Milton articulated "a theory of literature appropriate not only to his own personality but to his own historical moment." By means of her detailed analysis of the sonnets in the sequence, Patterson throws new light on Milton's literary practices, his conduct as a writer and his sense of self.

Extending the contextualization of Milton's works to include those of Thomas Hobbes and Abraham Cowley, Mary Ann Radzinowicz investigates the literary implications of allusion as an expressive device in the revelation of authorial intention. The point of focus for Radzinowicz is the biblical figure of King David as represented in 1 Samuel. In her analysis of the ways in which Hobbes and Cowley, on the one hand, and Milton, on the other, appropriate David into their respective works (both polemical/political and poetic), Radzinowicz demonstrates how the conflict between promonarchical and antimonarchical sensibilities calls into question any expectation of allusion as an ostensibly stable device. Both its fragility and its instability render it an extremely volatile figure indeed. The fact of its volatility, in turn, leads Radzinowicz to engage not only in a far-reaching analysis of the function of allusion in Milton's works but in an illuminating discourse on the theory of allusion as an expressive device.

If the first group of essays explores the psychological, political and literary dimensions of Milton's writings in general and the multiple transactions between author and reader that his writings demand, the second group of essays focuses primarily upon his major epic and the various contexts through which this work reveals itself as a fundamental source for the exploration of liminality in all its forms. It is the sense of copiousness as a rhetorical and literary phenomenon underlying these forms that is the subject of Diane McColley's tribute to *Paradise Lost* and the poet responsible for its making. In an essay that is itself tantamount to a poetic celebration of the author as God-like maker, McColley insists upon the "real presence" of Milton in his works. The manifold vocations of the poet of *Paradise Lost* invite us to see him in his various guises not only as literary Milton but as musical Milton, pictorial Milton, ecological Milton, political Milton and theophanic Milton, among others. All these guises, one supposes, are encompassed by the concept of the poet's literary presence in his works. Arguing against what she calls the "critical dismantlers" of that presence, McColley reveals how the copiousness that infuses Milton's poetic universe "continually unfolds mutually enhancing significances." In its own copiousness, her essay is a paean to all that is implied by the epithet "literary Milton."

As an aspect of the literary presence of Milton in *Paradise Lost*, Diana Treviño Benet concerns herself with the infernal council scene in book 2. There, she reassesses the conduct of the council scene through recourse not only to Milton's own text but to contemporary prose pamphlets and broadsides that portray councils in Hell. Doing so, Benet opens up new avenues of interpretation through which one is able to understand the council scene itself and the limina that define its boundaries. Specifically, she suggests the affinity that the scene shares with the political milieu of which Milton as poet and as polemicist was so much a part. Within the political context that Benet discerns in the scene, Satan emerges as a new personage. He becomes Milton's "portrait of the contemporary politician in action."

Moving from this portrait of Satan in book 2 to the portrait of Adam and Eve in book 4, Michael Lieb undertakes to revaluate the way in which the Miltonic text undermines any automatic conflation of appearance and reality even in the so-called prelapsarian world. As Lieb argues, the act of reading the paradisal text is perpetually problematic because appearance and reality in the world that Milton portrays defy any attempt to suggest their concurrence. Instead, all notions of a categorical liminality that immediately distinguishes between prelapsarian and postlapsarian points of view are held as immediately suspect. The problematic bearing of the paradisal text is founded upon both intratextual and intertextual considerations. The first (intratextual) arises as the result of the relationship between the portrayal of Adam and Eve in book 4 and the earlier portrayal of Sin and Death in book 2, and the second (intertextual) arises as the result of the relationship between the paradisal text of Milton's epic, its biblical antecedents, and its exegetical afterlife. All conspire to undermine any notion that reading the paradisal text is one in which appearance and reality automatically correspond.

The questions of gender to which Lieb's essay gives rise are interrogated with renewed vigor in Joseph Wittreich's exploration of contradictory gender discourses in *Paradise Lost*. In his analysis of those discourses, Wittreich demonstrates how Milton's epic, as a foundational text for the myths imbibed by modern culture, not only appropriates and transforms the mores of the past but produces its own ideologies that, on the one hand, appear to align it with patriarchy and misogyny and, on the other hand, cause it to be in opposition to both. An epic "in dialogic rather than monologic relation to hermeneutic traditions," *Paradise Lost* thereby becomes "a repository for overlapping, incongruent discourses, as well as a site from which to observe not so much a received myth and dominant ideology as the crevices and contradictions within them both." It is the crevices and contradictions that Wittreich explores in depth as a way of revealing the extent to which the discourses upon which Milton's epic is founded will always elicit responses that run counter to one another. At the very core of Milton's epic resides a hermeneutics that fosters competing systems of interpretation and that encourages debate at every term. Such an outlook is perfectly consistent with Milton's stance as poet and as polemicist.

In his discussion of *Paradise Lost*, Stephen M. Fallon returns to the topic of allusion, in this case, the figure of Bellerophon. Tracing the emergence of Bellerophon as a figure of major import in classical mythology, Fallon suggests the extent to which this figure represented for Milton two extremes, that involving the potential for great achievement and that involving the potential for great error. Projecting his own desires and aspirations on Bellerophon, Milton was faced with the choice of moving toward either extreme. On the one hand, he is confident in his claim to prophetic status and, on the other, he is faced with doubts and misgivings that risk undermining such a claim. At the core of his anxieties is the fear of rendering himself guilty of the presumption of Bellerophon as implied by the proem to the seventh book of Milton's epic. Exploring the implications of the Bellerophon allusion in this proem in depth, Fallon draws upon the insights provided by John T. Shawcross's distinction between the "reader's text" and the "author's text" in order to suggest the full bearing of Milton's allusive practices.

Moving from book 7 to book 10 of *Paradise Lost*, Jason P. Rosenblatt explores in depth the biblical and dispensational implications of Adam's long and revealing postlapsarian soliloquy. As Rosenblatt reflects on the significance of this soliloquy, he discovers a corresponding transition in Milton's own thought from a sympathy with the religious predilections of the Torah with its emphasis upon Mosaic law to an acceptance of the full bearing of the Pauline outlook embodied in the New Testament. Within the context of Milton's epic, it is the prelapsarian world of paradise in which the Mosaic law coexists with natural law in a state that is entirely benign. But this state does not last: in the postlapsarian world, faith and law are at odds. In Pauline terms, one supersedes the other. In keeping with the theory of limina that Shawcross puts forward in *Intentionality and the New Traditionalism*, one might suggest that Rosenblatt's essay concerns itself with the effects of passing from threshold to threshold as the result of the violation of a prohibition that causes an earlier dispensation to give way to a newer dispensation. As he focuses upon the language that constitutes Adam's soliloquy, Rosenblatt demonstrates that Milton's dispensational concerns possess a decidedly literary bearing.

Rounding out the volume as a whole, Barbara K. Lewalski's essay concerns itself with the relationship between Milton's theories of learning and the dissemination of knowledge made evident in the tractate *Of Education*, as well as other prose works, and the application of these theories in *Para-*

dise Lost and *Paradise Regained*. Lewalski establishes a context for her investigation through an examination of Milton's
association with Samuel Hartlib and the Hartlib Circle. As
a result of this examination, she concludes that both in his
prose tracts and in his epics, Milton is in dialogue with but
not necessarily in close accord with the educational programs and projects of the Hartlib Circle. It is particularly
in the exploration of the terms of this dialogue that the
movement from context to text illuminates the literary implications of Milton's educational theories. As it draws the
collection to a close, Lewalski's essay, moreover, suggests
the extent to which the volume as a whole has, in effect,
been concerned with the nature of education in its various
forms. Those forms encompass Milton's literary presence in
his works and the correspondence between the text of his
works and the dynamics through which his text emerges.

As an overview of what the essays in the collection seek
to accomplish, the foregoing should provide a sense of the
scope and direction of a volume that draws directly on the
life, work and accomplishments of John T. Shawcross. In
that sense, this is as much a commemorative endeavor as
it is a critical and scholarly enterprise. Shawcross's works
and "presence" in the profession have had a profound impact
on the world of Milton scholarship. Those whose essays
appear in this volume are only a representative sampling
of individuals who gather to celebrate a major force in the
field of literary studies in general and Milton studies in
particular.

There is indeed so much to celebrate. One need only
glance at the List of Publications of John T. Shawcross on
John Milton (see page 257) to confirm the impression. Despite
its length, this list, *mirabile dictu*, is only partial: it does
not include the extensive work in other areas of the literature of seventeenth century England nor in areas well beyond
the confines of the seventeenth century. The work on Milton
alone, however, is sufficiently daunting. In a career of
publications spanning nearly four decades, Shawcross has
written on just about every aspect of Milton's life and *oeuvre*.
There is almost nothing upon which he has not left his

mark. Biography, bibliography, text, literary criticism and interpretation: all these areas of endeavor and more fall within his purview. In part, this fact has already been accorded "official" recognition by the Milton Society of America, which named Shawcross Honored Scholar in 1981.

His edition *The Complete Poetry of John Milton* (1971) is both comprehensive and standard; his coedited collection of essays on Milton's prose, *Achievements of the Left Hand* (1974) reignited interest in that crucial area.[2] His studies of the major poems are seminal. *With Mortal Voice: The Creation of Paradise Lost* (1982) and *Paradise Regain'd: 'Worthy T'Have Not Remain'd So Long Unsung'* (1988) are two complementary volumes that are not only models of literary criticism in themselves but astute statements concerning the means by which the diffuse epic, on the one hand, and the brief epic, on the other, are to be most profitably understood as distinct works of art.[3] (In the same vein, a volume on *Samson Agonistes* will be forthcoming shortly.) Extending his reach well beyond the seventeenth century (as well as beyond the shores of England), moreover, Shawcross has discoursed wisely on the issue of reception theory in his volume *John Milton and Influence: Presence in Literature, History and Culture* (1991).[4] His critical reach does not end there, however. Most recently, he has produced what amounts to the most important psychobiographical study of Milton that we currently possess. This is his current new book *John Milton: The Self and the World* (1993).[5] Here is not simply literary criticism, not simply biography: here is a profoundly important analysis of the innermost workings of Milton's mind and heart, a study of the forces that shaped his personality, a taxonomy of the process through which he matured and produced his writings.

Shawcross's most important project for well over two decades, in many respects, is his ongoing series of bibliographies and compilations detailing all manuscripts, editions, studies, critical statements, allusions, quotations and the like concerning Milton's life and works during the seventeenth and eighteenth centuries. With the publication of *Milton: A Bibliography For the Years 1624-1700* (1984) and

Milton: A Bibliography ·For the Years 1624-1700: Addenda and Corrigenda (1990), a portion of this massive undertaking has been made available, that covering the seventeenth century.[6] (The 1984 volume is the recipient of the James Holly Hanford award of the Milton Society of America for the most distinguished book published on Milton that year.) In process are additional volumes that will deal with the eighteenth century. It is difficult to overestimate the importance of this ongoing project not only for the field of Milton studies, but for the history of reception and influence in general. When completed, this project will have effectively altered the landscape of what constitutes "Milton studies" and "Miltoniana." Already pointing the way are the complementary and immensely useful collections that distinguish Shawcross's list, *Milton: The Critical Heritage* [1624–1731] (1970) and *Milton: The Critical Heritage, 1732–1809* (1972), which are not only compilations of relevant material but books that contain immensely important essays on the whole issue of influence.[7]

Even more than his scholarship attests, however, Shawcross's personal presence in the profession is immeasurable. Through his writings, through his teachings, and through his counsel, he has shaped many careers. He has given of himself personally to so many individuals, students and colleagues alike.

One incident in particular is worth recording here. At a Modern Language Association session on Milton a number of years ago, the room was packed with attendees. The panelists had completed the reading of their papers, and during the discussion period that followed, the chair of the panel looked across the room and asked, "What do you think, John?" Who knows how many "Johns" were assembled in the room on that occasion! But everybody knew to whom the question was addressed. Shawcross knew as well, for, without hesitation, he responded to the question.

It is our hope that the collection of essays that follow will contribute to the field of Milton studies, in some small way, after the example of John T. Shawcross.

1 • The Toad at Eve's Ear
From Identification to Identity

Regina M. Schwartz

The text is an experience that the reader undergoes;
it is an experience whose lineaments, however, have
been laid out by the author.

— John T. Shawcross

In April of 1982, when a Jewish woman in her late twenties from Dayton, Ohio was preparing for her Ph.D. oral exams at the University of Virginia and came to that point in her study of the life of John Milton when he lost his sight, 1652, she became unable to see. While this blindness passed in a day, nonetheless, we must ask what mechanism of intense identification caused it to happen. Milton is supposed to be alienating for women: he's been enshrined as a paradigm of male misogynistic culture. A Puritan who speaks of redemption through Christ from the first sentence of *Paradise Lost* to the last of *Paradise Regained* should be alienating for a Jew; identifications with a nationalistic Englishman, for an American who considers herself a citizen of the world, and with a seventeenth century religious poet, for

1

a twentieth century secular critic, are no less troubling. Here I will argue that this event was not just the symptom of a romantic overactive imagination in a young scholar, but the logical consequence of a mechanism of identification that his poetic processes assist in creating and controlling. Simply put, I identify with Milton not only because I want to but also because he wants me to. I have since heard over and over from many quarters that all Miltonists identify with Milton. These Miltonists do not look like one another and they certainly do not look like Milton: they are old and young, women and men, painstaking bibliographers, meticulous historians, inspired biographers, and theological and philosophical types; they include in their ranks feminist and gay critics, psychoanalytic critics, poststructuralist critics, marxist critics, canon-busters and canon-defenders, Catholics, Protestants, Jews, Hindus, and atheists; British, Japanese, Canadian, U.S. and Indian scholars, redheads, blonds, brunettes, black, gray, white-haired, long haired and little haired scholars—all of whom have something in common because they all think that they are John Milton. What is this phenomenon of identification about?

IDENTIFICATION AND DISSEMBLING

In the middle ages, the pervasive principle that organized expressions of piety was the *imitatio Christi*, the notion that the imitation of every gesture, every event, every word, and every thought in the life of Christ disciplined the life of the faithful toward salvation.[1] "Whoever desires to understand and take delight in the words of Christ must strive to conform his whole life to Him . . . Lofty words do not make a man just or holy; but a good life makes him dear to God."[2] *Imitatio Christi* was the soul of monastic piety. The Reformation turned the walls of that monastery inside out, making the discipline of the literal imitation of Christ part of the everyday life of the layman. To imitate the life of Christ was to identify with him, to be Christ-like. Much of the discipline that had been dramatized in external ritual became internalized as the province of an inner spiritual life. To be Christ-like was to feel Christ-like. In such an atmosphere, what constituted a successful imitation and what constituted a bad one—even a parody—was increasingly difficult to ascertain, as many soul-searching agonized spiritual autobiographies of Reformers attest.

In this atmosphere, Milton wrote an epic that explores the permutations of identification, imitation, and identity. In contrast to *identity* which is basically an ontological category—two things share identity when they are of the same substance, the same essence—*identification* is an epistemelogical category, one which presupposes ontological dissimilarity. One can only "identify with" another if one is *not* that other—at least two persons, a Self and an Other, are required. But such identification seeks to overcome dissimilarity, if only momentarily and sporadically, to imagine the Self as the Other—even as it knows better—to will the Self as similar, even while acknowledging the difference. At a further ontological remove is *imitation*, chiefly external mimicry that may or may not be accompanied by inner spiritual identification. One way of describing the Reformation's appropriation of the *imitatio Christi* tradition is that it set out to turn the *imitation* of Christ into *identification* with Christ, the outward and visible signs of likeness into the inward and spiritual feeling of identification.

Milton was uneasy about identification. It lay open to so much error: one could identify with the wrong object, one could not truly identify at all but merely imitate, one could even dissemble. In fact, with dissimilarity being a precondition for identification, it has a kind of dissembling built into its very structure: I identify with you but I am not you. Identification is a lying likeness. Belial has made this dissembling his hallmark:

> up rose
> Belial, in act more graceful and humane;
> A fairer person lost not Heav'n; he seem'd
> For dignity compos'd and high exploit:

> But all was false and hollow; though his Tongue
> Dropt Manna, and could make the worse appear
> The better reason.
>
> (2.108–14)[3]

The first step in each foray Satan makes to tempt human-kind is to assume a false identity. On his mission of destruction, he begins to explore the whereabouts of the new world,

> But first he casts to change his proper shape
> Which else might work him danger or delay:
> And now a stripling Cherub he appears,
> Not of the prime, yet such as in his face
> Youth smil'd Celestial, and to every Limb
> Suitable grace diffus'd, so well he feign'd.
>
> (3.636–39)

Even "the Eyes of God"—the archangel Uriel—are unable to see through the ruse, so effective is this dissembler.

> So spake the false dissembler unperceiv'd;
> For neither Man nor Angel can discern
> Hypocrisy, the only evil that walks
> Invisible, except to God alone.
>
> (3.681–84)

If hypocrisy is the invisible evil and the narrator wants to see things invisible (to mortal sight) that are ostensibly good, the necessity of discerning between these invisibles is urgent. Nonetheless, with hypocrisy so hidden, it is no wonder that Eve could not penetrate the disguise of the angel who flattered her in her dream: "stood/One shap'd and wing'd like one of those from Heav'n/By us oft seen" (5.54–56). The dissembling finally issues in the terrible ruse of a talking snake at the Fall. In Genesis, that snake was a snake, not someone else disguised, but in *Paradise Lost*, Milton makes him ontologically fraudulent—and makes Adam instinctively if vaguely aware of it.

> how hast thou yielded to transgress
> The strict forbiddance, how to violate

> The sacred Fruit forbidd'n! some cursed *fraud*
> Of Enemy hath beguil'd thee, yet unknown,
> And mee with thee hath ruin'd.
>
>> (9.904–06; my emphasis)

It is into this hazardous world, where things that are not what they seem ("seem" is used over a hundred times in the poem) lead to the catastrophic destruction of human-kind, that Milton acknowledges—courageously, in this light—that language itself, even his language, even the language he puts in the mouth of an authoritative angel, lies.[4] Words do not partake of the identity of their referent; they are dissimilar from what they attempt to convey, at best, a mere likeness which falls short of conveying the full truth.

> what surmounts the reach
> Of human sense, I shall delineate so,
> By lik'ning spiritual to corporal forms,
> As may express them best.
>
>> (5.571–74)

Of course, this is only a question about the untrustworthiness of language, not an assertion. And it quickly veers into the opposite sentiment: that the spiritual and the corporeal are alike, that heaven and earth may not be so ontologically distinct.

> though what if Earth
> Be but the shadow of Heav'n, and things therein
> Each to other like more than on Earth is thought?
>
>> (5.574–76)

The angel's "lik'ning" spiritual to corporeal is countered by his hint that they may *be* alike and by his earlier assurances that the corporeal is on a continuum with the incorporeal, that bodies turn into spirit: "from these corporal nutriments perhaps/ Your bodies may at last turn all to spirit,/ Improv'd by tract of time, and wing'd ascend/ Ethereal" (5.496–99). This in turn could become the ground for a more trust-worthy, secure understanding of language, one that sees lan-guage as ontologically anchored.

Milton seems to have just that predilection, to want to depict identity—the ontological category—as more trustworthy than mere identification. Genuinely the same, partaking of the same identity, this dialectic can even allow room for a productive play of differences. Eve, the Mother of Life, is also the bone of Adam's bone, the flesh of Adam's flesh, part of Adam's very substance. When Eve fails to recognize that identity, Adam explains it to her:

> Whom fli'st thou? whom thou fli'st, of him thou art,
> His flesh, his bone; to give thee being I lent
> Out my side to thee, nearest my heart
> *Substantial Life*, to have thee by my side
> Henceforth an individual solace dear;
> Part of my Soul I seek thee, and thee claim
> My other half.
>
> (4.481–88; my emphasis)

This is not identification; it is identity. And Adam is at pains to distinguish that identity from the identification Eve has mistakingly made of herself with the watery image she has just seen: Eve learns that she is not the reflection of herself, but the substance of Adam. "Substantial Life"—not accidence but substance—is a term that resonates with Reformation controversies about the eucharist. Such substantial identity is shared not only by Adam and Eve but by the Father and Son, echoing the Nicene Creed: "Beyond compare the Son of God was seen/ Most glorious, in him all his Father shone/ Substantially express'd" (3.137–39). And Milton extends the theological doctrine that the incarnation partakes of divine substance into a cosmological principle: God is substantially expressed in his entire creation; in his world everything partakes of—literally eats—everything else. Despite the Reformers' vehement rejection of transubstantiation with their slurring characterizations of it as cannabalistic, Milton has radically delineated an entire eucharistic universe, one engaged in ceaseless acts of transubstantiation.

> whatever was created, needs
> To be sustain'd and fed; of Elements
> The grosser feeds the purer, Earth the Sea,

Earth and the Sea feed Air, the Air those Fires
Ethereal, and as lowest first the Moon;
Whence in her visage round those spots, unpurg'd
Vapors not yet into her substance turn'd,
Nor doth the Moon no nourishment exhale
From her moist Continent to higher Orbs.
The Sun that light imparts to all, receives
From all his alimental recompense
In humid exhalations, and at Even
Sups with the Ocean.

(5.414–26)

In such a universe, God would not only turn into man, a
wafer into Christ's flesh or wine into his blood; this eucharist
moves in the other direction too, turning flesh into spirit,
corporeal into spiritual—enabling an angel to turn human
food into spiritual nourishment. Raphael explains that

                    though in Heav'n the Trees
Of life ambrosial fruitage bear, and vines
Yield Nectar,

    .   .   .   .

            yet God hath here
Varied his bounty so with new delights,
As may compare with Heaven; and to taste
Think not I shall be nice. So down they sat,
And to thir viands fell, nor seemingly
The Angel, nor in mist, the common gloss
Of Theologians, but with keen dispatch
Of real hunger, and concoctive heat
To transubstantiate.

(5.426–38)

Milton's direct hit here may well be against scholastic glosses
on angelology, but his pointed use of "transubstantiate" has
deeper implications, given the Reformation debates about
it. The association with the eucharist is strengthened by the
ensuing invocation of alchemy, the science of transforming
substances:

                    what redounds, transpires
Through Spirits with ease; nor wonder; if by fire

> Of sooty coal the Empiric Alchemist
> Can turn, or holds it possible to turn
> Metals of drossiest Ore to perfet Gold
> As from the Mine.
>
> (5.438–43)

But why the doubt? If the angel is asserting that his transubstantiation of paradisal food is as sure as the Alchemist's
conversion of the drossest ore to gold, why hedge with "the
Empiric Alchemist/ Can turn, or holds it possible to turn/
Metals..."? Are the claims of alchemical science suspect?
and if so, what is the consequence for the comparison to
this universe in which everything is converted into everything else?

Soon we will see this suspicion of alchemical transubstantiation deepen into a suspicion of the very notion of
corporeal identity Milton has been elaborating.[5] At the crisis
in the poem, the very moment when Adam chooses to
disobey, ushering in his Fall and that of humankind after
him, Adam invokes identity—the sharing of substance—as
his reason, chillingly aware of the consequences of his choice.

> Certain my resolution is to Die:
> . . . . .
> Should God create another Eve, and I
> Another Rib afford, yet loss of thee
> Would never from my heart; no no, I feel
> The Link of Nature draw me: Flesh of Flesh,
> Bone of my Bone thou art, and from thy State
> Mine never shall be parted, bliss or woe.
>
> (9.907–16)

The principle that Raphael has explained as informing the
ontology of the entire universe, from the creation of life to
the first marriage vow (bone of my bone, flesh of my flesh)
becomes the ground of our undoing. Because Adam does not
feel distinct from Eve, his will cannot be distinct from Eve's.
Alarmingly enough, this identity with Eve makes Adam feel
unfree to choose.

> I with thee have fixt my Lot,
> Certain to undergo like doom; if Death

Consort with thee, Death is to mee as Life;
So forcible within my heart I feel
The Bond of Nature draw me to my own,
My own in thee, for what thou art is mine;
Our State cannot be sever'd, we are one,
One flesh; to lose thee were to lose myself.

(9.951–59)

Such thinking reveals that Adam has already lost himself.

Transference and Interpretation

This brings us full circle. At first it seemed as if Milton were more confident about relations of identity, of one flesh, than about identification between two dissimilar entities whose very dissimilarity he found untrustworthy. But perhaps it is not that simple, perhaps both identity and identification have their respective dangers—besides, danger is not something that Milton would shirk: he "cannot praise a fugitive and cloistered virtue, unexercised and unbreathed, that never sallies out and sees her adversary." If Milton is nostalgiac for a notion of corporeal identity that would guarantee that all partakes of God, that all is part of All, he is also so deeply committed to free will that in his theology even this universal identity—the oneness of All—was freely willed at the creation rather than "necessary."

> bid the Deep
> Within appointed bounds be Heav'n and Earth,
> Boundless the Deep, because I am who fill
> Infinitude, nor vacuous the space.
> Though I uncircumscrib'd myself retire,
> And put not forth my goodness, which is free
> To act or not, Necessity and Chance
> Approach not mee.

(7.166–73)

When this same freedom is extended to mankind, it becomes the ground for genuine faith, that is, for a faith that is chosen.

> Not free, what proof could they have giv'n sincere
> Of true allegiance, constant Faith or Love,
> Where only what they needs must do, appear'd,
> Not what they would?
>
> (3.103–06)

Without such freedom, mankind had "serv'd necessity, / Not mee" (3.110–11). And so, paradoxically, the "high Decree / Unchangeable, Eternal" ordained not predestination, but freedom itself (3.126–28). This freedom is contrasted not only to "what they needs must do" but also to appearance, for appearance, dissembling, and fraud can induce false identification, compromising the ability to choose freely. The Son brings this crisis of divine justice, omnipotence, human freedom, and dissembling to a head when he puts the pointed question to the Father: should man be condemned for having fallen for fraud?

> should Man finally be lost, should Man
> Thy creature late so lov'd, thy youngest Son
> Fall circumvented thus by *fraud*, though join'd
> With his own folly?
>
> .   .   .   .   .
>
> So should thy goodness and thy greatness both
> Be question'd and blasphem'd without defense.
>
> (3.150–66; my emphasis)

When fraud, with hypocrisy, walks invisible, how can mankind be blamed for an error in judgment? How can he identify with the correct object when paradise includes dissemblers? The father answers with his grace:

> Man shall not quite be lost, but sav'd who will,
> Yet not of will in him, but grace in me
> Freely voutsaf't;
>
> .   .   .   .
>
> And I will place within them as a guide
> My Umpire Conscience, whom if they will hear,
> Light after light well us'd they shall attain,
> And to the end persisting, safe arrive.
>
> (3.173–97)

Here, free will is coupled with grace, and as many Milton critics have noted, the passages that emphasize grace so strongly—when Adam and Eve repent, "Prevenient Grace descending had remov'd/ The stony from thir hearts, and made new flesh regenerate grow instead" (11.3–5)—seem to contradict a theology of free will.[6] But, as Dennis Danielson has persuasively argued, we would be better to think of a dialectic of divine and human powers rather than a contradiction between them. Somehow, planting an umpire conscience does not mitigate free choice. Together, divine initiative and human freedom forge the staff of eternal life.

A similar dialectic of power describes the dynamics of transference, the mechanism of identification elaborated in the discourse of psychoanalysis. Transference can be characterized not only as identification with the analyst, but by submission to the analyst as master-interpreter, even by a loss of self and free will. Freud rejected hypnosis on those grounds, for hypnosis quiets the patient's conscious will, inducing him to relive in the present rather than remember events, placing them in the past. But this picture became vastly complicated when he came to see transference as virtually a waking hypnosis. When Freud discovered transference, he feared it would disrupt the analytic process: in transference, the patient confuses a past event with the present and a person from the past with the analyst: "a whole series of psychological experiences are revived, not as belonging to the past, but as applying to the person of the physician at the present moment. Some of these transferences have a content which differs from that of their model in no respect whatever except for the substitution."[7] Transference therefore challenged his confidence that remembering—the "talking cure" which brings a past injury to conscious recollection and places it into a narrative of the past—was distinct from repeating, a compulsive, pathological effort to reenact, an unsuccessful effort to revise the past injury. Elsewhere I have argued that Milton articulates these alternates in the two myths of the Fall, angelic and human, in *Paradise Lost*.[8] Satan compulsively repeats his injury with human substitutes and his "reiterated crimes"

continue to "heap on himself damnation." Even when he
admits that he cannot repair his injury, he resolves to injure
others:

> Nor hope to be myself less miserable
> By what I seek, but others to make such
> As I, though thereby worse to me redound.
>
> (9.126–28)

Ironically, this effort to redo the past is not so much a kind
of memory as it is a willed forgetting, a refusal to admit
that the past is in the past and hence not recoverable. Satan's
refusal to remember "his making" is symptomatic of the
forgetting that issues in endless repetition: forever reaching
for the apple in hell that turns to ashes, Satan condemns
himself to repeating the same fruitless gesture to the same
futile conclusion. In contrast, the human pair confess, repent,
and are saved from an endless repetition of their fall. Adam
"remembers with what mild and gracious temper" their
judgment was delivered and proposes that they return to the
place of judgment, not to reenact the injury to set it right,
but to recall it in confession, contrition, and repentance,
thereby enabling a new beginning. The human pair engage
in the "talking cure," as it were, instead of compulsively
repeating. But this neat distinction between remembering
and repeating that Freud, Milton (and Schwartz) have been
drawing is confused by transference: by the paradox of reliving
the past in the very context of trying to remember it.

The confusion deepens when we look at hypnosis. Freud
experimented with hypnosis, using it not for direct suggestion but for memory's purposes, to "reimmerse the patient
into that 'hypnoid' state during which a traumatic event
supposedly had become embedded in the psychic mechanism like an internal foreign body."[9] In that state, the patient
would tell his or her story and Freud saw this as bringing
about an emotional purge, a catharsis made possible because
the patient was not simply narrating a story, but acting out
a drama. Freud writes in the Preliminary Communication
to *Studies in Hysteria* that "Recollection without affect
almost invariably produces no result. The psychical process

must be repeated as vividly as possible; it must be brought back to its *status nascendi* and given verbal utterance."[10] As Mikkel Borsch-Jacobsen describes it, "repetition in *statu nascendi*, in the state of being born, is clearly not remembering; it is neither telling a story nor representing a past event *as past*. It is, as Freud and Breuer also write, reliving the event, with all the intensity of the first time, by repeating it *in the present*."[11] Hypnosis would make devils of us all.

The ambiguity between remembering and repeating continues in Freud's work until he decisively abandons hypnosis. For him, "true" psychoanalysis was born with this rejection of hypnosis (along with all suggestive practices) in favor of telling—not reliving—the story. From this so-called "remembering," the patient could expect the relief of symptoms. Nonetheless, the distinction between reliving, with its rekindling of the emotions, and remembering, as a narrative without the emotional component, continued to be troubling: Freud came to regard the transference—even though it is a waking phenomenon—as characterized by the same suggestibility, dependence, and submission of the self that mark hypnosis—in Miltonic terms, the same threat to free will.

In *Paradise Lost*, Satan is a hypnotist. He shares that distinction with Belial who "charms the senses" and with the epic poets of Hell: "Thir Song was partial, but the harmony/ (What could it less when Spirits immortal sing?) / Suspended Hell, and took with ravishment / The thronging audience" (2.552–55). But Satan does not only rely on the suggestibility of words; he makes his suggestions to his patients/victims when they are in a deep sleeplike trance:

> Squat like a Toad, close at the ear of Eve;
> Assaying by his Devilish art to reach
> The Organs of her Fancy, and with them forge
> Illusions as he list, Phastasms and Dreams.
>
> (4.800–03)

What Satan is planting, of course, is the suggestion that Eve disobey the command: "Taste this,"

and be henceforth among the Gods
Thyself a Goddess, not to Earth confin'd
But sometimes in the Air, as wee, sometimes
Ascend to Heav'n, by merit thine, and see
What life the Gods live there and such live thou.

(5.77–81)

In an apt description of hypnosis, Adam explains to the discomfited Eve that reason retires into her private cell when Nature rests; that is, in a trance, consciousness retires. Weakening her will, the suggestion planted by the hypnotic toad prepares Eve for her meeting with the insinuating snake when she is awake. And even that waking seduction proceeds by suggestion: "his words replete with guile / Into her heart too easy entrance won" (9.733–34).

How is this hypnotic threat to Eve's free will different from robbing her of it? How are divine trances different from demonic ones? How does planting an Umpire Conscience compromise free will? Certainly God does his share of suggestion planting too. How, then, does Milton distinguish grace from hypnosis? In the Genesis account, Adam falls asleep once, for a rib to be taken from his side, but Milton adds another trance to Adam's birth narrative. Adam assumes consciousness, asks how he got there, who made him, and

when answer none return'd,
On a green shady Bank profuse of Flow'rs
Pensive I sat me down; there gentle sleep
First found me, and with soft opression seiz'd
My drowsed sense, untroubl'd, though I thought
I then was passing to my former state
Insensible, and forthwith to dissolve.

(8.285–91)

His trance is characterized as a dissolution, a return to his preconscious state. Next, Adam is planted with a suggestion by God that counters the suggestion to Eve by the Toad: he too is introduced to the forbidden tree but instead of hearing "taste this," he is warned not to eat of its fruit and told the consequences of disobedience. There are other

significant differences between these accounts of hypnosis.
While Adam is in a trance, he awakens from it before he
is given his instruction, making his submission to his in-
structor a waking, not an entranced, one. Furthermore, when
Adam awakens from the dream, he finds it all real—while
Eve's dream had dissipated into fantasy.

> whereat I wak'd, and found
> Before mine Eyes all real, as the dream
> Had lively shadow'd: Here had new begun
> My wand'ring, had not hee who was my Guide
> . . . . . appear'd,
> Presence Divine. Rejoicing, but with awe,
> In adoration at his feet I fell
> Submiss.

> (8.309–16)

We are faced with Freud's dilemma: if Eve's case is closer
to (entranced) hypnosis and Adam's to (waking) transference,
are they so very different with regard to the issue of a subjected
will? Again, how free is Eve's will in light of the hypnotic
suggestion planted by the toad that she disobey? And how
free is Adam when even waking he is "submiss" to the
divine will that he obey?—submiss to a Guide who, we
should note with some alarm, "appear'd," surely, not dissembling "Grace" in theological parlance and "transference"
in psychoanalytic parlance begin to coalesce: in one, the
faithful accepts the divine will as his own; in the other, the
patient concedes his will to the suggestions of the analyst.
In both, free will can seem imperilled.

I am moving freely between psychoanalytic and theological discourses, even combining them, because I regard them
as two vocabularies engaged with the same fundamental
issues.[12] Investigating the processes of defining the Self in
relation to the Other (including the Other that is not
immanent), life in relation to death, will in relation to
determinism, identity in relation to difference: these are
among the provinces of the parallel and inevitably overlapping discourses of theology and psychoanalysis. Dealing here,
then, with not two but three different modes of language—

literature, psychoanalysis, and theology—and three different modes of knowledge—variously called identification, transference, and imitatio Christi, we should not be surprised to discover that the dynamics that structure them are similar. The virulence with which psychoanalysis rejects religion is only symptomatic of its co-optation, of its becoming a new religion.

The power differential—in which the analyst is the master-interpreter and the patient submissive—is precisely the ground on which Freud has been critiqued. His difficulty in coming to terms with the transference in the Dora case, in understanding the failure of his treatment, stemmed from his belief in his role as master-interpreter.[13] In later work, when he no longer underestimated the vital importance of the transference, he regarded it as chiefly a weapon of resistance to therapy: "This transference alike in its positive and negative form is used as a weapon by the resistance; but in the hands of the physician it becomes the most powerful therapeutic instrument and it plays a part scarcely to be over-estimated in the dynamics of the cure."[14] Its importance in the cure stems from his observation that the patient "cannot remember the whole of what is repressed in him, and what he cannot remember may be precisely the essential part of it . . . He is obliged to *repeat* the repressed material as a contemporary experience."[15] This repetition occasioned by the transference may be the analyst's only access to valuable information from the patient's past. Nonetheless, Freud stresses the need for the analyst's interpretive strong hand, the need for the analyst "to keep this transference neurosis within the narrowest limits: to force as much as possible into the channel of memory and to allow as little as possible to emerge as repetition."[16] Lacan's rereading of the transference stresses that power is a dialectic between analyst and patient: "the discovery of transference is the discovery that the power in analysis is not the analyst's power, but something very powerful that happens between subjects."[17] Lacan formulated the notion that the patient projects onto the analyst the role of "the subject-supposed-to-know," the one vested with authoritative insight, and proceeds to elaborate "what he thinks the analyst thinks" in his own mind, the site of the important interaction. Clearly, such a transference relationship is not confined to analysis but occurs whenever we vest others with supposed knowledge, frequently within institutionalized structures of interpersonal relations. Foucault saw it as the structure of confession, for instance, one later taken over by analysis:

> If one had to confess, this was not merely because the person to whom one confessed had the power to forgive, console, and direct, but because the work of producing the truth was obliged to pass through this relationship. . . . The truth did not reside solely in the subject who, by confessing, would reveal it fully formed. It was constituted in two stages: present but incomplete, blind to itself, in the one who spoke, it could only reach completion in the one who assimilated and recorded it. It was the latter's function to verify this obscure truth: the revelation of confession had to be coupled with the decipherment of what it said. The one who listened was not simply the forgiving master, the judge who condemned or acquitted; he was the master of truth. His was a hermeneutic function.[18]

The power that Foucault recognized as conferred upon the Confessor is, in Milton's epic, conferred upon God the power to forgive, console, direct, and produce truth—as "forgiving master, judge who condemn[s] or acquit[s], and master of truth." But that power is not unidirectional: Adam chooses to submit his will to divine will, Satan does not; the choice is, nonetheless, a real choice and the freedom—even to identify one's will with the will of God—a real freedom. Grace is offered freely, but not irresistibly. Man can accept or reject it. Freedom and grace participate in a dialectic; grace may illumine the mind and incline the heart, but reason is choosing. Arminius's description of grace is strikingly like Foucault's Confessor and Lacan's subject-supposed-to-know, if we precede it with "the faithful believe that," if, that is, we accede some power to the faithful in this transference:

> grace is simply and absolutely necessary for the illumination of the mind, the due ordering of the affections, and the inclination of the will to that which is good. It . . . infuses

good thoughts into the mind, inspires good desires into the affections, and bends the will to carry into execution good thoughts and good desires. This grace goes before, accompanies, and follows; it excites, assists, operates that we will, and co-operates lest we will in vain.[19]

Man freely consents to grant authority to another, to the transcendent subject-supposed-to-know, consenting thereby to law, to grace, and especially to his own freedom. In this way, transference becomes a master trope for Milton's theology. The transference, that complex structure of relations in which one confers knowledge and authority to another and then identifies with him, in which persons and events from the past are confused with the ones in the present, becomes the engine that drives the processes of identification—both for the actors within *Paradise Lost* and for the readers of *Paradise Lost*. Will Eve identify with Satan's narcissism or with Adam's filial piety? Will Adam identify with a fallen Eve or with the will of God? Will Satan genuinely identify with Christ or merely parody him? Where will the reader's identifications come to rest? With Eve at her impassioned argument for freedom as she separates from Adam? With Adam in his passionate declaration of devotion to Eve at her fall? With Satan, courageous in defeat in hell? With a blind narrator who sees things invisible to mortal sight? With John Milton, whoever he is?

READING AND IDENTIFICATION

In an important discussion of the relation between literature and psychoanalysis in which she advocates that neither discourse be subordinated to the other, Shoshana Felman observes that if "the literary critic occupies ... the place of the psychoanalyst (in the relation of interpretation)" she is in "the place of the patient (in the relation of transference)."[20] To pursue the implication of that insight: the reader grants the text the authority of the subject-supposed-to-know, making the text "the very place where meaning and knowledge of meaning reside."[21] Transference thereby becomes the master trope for Milton's poetic practice. The reader consents to that poetics, consenting thereby to the knowledge-ableness of the narrator and the dynamics of identification established by him. John T. Shawcross maintains "that what the author does and what the author intends to do are important issues for anyone interested in the creative process, as well as for a means to understanding a literary work, and that what the reader elicits from a literary work is a major factor in determining what the author does or does not do."[22] What readers have thus far elicited from *Paradise Lost* are multiple and shifting identifications, but ones that also seem to settle on identification with the narrator and with Milton as narrator. How does this process work and what might be its attractions?

We are told repeatedly that the whole universe is one: presumably this ontology includes in its purview Milton and the reader.

> O Adam, one Almighty is, from whom
> All things proceed, and up to him return
> If not deprav'd from good, created all
> Such to perfection, one first matter all.
>
> . . . . .
>
> And from these corporal nutriments perhaps
> Your bodies may at last turn all to spirit,
> Improv'd by tract of time, and wing'd ascend
> Ethereal, as wee, or may at choice
> Here or in Heav'ny Paradises dwell;
> If ye be found obedient.

(5.469–501)

When the narrator suggests that he is also one with the author, he only corroborates just this understanding of identity; for however sophisticated our notion of "persona" and "epic narrator," John Milton took pains to present himself in his epic—his blindness, his clime, his political crisis, his religious vision, his poetic inspiration. If there is a construction of selfhood at work here, it is not only of the narrator but also of Milton. So strong is this sense of Milton's presence in the epic that the next major English epic—Wordsworth's

Prelude—is unabashedly autobiographical.

When Milton becomes uneasy and begins to make us uneasy about the implications of this idea of identity for our freedom—careful as he is to include the caveat that the sublimation of matter to spirit to Godhead depends on obedience—he seems to embrace identification only to elaborate its hazards: misidentification, false identification, and downright dissembling. Within the epic, Milton depicts the problem of salvation as a process of choosing the right object of identification. Initially, Eve identifies with Satan's narcissism and ambition but then she elects to redirect her identification to another, to Adam, and through him, to divine will. That process was presaged in her birth narrative when her initial identification was with her shadowy image in the water until a warning voice led her to her Other who grasps her hand to guide her. I want to suggest that it is that voice and that hand that become the emblems of the direction offered not only to the untutored Eve but to the untutored reader; we make our choices, like Eve, with a warning voice and a guiding hand, those of John Milton. Making reading an activity in which the reader is engaged in choosing identifications, he exposes his work to the danger that the reader may identify with the wrong character at the wrong juncture in his or her moral life: with Eve at the Separation, with Adam at the Fall, with Satan in Hell. But for all of this freedom of choice granted the reader—and certainly the history of Milton criticism has manifest the success of the strategy through the wide range of identifications that have been recorded—the reader comes to rest, whatever else her sympathies, with Milton himself. And this is his doing. He has guided that transference. The narrator/Milton offers a vision of grace and free will, and his poetic process, guiding our identification with a warning voice and a gentle hand—even as we are left the freedom to refuse it—enacts the very vision he recommends. If we cannot *be* him, we must identify *with* him for such identification holds out the promise of our own freedom.

As we have seen, Milton's Arminianism offers just such a dialectic, that unique combination of grace and freedom, guidance and choice, while his antinomianism posits just such identification; the will of the faithful is identified with divine will but suffers thereby no loss of will. His poetic process is now coincident with his theology. For Milton lays down an ethical imperative in his epic: his verse is inspired by the divine Muse; to identify with him—with his voice, with his vision—is to identify with the will of God, who, after all, wills our freedom.[23] No wonder that so many readers want to think of themselves as John Milton.

For a religious writer and thinker like Milton, the dialectic Shoshana Felman describes between literature and psychoanalysis should include a third term as well, theology: "In the literary critic's perspective, literature is a subject, not an object; it is therefore not simply a body of language to interpret, nor is psychoanalysis simply a body of knowledge with which to interpret, since psychoanalysis itself is equally a body of language, and literature also a body of language . . ."[24] Like literature and psychoanalysis, theology is also a body of language and a body of knowledge. If Milton invites us to identify with him in order to identify with the will of God, his invitation is issued through his poetry, and if it is accepted, it is through the reader's transference onto and faith in that poetry. What in us is dark illumine, what is low, raise and support.

2 • That Old Man Eloquent

Annabel Patterson

> As soon as anything becomes poetic, it does transcend
> the chaos of the everyday world, and indicates an ability
> on the part of the author to transcend or transform it—
> to have his mind on consonance as well as party politics,
> and to hold action and contemplation in some kind
> of fusion where all is simultaneously ill and well.

It was not so very long ago that claims like these, for
the difference between "the poetic" (or "the literary")
and other kinds of writing, were taken as axiomatic. This
version of old New Critical doctrine, however, arrives more
intricately mediated than most. One should imagine it framed
by a double set of quotation marks, since I am here citing
Anna Nardo (in 1979) citing Joan Webber (in 1968), who
herself was adapting the anticontextual aesthetics she inherited to the subject that then engaged her—Milton's
polemical prose. As Nardo transmitted her predecessor's
dilemma a decade later, Webber wondered how Milton
"sustained his vision" of the poetic life during the years he
thrust his fighting words into the arena of church reform
and political revolution; she concluded that his vision was
sustained in the digressive spaces within those pamphlets

where Milton spoke of his poetic vocation, and thereby "evoked a timeless world where contemplation and harmony are possible."[1]

For Nardo, whose own project was to render an account of Milton's sonnets as a coherent poetic program, their origin as occasional poems notwithstanding, Webber's faith in Milton's faith in the timeless was exemplary; pondering what exactly Webber might have meant by that "kind of fusion where all is simultaneously ill and well," we might rather suspect evidentiary perversity. The intractability of the material that Webber had to deal with (in order to understand the anti-prelatical pamphleteer) breaks through the ideal hypothesis (that one can fly above the clouds) and reveals that vocationalism is itself a distillation of turbulence.

Almost a decade and a half later still, the difficulty in distinguishing between what is timeless and what time-bound appears still more intractable, not least because I write to honor a venerable Miltonist who desires that this book of essays on Milton, linking in commemoration two scholars three hundred years apart, will focus on the literary Milton. But what is literature? This question must surely provoke a rather different answer today than either that assumed by Joan Webber, or its diametrical opposite as demanded by Jean-Paul Sartre in the aftermath of the Second World War, that literature redefine itself so as to privilege political engagement.[2]

It is, of course, unfair to both Webber and Nardo to imply that their own theory of "literature" was time-bound. While the term "transcendence" irresistibly signals a poetics derived from Romanticism and given a new lease on life by certain forms of New Criticism, each took large steps in expanding the idea of the literary Milton in a direction of which Sartre might actually have approved. In Webber's case "literature" was discovered in Milton's polemical prose pamphlets by making them the subject of poetic (stylistic) analysis, and by focusing on the poetic psyche, the "Eloquent I" that Milton himself placed at their center, by his use of first-person pronouns and autobiographical excursions. In Nardo's case "literature" already existed (what can be more unequivocally literary than a sonnet?), but it was rendered more literary by the concept of an overarching intellectual program under which could shelter a seeming hodge-podge of poems, written over a quarter of a century, often in response to specific frustrations. For Nardo, there was an overarching coherence binding these fragments together, the notion of an "ideal community" of idealists, past and present. "Each sonnet," wrote Nardo, "details a unique engagement with a person, event, or partisan issue of the day, but each also asks its readers to consider this one moment in the light of man's ongoing fight against barbarity":

> At the center [of the ideal community] is an individual—free and virtuous, with a calm and humble faith. Surrounding this "upright heart and pure" are the groups of significant "others" that form the society that Milton envisioned: a beloved woman, the home, friends male and female, the nation, and Protestant Europe. Embracing all, of course, is a totally provident and beneficent God.[3]

This program has more in common, in terms of its aesthetic presuppositions, with that of Mary Ann Radzinowicz than Nardo was willing to acknowledge; for Radzinowicz was also committed to the view that Milton created that most New Critical of values, a unified structure, when he gathered his sonnets together for publication. Even though his *Poems of Mr. John Milton* (1645) contained only those sonnets now numbered 1 through 10, and even though the 1673 edition of his collected works omitted (presumably for prudential reasons) the "commonwealth" sonnets 15, 16, 17 and 22, Radzinowicz, like Nardo, believed that Milton, retroactively and quite deliberately, created a sonnet "sequence" composed of individual "clusters," whose interrelations can now be securely determined:

> Milton intended each sonnet to bear its individual meaning; he grouped the sonnets by interlinked cross-reference and wrote them at distinct periods, often several years apart, so that a thematic meaning emerges within subgroups. He then printed them retrospectively, breaking chronology for other

effects, and brought them together so that a final polyphonic harmony would be apparent in them.[4]

Radzinowicz saw the final structure as a narrative of maturation: from Milton's "youthful confident sense of the irresistibility of virtue and the certainty of election" (sonnets 1–7), to studies of the "ethics of purity" (8–10), to those of Milton's "most revolutionary period" that consider the consequences of writing the divorce tracts (11–14), to those (not quite identical with the group unpublishable in 1673) in which Milton "labored to prevent the revolution from failure" (15–18), to the last and most purely autobiographical group, which "as a whole records calm of mind and assent to the temporal circumstances of the period."[5]

No doubt for reasons of which I remain unconscious (and no doubt fortunately so) I cannot equate the "literary" exclusively with any of the values adumbrated so far: whether Webber's transcendence and consonance, Radzinowicz's "polychronic harmony," or Nardo's "free and virtuous" individual with his "calm and humble faith," secure in reliance on "a totally provident and beneficent God." For me, what constitutes the literary Milton as exemplified by his sonnets is a more embattled and less optimistic notion; though (as will become clear as I attempt to describe it) it shares with each of these three fine readings of Milton a point of convergence. With Webber I share the belief that one cannot understand Milton without taking into account the eloquence of his psychological self-presentation— although I would push psychology lightly in the direction of psychoanalysis. Milton's sonnets, like much of his mid-century pamphleteering, are full of disingenuities and repressions, whose centrifugal pressure makes their small shells always on the verge of explosion. With Radzinowicz I share the conviction that Milton's sonnets came retroactively to tell the story of his life and political career,[6] not least in the history of their printing; but their implied narrative is less a *bildungsroman*, more an undoing, than the one proposed by her five clusters. And I share with Nardo the conviction that Milton in his sonnets created the community

with which he wished to be identified; but its most important members were dead, some very long dead indeed, and
hence only available as a community in which he might
participate in a highly restricted sense; while their value to
him, as models, had itself to be constructed in a restricted,
highly selective, manner. The story that Milton made his
sonnets tell was indeed that of the "ongoing fight against
barbarity," but we learn of the defeats in that campaign as
much or more than the victories.

There is nothing casual, however, about the way that we
learn. At the center of my own argument is a definition of
the "literary" that resituates an old New Critical term,
"difficulty," in an aesthetics recharged in the 1990s with
respect for historical knowledge. One can scarcely doubt
that Milton's own aesthetics was so charged, or became so
when he entered the field of pamphlet warfare; but in the
sonnets, for reasons we will need to reconstruct with some
delicacy, he offers historical knowledge as simultaneously
a bait, the reward that will make the sonnet give up its
intellectual goods to the scrupulous and worthy reader, and,
conversely, as something finally unreliable, if not entirely
unavailable. He constructs a sonnet *sequence*, peppered with
signs that autobiography and chronology are its very themes;
but he ensures that it will remain impossible for his readers
to date them with any certainty. I take this provocative
behavior to constitute a poetics, not of the timeless, but of
sequentiality itself: of what it means, philosophically, to be
timebound, bound by what one has said and done, written
and published, previously; and bound to follow, belatedly,
those who have gone before.[7]

OCCASIONALITY

This reconnaissance of the critical tradition has perhaps
grouped too casually together ideas of sequence that should
be kept distinct. The first proposition is that Milton arranged his sonnets in strict chronological order based on the
moment of composition. This hypothesis, closely related to

the conviction that the sonnets were all "occasional," would surely not have dominated the criticism so clearly, generating only mild or sporadic dissent, without the testimony of the Cambridge manuscript, which gives firm occasions for all but two sonnets in what, looking at the final structure we ourselves have produced, is manifestly the middle of the sequence: sonnets 8, 11/12, 13, 14, 15, and 16 all carried manuscript titles that stated or implied a precise dating, one that matches the poem's position in the sequence. Yet those temporal markers that originally locked the poems into their occasions were *omitted* from the editions of 1645 and 1673. The effect is to render the occasion indistinct, the chronology harder to reconstruct, or even the referent mysterious.

Thus sonnet 8 carried in the manuscript two versions of the same title: "On his dore w*hen* ye Citty expected an assault," in the hand of a copyist, subsequently deleted, and below it in Milton's own hand, "*When* the assault was intended to ye Citty." Both versions contain not just a sign of time but a sign of *the times*. The precise formulation must have been important to Milton, or he would not have corrected it. The effect of the correction, while de-literalizing the poem's talismanic function, is to give the "when" more prominence. Yet (whether or not at the same time) Milton *deleted* the manuscript's marginal dating of 1642—a change of mind that inspired E. A. J. Honigmann to posit another occasion altogether, not the Royalist assault on London expected on 13 November 1642, but another alarm in May 1641.[8]

But for readers in 1645 the question was moot, since the sonnet appeared before them *almost* stripped of its uneasy ricochet between local wartime news and the claims, from time *almost* immemorial, for poetry's protective function:

> Captain or Colonel, or Knight in Arms,
> Whose chance on these defenceless dores may sease,
> If deed of honour did thee ever please,
> Guard them, and him within protect from harms,
> . . . . . .
> Lift not thy spear against the Muses Bowre,
> The great Emathian Conqueror bid spare

> The house of Pindarus, when Temple and Towre
> Went to the ground: And the repeated air
> Of sad Electra's Poet had the power
> To save th'Athenian Walls from ruine bare.[9]

I say "almost," because, with the title gone, the poem's challenge to the reader becomes better balanced. Knowledge of ancient history is required to answer the question: who was "the great Emathian Conqueror?" (Alexander) and when did he spare the house of Pindar? (during the destruction of Thebes in 335 B.C.) I submit that this act of historical reconstruction, which has to be repeated for "sad Electra's poet," generates more interesting questions about the contemporary situation and the reticence with which it, too, is described (whose "defenceless dores" are they, and why is history repeating itself?) than the question debated by Honigmann and the *Milton Variorum*,[10] of when precisely Milton would have reason to fear Royalist retribution for statements made in his pamphlets. It is not just, as Woodhouse and Bush sensibly remark, that the sonnet "uses the occasion for general reflections on the place and power of poetry in war-time," but that its withholding of historical transparency—its demand that the reader *earn* the rewards of a historical perspective—is part of its argument and its power.

Sonnet 12 (number 11 in the Cambridge manuscript) also carried an occasionalist title, "On the detraction which follow'd upon my writing certain treatises." But here the clear indication of sequentiality (the sonnet follows the detraction which followed the treatises) is accompanied by vagueness as to which treatises they were. Since sonnet 11 (numbered 12 in the manuscript, and there carrying the title "On the same") mentions by name *Tetrachordon*, published 4 March 1645, we assume that "certain treatises" referred to the four divorce pamphlets as a group; but why was Milton not more helpful, and why was even that limited helpfulness reduced when sonnet 12 appeared in the 1673 edition without the manuscript title?

Once again, without the manuscript title, the effect is not

to move the sonnet towards some transhistorical realm, but to focus attention on the mysterious structural relation between past and present, as in sonnet 8, which is arranged in reverse order of expectation in octave and sestet. Without the reference to "my writing," the passive construction of the event ("A Book *was writ* of late call'd *Tetrachordon*") generalizes the issue. Instead of a temporary need for self defence, the opening lines pose the problem of cultural innovation and the difficulty of placing a "Subject new" before a receptive audience. Moreover, there is a smaller temporal sequence invoked within the frame of the up-to-the-moment opening: a book "was writ *of late*," "it walk'd the Town a while," but "now" already it is "seldom por'd on," topical no longer. How short a time it takes for present occasion to become recent past—a troublesome concept that must inflect with slight irony the temporal marker in the opening line—"of late." That word "late," as we shall see, will acquire infinitely greater resonance when the sonnet takes its middle place in the different sequence of twenty-three.

And the last three lines are an epitome of Milton's troublemaking. Not only do they require one to know *when* it was that Sir John Cheke tutored the young King Edward VI in Greek, and the intellectual controversy generated by his changing the pronunciation of Greek at St. John's College, Cambridge (an innovation suppressed by bishop Gardiner in 1542); it is also extremely unclear what they actually assert about the relationship between the recent past and an earlier era, with respect to the climate for intellectual innovation. On the one hand Milton asserts a symmetry between the 1540s and the 1640s ("Thy age, *like* ours") and on the other his negative syntax ("Thy age . . . Hated *not* Learning") seems to require a contrast between them. The *Milton Variorum* dutifully studies this crux and the scholars who have wrestled with it;[11] but it passes lightly over what is perhaps the most interesting aspect of Milton's implied comparison of himself to Cheke—the fact that his reactionary pamphlet, *The Hurt of Sedicion*, berating the Norfolk followers of Robert Kett in 1549, had in 1641 been reissued by the Royalist Gerard Langbaine as *The True Subject to the Rebell*, with clear application now to the Long Parliamentarians.[12] If, then, Milton aligned himself with Cheke on the subject of Greek, he could only have done so by the use of a very selective memory.

Sonnet 13, appearing first as a rough autograph draft in the Cambridge manuscript, originally carried Milton's title, "To my friend Mr. Hen. Laws Feb. 9. 1645" (that is, 1646). This gives a very different chronology from that implied by the second title added by an amanuensis to Milton's fair copy: "To Mr. Hen: Laws *on the publishing* of his Aires," since Lawes' *Ayres and Dialogues* were not published until 1653; unless one posits, as does the *Milton Variorum* (399), that the poem was written in anticipation of a publishing event planned for 1646 but subsequently delayed. Critical ingenuity is required to explain the disparity; but for our purposes the most important point is that, while the 1673 edition in this rare case did retain a sonnet title, it was one innocent of dating: "To Mr. H. Lawes, on his Aires." As for sonnet 14, were it not for the survival of the Cambridge manuscript, which identified the elegy as "On ye religious memorie of Mrs. Catharine Thomason my christian freind deceas'd Decem. 1646," we would never have been able to guess that behind its baroque catalogue of religious conventions ("Purple beames/and azure wings") lurked the historical profile of *two* remarkable people: Katharine Hutton, who in the early 1630s married George Thomason, who created the great collection of Thomason Tracts, containing virtually everything that was published in England from 1640 to 1660, including unlicensed materials. Milton apparently donated several of his own pamphlets to the collection, which appear there with the words "Ex Dono Authoris." Mrs. Thomason herself owned a considerable library, and Nardo speculates that she may well have assisted her husband in the difficult and sometimes dangerous work of collection.[13]

Sonnets 15 and 16 were two of the four "commonwealth" sonnets omitted from the 1673 edition. Whose decision that was, if caution were the motive, we cannot tell. In the

Cambridge manuscript both carried specific autograph datings, in titles that never made it into print: "On ye Lord General Fairfax at ye seige of Colchester," that is to say, the summer of 1648; and "To the Lord Generall Cromwell May 1652/On the proposals of certain ministers at yr Commitee for Propagation of the Gospel." Both titles were deleted in the manuscript, indicating perhaps that Milton himself planned to publish them. In both, but especially in the sonnet to Cromwell, the erasure of the title allows a broader interpretation of the war/peace dialectic they share. In sonnet 16 the heroic references to the battles of Dunbar and Worcester (September 1650 and 1651) are allowed to set the historical context for the poem, rather than the parliamentary Committee for the Propagation of the Gospel established on 18 February 1652, of which Cromwell was a member; and the references to "new foes," "secular chaines" and "hireling wolves" in the last four lines acquire an ambiguity comparable to the famous "two-handed engine" of *Lycidas*.

The testimony of the Cambridge manuscript, then, produced the mainstay of the argument for a strictly chronological sequence: sonnet 8, dated 1642, and inviting a tighter dating of November of that year; sonnets 11 and 12, with an implied dating of 1645; sonnet 13, dated February 1646; sonnet 14, dated December 1646; sonnet 15, with an implied dating of summer 1648; sonnet 16, firmly dated May 1652. And yet the testimony of the manuscript is at odds with Milton's subsequent intentions, which include, I argue, an intention to mystify, rather than clarify, their historical context.

AUTOBIOGRAPHY

Surrounding this central group in which "signs of the times" predominate, though not exclusively, are two clusters of sonnets in which the personal, the introspective, and the autobiographical are the manifest themes: sonnets 1 and 7, framing the five Italian sonnets; sonnets 19 through 23, meditations on friendship, the late shape of his career, friendship in a "hard Season," and the death of wives. Here, apparently, Milton *started* with a decision to mystify chronology. These sonnets abound with mythical (I am tempted to say false) datings—hints of a time scheme against which the poet is measuring himself; yet they have all proved virtually impossible to date with any certainty. And what also becomes visible when the entire sequence is in place is an anxiety spreading from the ambiguous semantics of "late," as Milton deploys the word in different ambiences; an anxiety not unconnected with the fact that he conceives of his friends, male and female, in terms of their fathers or grandfathers.

On the grounds of their resemblance to Elegy 5, which Milton himself dated "Anno Aetatis 20," the Italian sonnets have been hypothetically dated 1630, at the end of which year Milton became twenty-two, though no doubt the hypothesis was influenced by their preceding sonnet 7, which locates itself in relation to his "three and twentieth year." What we don't know for certain is whether that "three and twentieth year" is 1631, at the end of which he *became* twenty-three, or 1632, during most of which he *was* twenty-three.[14] What we certainly don't know is whether sonnet 1 actually preceded sonnet 7 in terms of composition. Sonnet 1, "O Nightingale," is in one sense the most timeless of the entire sequence, in being the most conventional. In its appeal to "propitious May," to the bird of love against the "rude Bird of Hate," and its assumption that sonnets are about "success in love" or alternatively failure, sonnet 1 could be readily assigned to almost any Elizabethan sonneteer; that is, until one recognizes the peculiarly Miltonic coloring of the appeal:

> Now *timely* sing, ere the rude Bird of Hate
> Foretell my hopeles doom in som Grove ny:
> As thou from year to year hast sung *too late*
> For my relief . . .

In what sense, the poem provokes us to ask, can the traditional song ever be sung "too late"; and, as a different kind of question, why would a 22-year-old register the fear that he was too late for love, and complain, further, that his failure is of several years standing? The links between this predicament and that of sonnet 7, which complains of his "*late* spring" and his unproductivity ("no bud or blossom show'th") compared to "some more *timely*-happy spirits" cannot be overlooked once the sequence is established, suggesting a development from a sexual conception of success to a religious-vocational one; but there is theoretically nothing to obviate the possibility that sonnet 1 was written much later—[15] perhaps in the late spring of 1642, the year in whose summer Milton suddenly came home "a married man, that went out a bachelor," or even that of 1643, when, Mary Milton having gone back to her father, Milton began to write the *Doctrine and Discipline of Divorce*. Suppose that were true, we would have to recognize the order created in the 1645 *Poems* as a fiction designed to conceal. Beneath the timeless texture of nightingale and cuckoo and their ancient rivalry, behind the timebound structure of poetic auto-biography, would be *another* story in which youthful dedi-cation to the "great Taskmaster" and youthful asceticism ("strictest measure") gave way to (were followed by) adult sexual frustration; a story that would actually better explain the language of sonnet 1 ("too late for my *relief*") and the threat of the cuckoo's song, more appropriate as a threat to the married man than to the university undergraduate who still, in all probability, considered a career in the church. This hypothesis is compatible with the theory of William Hunter, that his "three and twentith yeer" carried for Milton a special timebound force because "the age of twenty-three had been appointed by the Canons of 1604 as the earliest date for one's ordination as a deacon," and that, while fifteen of his twenty classmates had already been ordained, Milton was still hesitating over his decision.[16]

Let us now consider the opening proposition of sonnet 19: "When I consider how my light is spent,/Ere half my days." It was sonnet 19 that provoked Jonathan Goldberg's deconstructive exercise at the expense of Milton scholar-ship, which has wrestled with the problem of dating this poem only to produce at least four possibilities: 1642, 1644, 1651 and late 1655. Only the first of these hypotheses takes into account what Milton was likely to have meant by "ere half my days," which on the basis of the biblically sanctioned life span, threescore years and ten, would have implied some time before 1643, the year in which Milton became thirty-five. Indeed, if he figured a more modest longevity, such as the sixty-four years he actually achieved, this would push the sonnet back to 1639/40, when he returned from his continental tour and situated himself in London as a private schoolmaster. In such a profession, that "one Talent which is death to hide" was relatively useless; that is, if we suppose this to refer to "the strong propensity of nature" to write something truly memorable and enduring, that Milton refers to in *The Reason of Church Government* in 1642. It is the temptation to read "light" unmetaphorically and hence the assumption that when Milton declares his light "spent" and "denied" he refers to the approach of his blindness that led Honigmann to posit 1644 (the first signs of optical distress), others to posit late 1651, when his blindness became complete, and to so confuse William Riley Parker that he ricocheted back and forth between 1651–52 and 1655. On the other hand, if one assumes that the sequence is truly chronological, then sonnet 19, which follows that "On the late Massacher in Piemont," must also have been written later than the spring of 1655, when that massacre occurred, and Milton became forty-seven. If we suppose that Milton did in fact write sonnet 19 in 1640 or thereabouts (a surmise compatible with the vocational hesitations expressed in *The Reason of Church Government* but not with the conviction, expressed in the *Second Defence* of 1654, that he had already demonstrated his talents and "erected a monument that will not readily be destroyed"), we must also suppose that by rearrangement he either subordinated autobiography to a very different structure, or that he intended to live into his early nineties! Yet since the rearrangement occurs in the 1673 edition of his poems, surely prepared in the knowledge that he was running out of time in the most absolute sense, if we must choose one of these hypotheses we must choose the first. I believe we must choose. To Radzinowicz, as I have said, sonnet 19 ushers in a "final group" of autobiographical poems which "as a whole records calm of mind and assent to the temporal circumstances of the period of their composition," a sentence which now collapses under its own and Milton's ambiguities. To Goldberg, committed to the postmodern split subject and a Derridean concept of temporality, "When I consider" "would have been written and rewritten over a number of years, and could not be resolved into a single chronological placement."[17] Situating myself somewhere between them, I suggest that Milton *wrote* the sonnet in the early 1640s; but then resituated it, sometime in the late 1650s, in a sequence formed by hindsight, which is scarcely the same as a deconstructive "revision." In that hindsight, sonnet 19 becomes part of the introspective frame to the occasionalist center. The spent light becomes a reference to blindness. The vocational doubt includes the once triumphant achievement of the regicide pamphlets and the two *Defences*. Indeed, it reverberates with the vocational doubt expressed in 1655 in the *Pro Se Defensio*, that seldom-cited pamphlet in which Milton meditated aloud on the dubious fame those other contributions had brought him:

> My principle . . . is . . . that *if* as a youth in that literary leisure I then had I [sic] profited aught either from the instructions of the learned or from my own lucubrations, I would, in proportion to my poor abilities, employ all this to the advantage of life and the human race, *if* I could range so far. And *if* sometimes from private enmities public transgressions are wont to be censured and oft corrected, and *if* I have now, impelled by all possible reasons, prosecuted in a most just vituperation not merely my personal enemy, but the common enemy of almost all mankind . . . *whether* I have done this with that success which I ought . . . I do indeed hope (for why should I distrust?) that herein I have discharged an office *neither* displeasing to God, unsalutary to the church, nor unuseful to the state.[18]

In the frame of this diffident syntax, Milton's plaintive parenthesis, "Cur enim diffidam?" ("Why should I distrust?")[19]

resonates poignantly both with sonnet 19 and with sonnet 22, "Cyriack, this three years day these eys," with *its* misleading chronological marker, so seemingly precise, so open to subsequent conjecture.[20]

Given the reverberations between "late" as a marker of historical topicality and as a confession of belatedness or retardation, what are we to think of the "late espoused Saint" of sonnet 23, whose identity has remained in doubt because Milton chose not to specify whether it was Mary Milton or Katherine Woodcock Milton whom he mourns, and what kind of lateness is involved? Not only the woman's name-lessness but Milton's syntax seems to prevent the banal reading, "My late wife," on the same level of reference, only in reverse, as the "late Massacher in Piemont" (the meaning not that his wife has come into existence at a specific moment, but at that moment been erased from history). The doubt occurs in the interposition between "late" and "Saint" of the word "espoused," of the also presumably certain date of an espousal. Were they only recently (lately) married, in which case it must have been Katherine Woodcock, whom Milton married in November 1656, and who died just over a year later? or were they married late (too late), in which case it might still be Katherine, or, by a more interesting understanding in the light of the other dating for sonnet 1, have been Mary after all, whom Milton married in June 1642, too late for his relief. Perhaps he came to adore her (late) before she died too soon, three days after the delivery of a daughter, just under a decade later. But the sonnet's reticence, not to say coyness, on the crucial question of its subject, permits every reader to indulge her personal fantasy as to how Milton resolved his relations with women.

THE POETICS OF HISTORICITY

At this point, then, we should look more closely at sonnet 10, the last of the sequence created in the *Poems* of 1645, which operates as a fulcrum between the two types of sequence discussed above: on the one hand, the sonnets that narrate, however evasively, the events that Milton thought of as symbolic or threshold moments of his personal life or his life conceived as a vocation; on the other, the sonnets that, while still autobiographical in a sense, broaden the narrative to engage the political history of his day. This sonnet is the fulcrum of my own argument also, that in constructing this sequence Milton articulated a specialized poetics, a theory of literature appropriate not only to his own personality but to his own historical moment and perhaps to ours also; that is to say, a theory of how literature cannot be understood *except* in the perspective of history, which in turn cannot be understood *except* by finessing the subjective/objective dilemma:

> Daughter to *that good Earl*, once President
> Of Englands Council and her Treasury,
> Who liv'd in both, unstain'd with gold or fee,
> And left them both, more in himself content,
> Till the sad breaking of *that Parlament*
> Broke him, as *that dishonest victory*
> At Chaeronea, fatal to liberty,
> Kill'd with report *that Old man eloquent*,
> *Though later born*, then to have known the dayes
> Wherin your Father flourisht, yet by you
> Madam, me thinks I see him living yet;
> So well your words his noble vertues praise,
> That all both judge you to relate them true
> And to possess them, Honour'd Margaret.

Here details that are inarguably literary—syntactical repetition and pointing, and the formal structure of the italianate sonnet—collaborate to reveal a failure of revelation: we learn from the closest of readings that "the text itself" is insufficient for the task of signification—that it points beyond itself to historical facts that the reader must go out and bring back if any cognitive event is to take place. This sonnet continues the theme of belatedness installed in sonnets 1 and 7, but translates it into the register invoked by sonnets 11 and 18, in which "late" points to a verifiable historical event. More precisely, the octave constructs the problem of historical knowledge as a set of interrelated questions for which there are certain answers. Like the question provoked by "my late espoused Saint"—"Which one?"—those provoked by Milton's markedly repeated "that" is also "which one?" Which good earl? (a question rendered more difficult of solution when the manuscript title, "To ye Lady Margaret Ley" was dropped). Which parliament was it whose breaking broke him? And to which old man eloquent from ancient history is Milton's good earl compared? But unlike sonnet 23, where the question, "Which one?" remains insoluble, sonnet 10 operates in the confidence that the fit reader will know what needs to be known.

Obviously, the answer to the first question is the readiest to hand, even today: James Ley, earl of Marlborough, father of the Lady Margaret to whom the sonnet is addressed. And the fact that he died on 10 March 1629 permits the certain recognition of "that Parliament" as the last of the Caroline parliaments, dissolved on 4 March 1629 by Charles I, after the demonstration, famous or notorious depending on one's own political inclinations, when the Speaker Sir John Finch was forcibly prevented from reading the royal order to adjourn until the Commons had passed resolutions against tonnage and poundage and innovations in religion. The dissolution inaugurated the period referred to either as the eleven years of Personal Rule or the Eleven Years' Tyranny, again depending on one's ideological take on these events. That Milton called it a "sad breaking" is not surprising, but the phrase admits the constitutional disaster without explicitly assigning blame to either the king or the party of Eliot, Coke, Selden and others. It is surprising, given how clearly his republican political theory had already developed, that Milton does not mention the Petition of Right; but the milder constitutionalist position was obviously more appropriate to a sonnet honoring Ley, who had made a career in the service of James I and Charles I.

Nevertheless, the third "that," requiring another historical solution from the far more distant past, adds a republican gloss. The dissolution of 1629 is the equivalent in political theory of the battle of Chaeronea in 338 B.C., when the Athenian democracy succumbed to Philip of Macedon, news of which is said to have caused the death of Isocrates, "that Old man eloquent" with whom Milton aligned himself in 1644 in the writing (and naming) of *Areopagitica.*

The rewards that accrue from restoring these facts to the spaces held open by those deictic substitutions ("that good Earl, that Parliament, that dishonest victory, that Old man eloquent") are, however, fallacious.[21] At least, the further one goes towards filling out the historical profiles this sonnet sketches so lightly, the more uncomfortable grows that knowledge. James Ley, born in the reign of Edward VI, was apparently an able municipal lawyer who had, however, first acquired a reputation at the beginning of James's reign. This was as commissioner of the great seal for Dublin, where he became generally hated for his severity against Catholic recusants. When James brought him back from Ireland to serve as attorney to the court of wards and liveries, Ley entered the profitable world of legal patronage. When Sir Francis Bacon vacated the attorney-generalship in 1617, Ley was reported by Buckingham to have offered ten thousand pounds for the vacant post, which, however, he failed to receive. At 69 years of age, and according to D'Ewes already "a decrepit old man,"[22] he married as his third wife Jane Butler, Buckingham's niece,[23] and so put himself in line for preferment from the favorite, resulting in his appointment as lord chief justice of the King's Bench in January 1621. In that capacity he presided at Bacon's trial in the House of Lords for financial corruption. In 1624 Ley retired from the bench to become lord high treasurer and a privy councillor, also under Buckingham's auspices, despite the fact that Ley had no financial experience and showed no aptitude for it.[24] He resigned the post four years later to his assistant, Sir Richard Weston, and Charles I thereupon made him president of the council. Six months later, according to Clarendon, he "was removed under pretence of his age and disability for the work."[25] He died, at 79 years of age, in the following spring. It is only on the basis of Milton's sonnet, and the coincidence between the date of his death, on 14 March 1629, that it has been attributed to political disappointment rather than simple decrepitude. The *Dictionary of National Biography* sums up Ley's career as follows:

> Ley, although a feeble statesman, was an able, erudite, and impartial judge . . . On the other hand, Sir James Whitelocke denounces him as "an old dissembler," who was "wont to be called 'Vulpone' " and says that he borrowed money of the judges when lord chief justice (*Liber Famelicus*, 108).[26]

In the ellipsis between these two contrary evaluations, the *Dictionary* inserts, unconscious of any irony, the first four lines of Milton's sonnet, with its apparent dissociation of Ley ("unstained with gold or fee") from such venality as Bacon had been charged with in 1622, and that led to his disgrace.

This hole opening up in the fabric of the ideal community under the pressure of historical inquiry is likely only to gape wider if we also pursue "that Old man eloquent" a little further. For Isocrates' legendary suicide after the battle of Chaeronea could not have been, as Milton's sonnet implied, because of its fatality to Athenian liberty, since his *Philippus*, written in 346 after an earlier round of hostilities between Philip of Macedon and Athens, initiated his campaign to have Philip assume rule over a united Greece; and, as the *Oxford Companion to Classical Literature* observes, this placed him in absolute contradistinction to that other eloquent old man who indeed lamented Chaeronea, Demosthenes. The reason for that suicide, if truly historical, would have been, therefore, "not that Philip had been victorious—thus rendering practicable the chief hope of Isocrates—but that Athens was still determined to resist him." Again, a citation of Milton's sonnet, innocent of any irony, appears at the end of this account; the *Milton Variorum* acknowledges the problem, but resolves it in the most high-minded manner possible:

> If this aspect of the matter were present to Milton, the implication would be quite different, namely, that the Earl's policy was to reconcile the King and Parliament (as his loyal and rewarded service of the crown would indeed suggest) and that his hopes, like those of Isocrates, were shattered. This seems better to fit the facts, while the condemnation

of Charles by the implied comparison of him to Philip seems better to suit Milton's own principles (and prejudices).[27]

The *Variorum* editors therefore chose to believe that Milton believed in the earl's idealism and integrity, while disagreeing with his allegiances; the closest they came to imagining Milton's sonnet might have been disingenuous was to wonder: "Is it possible that Milton wrote the lines in one sense and allowed Lady Margaret to read them in the other?"[28]

But what of Milton's relationship to Lady Margaret herself? Introduced by a wonderfully intricate turn from the octave, which ends with "that Old man eloquent," into the sestet, which begins with a phrase of which we should by now have learned to be suspicious, "Though *later* born . . . " the relationship is itself a figure of syntactical obscurantism. Of whose belated birth are we here informed?[29] Of the daughter to whom the entire sonnet is addressed, and to the definition of whose filial excellence, by way of an account of her parent, it is, in one long sentence, dedicated? Or to the writer of the sonnet who suddenly emerges in the first person in the ninth line, in charge of the only main verb:

> Though later born, then to have known the dayes
> Wherein your Father flourisht, yet by you
> Madam, methinks I see him living yet.

In fact, one need scarcely decide which of the two is "later born," since Milton (born in 1608) and Margaret, born when her father was about sixty, were almost the same age. That being the case, and if we take the term "flourished" conventionally, implying a man at the height of his powers and reputation, we can take the idea of belatedness more literally (and more critically) than an idealistic reading of the sonnet would suppose.

In what precedes, I have only recirculated "facts" that have been known to lurk between the lines of Milton's sonnet, and that have passed from Smart's edition, through Honigmann's, to the *Variorum*. The difference resides in my own late twentieth century refusal to sweep them under the rug of a high-minded idealism, which in turn has rendered

Milton's sonnet a historical document of another sort, one supposedly capable of giving testimony as to the earl's character and the cause of his death. It is worth emphasizing again what I noted above, that both the *Dictionary of National Biography* and the *Oxford Companion to Classical Literature* incorporate lines from the sonnet as if it had acquired documentary status; whereas such other documents as we can summon to Ley's evaluation render its testimony decidedly suspect.

Perhaps we should accuse Milton of nothing worse than excessive politeness. But there is one other "historical" document that bears upon sonnet 10 and complicates the story further. In his life of Milton, Edward Phillips provided his own account of the occasion for his uncle's writing this sonnet, and placed it unmistakably during the period of temporary separation between the newly married Milton and his young wife, when Mary Powell Milton had returned to her family in Oxford and refused to return at her husband's urging. "Our Author," wrote Phillips:

> *now as it were a single man again,* made it his chief diversion now and then in an Evening to visit the Lady Margaret Lee, daughter to[Lord]Lee, Earl of Marlborough, Lord High Treasurer of England, and President of the Privy Councel to King James the First. This Lady being a Woman of great Wit and Ingenuity, had a particular Honour for him, and took much delight in his Company, as likewise her Husband Captain Hobson, a very Accomplish'd Gentleman; and what Esteem he at the same time had for Her, appears by a Sonnet he made in praise of her, to be seen among his other Sonnets in his Extant Poems (emphasis added).[30]

There are discreet signs in Milton criticism that Edward Phillips here put the cat among the pigeons—that for all its courtesy sonnet 10 barely conceals a mildly scandalous situation, which some modern readers have refused to acknowledge. What is at stake is its timing in relation to two marriages: Milton's marriage to Mary Powell in the early summer of 1642, and its almost immediate interruption (when she returned to her family in Oxford and refused to come back to her husband) which lasted until the summer of 1645;

and Lady Margaret Ley's marriage to John Hobson on 30 December 1641, which brought her into proximity with Milton in Aldersgate Street. It has therefore seemed to matter to Miltonists when precisely the sonnet was written.

If by its placement last in the 1645 volume we believe it was written after sonnet 8, "When the assault was intended to the city," sonnet 10 postdates November 1642 and therefore would fit without strain into the period described by Phillips as following Mary Milton's departure, when Milton was "as it were a single man again." Phillips' account suggests the not uncommon pattern of a newly married couple accepting the friendship of a "single" man who visits them more assiduously than neighborliness requires; he in turn, while being attracted to the wife, finds their marriage vicariously stimulating while protecting him against any serious entanglement. But William Riley Parker, whether consciously or not attempting to keep this scenario at bay, proposed that the use of Lady Margaret's maiden name in the Cambridge manuscript could mean that the sonnet was composed *before* her marriage, which would put its final placement in chronological jeopardy;[31] and Honigmann welcomed that suggestion, though "it is admittedly an open question whether every lady with a courtesy title adopted her husband's name at this time." In fact, he went further in attempting to obscure Phillips' none too obscure intimations: "As I understand him," Honigmann wrote, "Phillips merely cited the sonnet as a general illustration of his uncle's regard for Lady Margaret: that Milton's friendship with Lady Margaret only began after his wife's departure, or that the sonnet was written after that event, is by no means indicated."[32] The phrase that indicates dating, "*now as it were a single man again,*" has somehow been separated from the sonnet, lest the author we cherish might be thought to have written a sonnet less high-minded than traditional criticism would prefer.

To me, the centrality of sonnet 10 (a little off the numerical center) is a case worth making. But to make it requires a conception of the split subject that "literature," as distinct from textuality, is peculiarly equipped to accommodate. In that conception, we try to tell the truth while putting our best foot forward; an objective which requires, or ought to require, continual retrospection and stocktaking. Milton took stock, publicly, more often than most. When Milton wrote sonnet 10, probably, he was busy reconstructing his life in defiance of the mistakes he admitted in the *Doctrine and Discipline of Divorce*; when he came to publish it, as the last of the sonnets in the 1645/6 *Poems of Mr. John Milton*, a volume that Louis Martz has persuasively described as Milton's leave-taking of his moral and intellectual apprenticeship,[33] he must have been at least partly conscious that irony had accrued to his relationship with the Lady Margaret, now that his wife had returned. When he republished it in 1673, other ironies must have attached themselves to "the sad breaking of that Parlament," and the "dishonest victory . . . fatal to liberty" whose later versions Milton had tried unsuccessfully to prevent in 1659/60. As history moved on, the *words* of the sonnet, its disingenuities notwithstanding, were capable of carrying the message to the Restoration that Milton claimed he had never stopped proclaiming, "though fall'n on evil days." If he was not, as he also proclaimed, "unchang'd" over time, he registered his changes with a subtlety that deserves our continued attention. Above all, at age 63, Milton would probably have smiled over the expanding meaning of "that Old man eloquent," with whose relationship to political liberty he had taken certain liberties in the early 1640s, as in *Areopagitica* he had mystified the Isocratean position on censorship. And as in the sonnets that follow the occasionalist, activist phase Milton invited his friends to consider "what may be won / From the hard Season" (sonnet 20), or to learn "To measure life . . . betimes" (sonnet 21), so his writings in their totality (an *oeuvre* if ever there was one) will continue to invite meditation, or theorizing, on the relation between lives and works, works and days and on what, finally, eloquence is.

3 • Forced Allusions
Avatars of King David in the Seventeenth Century

Mary Ann Radzinowicz

During the seventeenth century, Englishmen supposed that they could think of their own times and write clearly about them by recalling the rise of King David as represented in 1 Samuel. Within the five years from 1649 to 1654, when King Charles was defeated in the Civil War, tried as an enemy of the people and beheaded, and the victorious general Oliver Cromwell made all but king, three writers—Thomas Hobbes, Abraham Cowley and John Milton, two royalists and one republican—explained what they saw around them by reference to David. Each alluded to King David, having reviewed 1 Samuel to confirm his intuition of a telling similarity, colored by interesting differences, between David and either Charles or Cromwell. Allusions are instruments of a writer's intention; Hobbes, Cowley and Milton were explicit about their intentions in alluding to David. Nevertheless, in each case the actual allusions may be described as "forced" in both senses of that word, both strained and constrained. All three writers make strained or overwrought allusions in facing the awkward fit between scriptural David and his royal avatar Charles or his republican avatar Cromwell. To episodes in David's story chosen by their opponents to illustrate political points, they make constrained or obligatory allusions. This essay will describe the Davids of Hobbes, Cowley and Milton, and will discuss the intentions, the awkward fits, and the constrained choices in their allusions.

This paper, having shown how scriptural allusion was destablized by three writers in a common brief moment of history, will argue that, detailing David's rise, Scripture itself incorporates ideological conflict and hermeneutic complexity. Allusion to King David is inevitably forced due to ambivalences in the text; thus, strained or constrained readings of 1 Samuel are not defective, though they are unstable. Scriptural allusion is a special case of a general literary device. The Bible is called canonical in two senses: in the literary, a book of permanent value; and in the teleological, a measure and representation of value itself. Individual books of the Bible stake the same double claim: they are beautiful and relevant, they are illuminating and true. Generally, we assume that a seventeenth century reading of 1 Samuel took that text seriously, but on examination, that book not only generates and sustains contrary or ironic allusions, it compels them. Its ambiguity with respect to David's political rise is a source of power; the works of Hobbes, Cowley and Milton respond to the text's arresting inconsistencies.

David, as a literary character, interested the young Milton more than any other Old Testament human figure. When he listed in the Trinity Manuscript, his writer's notebook, the biblical subjects he intended to turn into tragedies, Milton chose more scenes from David's life than even from the lives of Adam and Samson—among them four episodes from David's rise to kingship.[1] But Milton wrote an epic for Adam and a tragedy for Samson, while in poetry he depicted David's sole achievement as genealogical, as a regal link in the chain of descent from Adam to Jesus. (In *Paradise Lost*, David establishes a "Royal Stock"; in *Paradise Regained*, he has left a heritable *"David's* Throne."| Only in polemical prose does Milton actually allude to David's rise to kingship, interweaving with episodes that were the common property of pro- and anti-monarchists in the seventeenth century those original episodes by which he first meant to "instruct and better the Nation at all opportunities," "teaching over the whole book of sanctity and vertu through all the instances of example" by means of "wise and artfull recitations" "in Theaters, porches, or what other place" (*YP* 1.819, 817, 820).

The story of David might interest any writer, it so strongly blends folklore, ritual, and history. The folk hero David is a giant-killer, chosen when seven elder brothers are rejected.[2] The ritual David embodies all the common motifs of enthronement psalms: the people's demand for a leader as the enemy gathers, his secret anointing, his divine support, his arrival on an ass, the enemy's defeat, his return with the Ark of the Covenant, his ecstatic naked dancing, his public anointing. The historical David presides over Israel's gradual change from pastoral tribalism to a nation-state.[3]

This vivid story, however, became the inspiration for seventeenth century allusion when its writers perceived a contemporary parallel either in David who acquired a kingdom, lost it, and regained it, or in David who came from obscurity to bring peace to the nation, taking power when the old king faltered. Then royalists like Hobbes and Cowley or republicans like Milton tilted David to flatter or attack Charles or Cromwell, or to support or critique the institution of hereditary kingship.

Allusion unites two texts within a context, and in this case unites an ambivalent scriptural text to polemical views of a transitional time. The first book of Samuel supports multiple, even incoherent political and literary interpretations because it incorporates multiple, even incoherent interpretations, as its narrator and personages struggle to reconcile their sense of destiny, or of God's promise, with their known historical realities.[4] Fragmented and ironic readings of such ambivalent texts are synonymous with what one might call "honest" readings. While suggesting that a destiny like David's shaped their own times, Hobbes, Cowley and Milton created Davids of striking dissimilarity. Hobbes's David is a historical administrator whose gifts of leadership brought into being a stable monarchy, reflecting God's detestation of anarchy; Cowley's David is a fearless cavalier to whom all hearts warm, male, female or divine, displaying the charm of royal power; Milton's David is as self-directed and shrewd as Hobbes's and as beautiful as Cowley's, but his deeds illustrate God's will that men use the freedom he gives them to create more freedom. As these varied representations compete for political credence, they reveal allusion to be a problematic means of securing one's intentions. The three writers make coercive allusions to their equivocal foundation text. They use what they presume to be stable currency to influence what they experience as a uniquely significant moment, sharing the sense of living in an era of profound change. Their allusions are destabilized, however, by the weight of the unusable the writers suppress in the canonical text, or by the quantity of the unprecedented they find in their own contexts; these allusions are further undermined by their counter-applicability.

All books of the Old Testament are ambiguous, since old traditions have been editorially reworked in them in attempts to create doctrinal coherence from historical data. The first book of Samuel has its own particular form of that common ambiguity, though it describes the years from Samuel the prophet to David the king of Judah in brilliant detail and clarity. It reads like an earlier history taken in hand by a gifted narrator, who dramatizes the tradition by endowing its persons with vitality and complexity; that narrator has an editor who knows the story is meant to show that God rules destiny but, not trusting the tale, interrupts it to editorialize. While 1 Samuel glorifies David and seems deliberately to play down Saul's achievements,[5] it gives enough detail so that Saul could be seen as the legitimate ruler, striving to hold a new kingdom together and widely supported by his subjects, but threatened by the unscrupulous rebel David, who kills all possible informers against him and, to gain power, even allies himself with the Philistines. Milton proposed to write two tragedies on the combined story of David's rise and Saul's fall, calling the first "Saul in Gilboa" and the second "David revolted" (*YP* 8.555). The doubling respects both the Bible's narrative detail and its insistence that God wills David's dynasty. Samuel's episodic plot and overdetermined message is unified by David's willingness to answer to Samuel's prophetic vision and to replace Saul under God's revisionary plan, by which the king is promised not only monarchic but messianic descent. That plan says that the king rules by God's assent. Writers of the seventeenth century expected Scripture to afford a helpful political model. But the thesis that the king rules by God's assent is deeply ambiguous. Hobbes and Cowley say that it means absolute kingship; Milton, provisional temporal rule under God.

Whoever sought authority from 1 Samuel in the seventeenth century would feel obliged to expound at least three crucial episodes in which the text derives the king's rule under God:[6] the people's demand of Samuel that God give them a king like other nations (1 Samuel 8), and David's refusal on two occasions to kill Saul, the Lord's anointed (1 Samuel 24 and 26). Allusion to these episodes was made necessary by their persistent use in controversy, by such writers, for example, as John Goodwin in *Anti-Cavalierisme* (1642), Samuel Rutherford in *Lex, Rex* (1644), John Gauden in *Eikon Basilike* (1649), Salmasius (Claude Saumaise) in *Regii Sanguinis Clamor ad Coelum* (1649) and so on. It was also to those episodes that the monarchists turned, casting David in the mold of heroic kingship; consider Hobbes in *Leviathan* (1651), and Cowley in *Davideis* (written between 1650 and 1654).[7] And to them Milton turned, drawing David as an admixture of destiny and free choice in *The Tenure of Kings and Magistrates* (1649), *Eikonoklastes* (1649), and *The First Defence of the English People* (1651).

In *Leviathan* Hobbes defends a self-perpetuating sovereign state by allusion to "the Supernaturall Revelations of the Word of God,"[8] and emphasizes the transfer of power from the prophet Samuel to the warrior-king Saul and on to the dynastic ruler David. He asserts his own orthodoxy in writing a work containing nothing "contrary to the Word of God"

(727; 651–52) and he insists on the congruity of his religion and his politics, though from his own day to ours readers have found his intentions equivocal.[9] He begins by asking: what is the source of scriptural authority? Hobbes denies that it rests on eyewitness reliability: "the Books of *Samuel* were . . . written after his own time . . . long after the time of David" (419).[10] Nor does its authority derive from an unbroken priestly mediation; Hobbes writes that "whosoever had the Soveraignty of the Commonwealth amongst the Jews, the same had also the Supreme Authority in matter of Gods . . . worship; and represented Gods Person . . ." (512). The Bible is authoritative when the sovereign of the commonwealth declares its authority and enforces an official interpretation: "for, whosoever hath a lawfull power over any Writing, to make it Law, hath the power also to approve, or disapprove the interpretation of the same" (427). Because he is the subject of a Christian king who authorizes Scripture, Hobbes regards 1 Samuel as a binding text, but he notes that an agnostic or resident alien "is not obliged to obey [God's Laws], by any Authority, but his, whose Commands have already the force of Laws; that is to say, by any other Authority, then that of the Commonwealth, residing in the Soveraign, who alone has the Legislative power" (426).

Its authority established, Hobbes offers his reading of Samuel: the book shows that "the Kingdome of God, instituted by Moses, ended in the election of Saul" (639). Before God instructed Samuel to comply with the Jews' demand for a king—but to warn them what kingship would be like (1 Samuel 8.9), he assured Samuel, in a verse Hobbes cited more often than any other involving kingship: "they have not rejected thee, but they have rejected me, that I should not reign over them" (1 Samuel 8.7). God lodged power in Saul as a royal commander-in-chief, "captain over my people Israel, that he may save [them from] the Philistines" (1 Samuel 9.16). When Saul grew unstable, Samuel transferred sovereignty to David. Hobbes explains: "in this sense the Spirit of God is said, upon the anointing of David, to have come upon David, and left Saul; God giving his graces to him he chose to govern his people, and taking them away from him, he rejected. So that by the Spirit is meant Inclination to Gods service; and not any supernaturall Revelation" (465). Hobbes concludes of the "Right of Kings": "This is absolute power . . . summed up in the words, you *shall be his servants* . . . [T]he people heard what power their King was to have, yet they consented" (258).

In support of the "absolute power" in kingship, Hobbes considers David's twice refusing to kill Saul, "God forbid I should do such an act against my Lord, the anointed of God" (1 Samuel 24.9; 26.11). Hobbes claims that the refusals confirm the grant of absolute power. David's prayer is not meant to show his rectitude but his intelligence in acknowledging that the king is God's representative. Hobbes writes:

> The Laws of God are none but the Laws of Nature, whereof the principall is, that we should not violate our Faith, that is, a commandement to obey our Civill Soveraigns, which we constituted over us, by mutuall pact one with another. And this Law of God, that commandeth Obedience to the Law Civill, commandeth by consequence Obedience to all the Precepts of the Bible, which is there onely Law, where the Civill Soveraign hath made it so; and in other places but Counsell; which a man at his own perill, may without injustice refuse to obey (612).

From 1 Samuel forward, Hobbes says, the Old Testament conveys one over-arching message: the history of man's obedience to the kingly stock of David until his descendent Jesus be born.[11]

Hobbes takes little interest in the character and motives of David;[12] his power and place, not his person and gifts, command Hobbes's attention. He admits neither to finding ambiguity in 1 Samuel nor to applying the text ambiguously to contemporary affairs. He explains Saul's dethronement psychologically, not theologically; it was caused by the melancholy that made him ask the Witch of Endor to predict his future. She had no prophetic power:[13] her "Imposture" was "guided . . . to be a means of Sauls terror and discouragement; and by consequent, of the discomfiture by which he fell" (458). Hobbes holds, "there is scarce a Common-wealth in the world, whose beginnings can in conscience be justified" (722). And of its endurance, he writes: "Presumption of a future Ratification is sometimes necessary to the safety of a Commonwealth as in a sudden Rebellion, any man that can suppresse it by his own Power in the Countrey where it begins, without expresse Law or Commission, may lawfully doe it, and provide to have it Ratified or Pardoned, whilest it is in doing, or after it is done" (724). Good kings or bad, Hobbes thinks "Humane Nature, and the Laws Divine, (both Naturall and Positive) require an inviolable observation of the mutuall Relation between Protection and Obedience" (728). While he does not say that Charles resembles David, he repeatedly says that Israel's choice of kingship was a willed removal of power from God to his human agents on earth, leading to the "commandement to obey our Civill Soveraigns" in sustaining that transfer (612).

In brief, Hobbes's use of King David is more opportunistic than literal. Had King Saul been granted a sweeter afterlife in biblical mythology, he would have provided as firm a foundation for Hobbes's absolutism as David came to. Hobbes ignores David's political progress within a long reign from boy hero or warrior king, through spokesman and defender of the faith, to monarch established in God's name and stead, such transitions being nothing to his argument; there, only power in the status quo counts. The people, having effectually instituted kingship by consenting even to its grimmest conditions, are given Saul; they retrospectively ratify David's claim to the crown. For Hobbes, David's importance is his coronation, not his evolution. While Hobbes notes that with David a threshold is crossed, his rational and teleological hermeneutic excludes unnecessary historical narrative.

Hobbes's biblical allusions may scarcely seem forced (in the sense of appropriated or strained only by non-Christians), but they are forced in the sense of being constrained. Hobbes supports the institutional arrangements of the Christian states by referring to a book in Scripture where kingship is displayed as arbitrary in inception and sustained by cunning, murder and stealth. Hobbes turns this paradox to his advantage. But Scripture likewise displays this kingship as inefficient and doubtfully predestined. Why should allusion to a slippery case history seem to Hobbes to prove anything at all? Is not the answer that his allusions to three standard episodes are obligatory responses to republican citations?

Cowley projected a twelve-book epic *Davideis*, but completed only four books, written between 1650 and 1654, before, during and after the publication of *Leviathan*. He planned, he tells us in a footnote to book 1, to begin with David's flight from Saul's jealousy and end with his inauguration as King of Judah (1677, 24). The completed books are rich in biblical flashback and scroll-forward, largely taken from 1 Samuel 18 to 2 Samuel 2, but drawing on the alternative account of David's rise in 1 Chronicles. Cowley's temporal disruptions, digressions, and amplifications imitate classical epic. The David at the center is represented, until book 4, as a hero of epic romance, ennobled by a perfect friendship and elevated by the pains of love. The third book, for example, is a typical epic rest-and-recreation book dilating on love themes.[14] David Trotter suggests that Cowley broke off *Davideis* because of his sense of conflict over both the genre and the ideology of the work. He argues that Cowley was stymied by the requirement that epic achieve sublimity, when he himself believed that "truth is truest poesy." Although he considered his "sacred" subject sublime and true,[15] Cowley felt tied to the conventions of epic machinery; they strained beyond endurance his sense of probability. Equally, Cowley was afflicted by political ambivalence: he hoped to identify David with Charles, his preferred ideal, but he saw how Cromwell, the head of a stable Commonwealth, might recall David, a regal model he would prefer not to accept as the will of history.[16]

I shall not try to guess why Cowley broke off the project *Davideis*, for Trotter well explains his problems. But clearly when he got to book 4, Cowley confronted ambiguities in the text itself on which his epic depended, and they help us to guess why he broke off *where* he did. In that book, Cowley takes up the first of the three episodes monarchists are constrained to treat. After various adventures in his flight from Saul, David reaches Moab's court, where according to Cowley the king asks him to explain "the Reasons of the Change of Government in Israel [and] how Saul came to the Crown" (1710, 433). David responds with the story of God's granting kingship to the people. He summarizes the four hundred years of biblical history from Joshua to his own day as years of private immorality and political anarchy. In a footnote *in propria persona* Cowley writes: "For all the Wickednesses and Disorders that we read of during the time of the Judges, are attributed in Scripture to the want of a King" (1710, 491, n9). Cowley then cites not quite the last words of the Book of Judges, "And in those days there was no king in Israel," omitting the last clause, "but every man did that which was right in his own eyes." The whole sentence ironically undermines the point Cowley finds in the first clause: that wickedness and disorder may be cured by doing what seems right in a king's eyes.[17] Cowley thinks his cropped verse endorses kingship wholeheartedly; but 1 Samuel registers both God's alienated warning and his compliance, and its sequel shows Israel's and David's difficulty in securing stability and morality. Cowley planned his epic to trace David's rise to kingship not of Israel but only of Judah, so as to end before David's disorderly sons did that which was right in their own eyes. As he cuts short the last words of Judges to quench their ambiguity, he stops before the disruptive and immoral squabbles over dynasty compromise David's kingship.[18] He presents his subject as unblemished:

> [W]hat worthier *subject* could have been chosen among all the *Treasuries* of past times, then the *Life* of this young *Prince*; who from so small beginnings, through such infinite troubles and oppositions, by such miraculous virtues and excellencies, and with such incomparable variety of wonderful actions and accidents, became the greatest *Monarch* that ever sat on the most *famous* Throne of the whole Earth? whom should a *Poet* more justly seek to *honour*, then the highest Person who ever *honoured* his Profession? whom a *Christian Poet*, rather then the *man after Gods own heart*, and the man who had that sacred pre-eminence above all

other *Princes*, to be the best and mightiest of that Royal Race from which *Christ* himself, according to the flesh, disdained not to descend? (1949, 70).[19]

David explains to Moab "the just and faultless Causes, why / The general Voice did for a Monarch cry" (1710, 439); the people feared both "foreign Thral" and civil war, the "frequent Curse of our loose-govern'd *State*" (1710, 437). But God detected bad faith within their dutifulness to him and, while acceding to their reasonable demand, hedged the institution of monarchy with warnings. In the course of justifying monarchy by reference to the genuine political problems involved in founding a nation state, David seems to Moab to overstate the dangers of kingship. Moab remonstrates:

> The good old Seer 'gainst Kings was too severe.
> 'Tis Jest to tell a People that they're Free,
> Who, or how many shall their Masters be,
> Is the sole doubt; Laws guide, but cannot reign;
> And though they bind not Kings, yet they restrain.
>
> (1710, 444)

David concedes that old men fear changes so much that "they believe, / All evils will, which may from them arrive." But Cowley explains the warning episode otherwise in a footnote. Unlike Hobbes, he denies that Samuel's words "This shall be the manner of the king that shall reign over you" and "ye shall be his servants" (1 Samuel 8.11,17), can be construed as establishing "the Right of Kings": "Neither did the People of Israel ever allow, or the Kings avow the Assumption of such a Power" (1710, 492). Cowley is constrained to allude to the episode so widely used to support monarchy, but ambivalently registers its ambiguity.

Cowley then represents David's worthiness to succeed Saul, confining his ideological pressure (in the latter part of book 4) to scattered brief passages with a Hobbesian flavor:

> The Crown thus sev'ral Ways confirm'd to *Saul*,
> One way was wanting yet to crown them all;
> And that was Force, which only can maintain

The *Power* that *Fortune* gives, or *Worth* does gain.
(1710, 459)

David manifests his worthiness by the magnanimity with which he characterizes Saul and Jonathan to Moab, quietly describing how God turned against Saul and foredoomed him. As an interregnum royalist Cowley has sought to make his material pleasingly contemporary without displeasing any powerful contemporary. The last scenes of book 4 show Saul and then Jonathan on the battlefield, in hyperboles conventional to secondary epic.[20]

In brief, Cowley's hermeneutic was scholarly and led to rationalistic footnotes on biblical cruxes, given without political or generic exaggeration. He chose and began to shape, however, a unit of action meant to honor David as the symbol of monarchy, perfect in magnanimity and forbearance. He broke off on the very threshold of David's refusal to kill "the Lord's anointed."

Milton relegated to political prose the four episodes from 1 Samuel he earlier meant to treat dramatically. He found those episodes marginal even in controversy, however, when he felt obliged to take up the politically hotter stories of the institution of kingship and David's mercy to Saul. But he did not entirely abandon them. The first episode, a story of duplicity and retribution, Milton entitled "Doeg slandering" in the Trinity MS. The first book of Samuel 22 tells how David flees from Saul's jealous rage to Nob, where Saul's chief herdsman Doeg sees Ahimelech the priest give him hallowed bread.[21] Doeg denounces them to Saul as co-conspirators and at Saul's command murders eighty-five priests of Nob, only Ahimelech's son escaping. The son reached David with the news and David laments his own role in the deaths. Milton both politicizes and moralizes the episode in *Christian Doctrine*: he calls David an involuntary magnet for "anyone that was down on his luck," and finds Doeg guilty of "calumny, which puts the worst construction upon everything" and servility in thinking that he owes the king "obedience in unlawful things."[22] Several dark considerations render Milton's title, "Doeg slandering," equivocal,

however. David neither warned Ahimelech that Saul thought
him an enemy nor stopped Doeg from returning to inform
on him; those silences led to the deaths of the priests.
Moreover, Saul demanded a reprisal so brutal that only the
outsider Doeg would execute it. Milton chose an uneasy
plot, stained with madness and expediency, shaped in the
Bible to exculpate David and condemn Saul, yet exposing
David's dangerous plausibility.

The episode Milton entitled "The sheepshearers in Carmel:
a pastoral" tells how, at Abigail's intercession, David stayed
his hand against her foolish husband Nabal, who had been
provokingly rude to him. He then married Abigail when God
(not he) killed Nabal (1 Samuel 25). In Scripture, the story
divides the two occasions when David spares Saul, where
he shows a spontaneous forbearance in contrast to the
forbearance he learned in the Nabal scene. That David is
taught virtue may have commended this scene to Milton.[23]
He cited it in *Christian Doctrine* to rebuke Nabal's discour-
teous tight-fistedness—his very name in Hebrew is a moral
onomastic, Ignoble One, an ultimate contrast to David (*YP*
6.731, 769).

Milton intended to make two tragedies out of the same
chapters that end 1 Samuel and proposed the titles "Saul
in Gilboa," emphasizing the end of Saul's story, and "David
Revolted," marking the beginning of his story. That stress
highlights not only the text's double perspective but also
its chiastic shaping of its material. Milton alludes to "Saul
in Gilboa" in *Eikonoklastes*, written in 1649, the year *Eikon
Basilike* appeared and he was assigned the task of answering
it. The first book of Samuel narrates Saul's fall in two scenes
set atop Mount Gilboa, where Saul is encamped as the
Philistine army assembles below. Fearing encirclement, Saul
asks God's guidance. When Yahweh is silent he consults
the witch of Endor; she raises Samuel from the dead. Samuel
reminds him that God deserted him for having spared the
Amalekite king and his herds in war, though God ordered
their annihilation. Samuel foretells the deaths of Saul and
his three sons in battle. In the second scene, the prophecy
is fulfilled: with his sons dead and the battle lost, Saul asks

his weapon bearer to kill him and, being refused, falls on his own sword.

Milton found it easy to turn Saul against Charles in *Eikonoklastes*, for in *Eikon Basilike*, supposedly the king's prison autobiography, but compiled and largely written by the Presbyterian clergyman Gauden,[24] Charles was shown piously quoting David's psalms. Milton depicts Charles as a Saul in David's clothing; he writes: "Most men are too apt, and commonly the worst of men, so to interpret and expound the judgments of God, and all other events of providence or chance, as makes most to the justifying of thir own cause" (*YP* 3.429). Saul first claimed that he obeyed God's command against the Amalekites but later confessed, "I feared the people and obeyed their voice." Milton writes of Charles:

> [He] for feare to displease his Court, and mungrel Clergy, with the dissolutest of the people, upheld in the Church of God . . . those Beasts of *Amalec*, the Prelats against the advice of his Parlament and the example of all Reformation; in this more unexcusable then *Saul*, that *Saul* was at length convinc'd, he to the howr of death fix'd in his fals perswasion; and sooths himself in the flattering peace of an erroneous and obdurat conscience, singing to his soul vain Psalms of exultation. (YP 3.434–35)

Milton turns Saul's dying sense of Heaven's desertion against Charles's pious self-pity; having used Saul to rebuke Charles, he reserves David either to symbolize the English people or exemplify the genuine love of God Charles only feigns. He repeatedly shows Charles "transported with the vain ostentation of imitating David's language not his life" (*YP* 3.555).

In 1 Samuel, the story "David revolted" is told in brief scenes variously set. When David enters the military service of King Achish of the Philistines, he is given the township Ziklag as a fiefdom. But when the battle against Saul is imminent, Achish's generals mistrust him and he is commanded to return to Ziklag. He arrives to find that the Amalekites have attacked in his absence and taken his wives and possessions. He consults Yahweh and is told to pursue them. He defeats them, kills the warriors, recaptures his own goods and divides the Amalekite booty, half to his own men in equal distribution, half to the elders of southern Judah, a generous and politically astute move. God answered David but not Saul; he required David only to pursue the Amalekites not to destroy their booty; David was the man after God's heart. Yet David's rise and Saul's fall bring equivocal benefits to God's people. Israel is once more subject to the Philistines; David, the secretly anointed, remains uncrowned at the end of 1 Samuel.

Milton balances David's rise against Saul's fall in *The First Defence of the English People*, the work also affording the strongest readings of the three kingship cruxes from 1 Samuel; he treats David less as a man after God's heart than as a self-made man, good at taking chances. But Milton will not, of course, consider Charles in the same breath as even a manipulative David. When Salmasius aligns them, Milton rounds on him:

> Again you set up comparisons between Charles and the good kings of Judah . . . saying "Take David who was both adulterer and murderer; you find nothing like this in Charles . . ." Dare you compare Charles with David, one full of superstitious fancies and a mere novice in the Christian faith with a king and reverent prophet of God, a fool with a wise man, a coward with a hero, a sinner with a saint? Can you praise the purity and continence of one who is known to have joined the Duke of Buckingham in every act of infamy? I warn you, you imitation Plutarch, to give up such foolish parallel lives for the future, lest I be forced to recount stories of Charles which I would otherwise gladly pass over. (*YP* 4.408–09)

The episodes of Saul's fall and David's rise are incidental to *The First Defence*, compared to the three crux episodes, but Milton lets us know how he read David's reception of the news of Saul's fall. In 2 Samuel, David learns of the deaths of Saul and Jonathan from an eyewitness Amalekite. The messenger, currying favor,[25] claims that Saul begged him to kill him and that he complied, a story at variance with the suicide version of 1 Samuel; David instantly orders his execution. In *Regii Sanguinis Clamor ad Coelum*, to which *The First Defense* was a reply, Salmasius argued that by ordering the execution, David acknowledged the absolute loyalty due to Saul as God's anointed. Milton entwines two contrary explanations—David either found the execution expedient or acted on an impulse of moral outrage: "Unless David, because of his supposed defection to the Philistines . . . was . . . attempting to divert from himself suspicion of having pressed the murder of the king, I cannot myself believe that David had any reason for this harsh treatment other than that man . . . gave the final blow to the king when the king was already mortally wounded . . ." (*YP* 4.404).

Milton more richly alludes to the three politically hot cruxes of 1 Samuel. He first treats the people's request for a king in *The Tenure of Kings and Magistrates* with the neutrality of one who holds God's best gift to man to be freedom. He implies that God would not bully his people even into political virtue: "God himself joyn'd with [the People] in the work [to set up a King if thy pleas'd]; though in som sort it was at that time displeasing to him, in respect of old *Samuel* who had govern'd them uprightly" (*YP* 3.209). After Charles's execution, however, Milton defends the regicides in a more tart reading: "God was wroth at their desire for a king, not in accordance with divine law, but in imitations of the gentiles, and he was wroth furthermore that they desired a king at all" (*YP* 4.351).[26] Milton considers kingship a backsliding into servitude but finds that God, in conceding kingship, conceded his chosen people the freedom to choose.

In *The Tenure of Kings and Magistrates*, Milton counters the monarchists' insistence on David's piety in twice respecting Saul's person, with his praise of David's "sanctify'd prudence" in twice mistrusting Saul's friendship: "David . . . when once he had tak'n Armes, never after that trusted Saul, though with tears and much relenting he twise promis'd not to hurt him" (*YP* 3.240).[27] In *The First Defence*, Milton rebuts Salmasius by showing that David's refusal to kill Saul arises from considerations other than an absolute and necessary obedience to God's anointed king.[28] His opening move, however, is to deny that David's act, whatever his motives, is exemplary to seventeenth century Englishmen:

> David would not act, being a private citizen; must therefore a council, a Parliament, a whole people at once refuse? He would not kill his foe by treachery; shall a magistrate therefore refuse to punish a criminal by law? He would not kill a king; and shall a senate therefore fear to touch a tyrant? He had scruples as to the slaughter of the Lord's anointed; shall a people then scruple to condemn their own anointed, especially one whose anointing, whether sacred or civil, had been washed off by continual warfare which had bathed him from head to foot in the blood of his citizens? (*YP* 4:402)

Then Milton doubts that "without popular support or magisterial command David was a proper and suitable person to slay Saul the king." Finally he depicts David as an opportunist:

> And even David, who for various reasons . . . would not slay the king his father-in-law, had no hesitation in gathering forces in his own defence and attacking or besieging Saul's cities . . . If Saul had tried to besiege Ziklag, bring ladders to its walls, and himself lead the attack, do you suppose David would have laid down his arms on the spot and betrayed his whole force to the anointed enemy? Hardly; he would have acted as we did [in bringing Charles to justice], for when he was driven to it by his own extremity he promised extensive aid to the Philistines who were his country's foes, thus doing to Saul what I believe we would never have done to our own tyrant. (*YP* 4.403–04)

I have chosen allusions to David in five works written within five years by two monarchists and one republican (though equally arresting avatars had already appeared and continued to appear in the century, most famously in Marvell and Dryden) in order to discuss allusion, seemingly a stable device, at the point at which its destabilization can yet be inferred. I want now to turn to the fragility of allusion, taking up the invitation of John Shawcross in *Intentionality and the New Traditionalism* to respect "allusion and all the connotative meaning that allusion will subtend," for "such 'devices' as allusion" provide "liminal means to enter into [a] work, the threshold over which one may step to enter the world of the literary work."[29] Choosing a biblical text deeply embedded in the culture of England, I have examined works asserting the relevance or contemporaneity of one common allusion, works drawn from a period aware of its unique importance but finding an instructive similarity to God's first chosen people. The conviction that allusion strengthens or guarantees a writer's analysis of his own times is strong there, at the moment of its crumbling. Hobbes, Cowley and Milton, writers worthy of serious attention as exegetes, found themselves forced to coopt for polemical purposes three scenes from the life of David, converting the symbolic hero of 1 Samuel—David on the threshold of kingship, anointed by God but yet to be enthroned by the people—into a figure of imperious power and equally of calculated free choice. If their allusions are devices chosen for their liminality, they are at the same time constrained by the needs of political debate.

But allusion buckles not just when it is forced to respond to previous conflicting allusions, but also under the strain of its own over-wrought inventiveness. Allusion is established by scanning a past work to confirm its similarity and difference from one's current self-representation of meaning. I suppose it may be triggered by intuitions containing many degrees of comprehensiveness. An allusive phrase may connote a good deal by recalling literary precedents. For example, in *Paradise Lost* Milton transfers to Christ the phrase "that be far from thee," alluding to the words in which Abraham and Moses challenged God to show justice; he thereby balances Christ's mercy against God's rectitude in the Dialogue in Heaven (3.154; cf. Genesis 18.25). An allusion to a genre may represent an ideal entry into a new work. Thus Milton's homage to "the three Tragic Poets unequall'd yet by any" points the reader-critic in a helpful direction in determining the shape and ethos of *Samson Agonistes*. The intuition of a recurrent pattern in human

experience itself may prompt an allusion. Perhaps his response to the tragic patterning in waves of loss and gain
directed Milton to shape an epic on the scriptural account
of the fall and promise in Genesis. Allusion to a personage
may both fall somewhere within that arc of comprehensiveness and contain degrees of comprehensiveness, from the
slight in an epithet to the comprehensive in a diagnosis. Sir
Thomas Browne alludes to Oedipus to show man as good
at riddles, Freud alludes to him to convey a universal stage
in human development. Allusion to a person may refer to
a single act of selfhood or to a history of deeds: David and
Goliath, David the man after God's heart.[30] The most comprehensive allusion to such a text as 1 Samuel would rely
on a faith in stable universal meaning.

I will end now with two twentieth century interpretations, convincing but opposed, to show how completely
allusion to David has been destabilized through the impossibility of crediting only one in the face of both. In "The
Histories of David: Biblical Scholarship and Biblical Stories,"
Regina Schwartz sets out the "ruptures" that throw doubt
on the pattern biblical scholarship represents as David's rise
and Saul's fall. She thinks that the text does not mean to
show the "development" scholars have found in it, but rather
to depict the endemic disorder of its own times. She writes:

> The institution of monarchy itself is presented from wildly
> divergent points of view, often broadly drawn. How can the
> narrative depict the 'development of monarchy' when it is
> unsettled about what monarchy is, what the nation is, and
> what it means for this entity called a nation to be ruled
> by this entity called a king? Rather than presupposing settled
> answers, the stories are intently interested in exploring such
> questions of definition.[31]

Schwartz traces the will to make coherent patterns back to
the predilections of nineteenth century historians. She
describes a disordered 1 Samuel. And she concludes: "When
we read the very discontinuities, duplications, and contradictions that biblical scholars want to smooth out, perhaps
we could take note of them, not at all surprised at the

instability in these stories: how could it be otherwise, when there is no stable ground from which to tell this story? We may even like ancient Israel's founding fiction better, not despite, but for all the cracks in its foundation" (210). Many of us would wholly assent but, wary of our postmodern predilections for cracked foundations, express our preference just as equably as Schwartz does hers.

For we may also be persuaded by a strongly patterned modern version of David. Amongst several anthropologists who have brought theories of social evolution to bear on the Bible, discovering its structures, Edmund Leach just as heartily rejects nineteenth century biblical scholarship as Regina Schwartz does, but finds an intricate pattern in First and Second Samuel as a response to the state of development of its society. He first documents the belief that God's gift of a promised land entailed endogamy, to make a people of pure blood and pure religion. He next shows evidence that the promised land was also thought of as a mixture of many peoples conquered and dominated by the Jews, who freely intermarried with them. Finally he shows the synthesis of these two beliefs in the figure of David: David's exogamous marriage to Bathsheba, morally bad, is thought in the enthronement of their son Solomon, to represent the preservation of a people of pure blood and religion, morally good. Leach summarizes:

> The historical parts of the Old Testament constitute a unitary myth-history which functioned as a justification for the state of Jewish society at the time when this part of the Biblical text achieved approximate canonical stability . . . The significance of history lies in what is *believed* to have happened, not in what *actually* happened. And belief, by a process of selection, can fashion even the most incongruent stories into patterned (and therefore memorable) structures.[32]

Many of us would agree that an adequate reading of a foundation text would be one that penetrated to its underlying patterns. But, wary of our enthusiasm for organization, we would hope also to honor the opposite impulse towards valuing in a text its uninstitutionalized elements. How can we then allude to but one David nowadays—the incoherent or the synthetic?

Allusion is certainly destabilized for us when the canonical text yields equally a sense of its certainty and its volatility. But allusion is also destabilized by being forced, in both senses of the word. Hobbes, Cowley, and Milton made historical and polemical allusions to David. Hobbes does not always convince his readers, contemporary or current, that he has recuperated from the Bible what he says he has; he has been read as an atheist recommending expedient belief, and as a Christian reformulating old truths in a changed time. Perhaps *Leviathan*'s meaning may be fixed only in the very way he said the interpretation of the Bible could be fixed—that is, by the authority of the sovereign. That conclusion is a modern view, if for the sovereign is substituted the magisterium or interpretive community. Perhaps Hobbes's allusions to Scripture are destabilizing because forced in the sense of constrained: that is, polemical devices seized on by a skeptic who wishes to convince his contemporaries by the means they themselves have shown they thought persuasive. Can Hobbes's allusion to monarchy be called forced in the sense of strained? Probably only by those who believe the Bible to have a single stable meaning and dislike his version. He coerces his readers by showing the Jews given only two political alternatives, slavery or anarchy; fearing for themselves more under anarchy than slavery, they dignify their choice as monarchy. It may seem that too little of the foundation text has been made to carry the burden of exceedingly large fears about his own day.

Cowley and Milton allude to other dissimilar but consistent Davids. Cowley's allusions are less constrained than Hobbes's or Milton's; he breaks off when he reaches the parts of the text most politicized, before he need explain David's mercy to Saul some years after England's severity to Charles. His allusions are more strained or overwrought than theirs. His David inhabits an encoded royalist tragicomic romance or masquing costume-epic. But Cowley is so far from being a negligible reader that he signposts his own allusive exaggerations in footnotes. Contrariwise,

Miltonic allusion to David is highly constrained and very little strained. The irony of the antithetical use of the crucial scenes is not lost on the writer whose favored polemical method is the point by point rebuttal of an opponent, on two occasions the opponent assigned him. Milton took advantage of the irony of counterallusions, in rebuking one such, Salmasius, for mistaking the false Samuel of witchcraft for the true: "you present us with no true Samuel, but like the witch, summon an insubstantial ghost, though I am sure that not even her hell-sprung Samuel was such a liar as to name what you call royal rights anything but unbridled tyranny" (*YP* 4.352). The effect of thrust and counterthrust polemic is also to destabilize scriptural allusion.

Allusion, then, is hard to control, hardest in times of most rapid intellectual change. The more comprehensive the proposed area of allusion, the stronger the probability becomes that the destabilization of foundation texts will render allusion not a threshold entry into a work but a will-o'-the-wisp in a bramble-thicket. Confined to simple echoes, allusion to David may remain stable though duplicitous. But since Scripture has ambiguous strands and the Commonwealth contrarious readers, the applicability of the text to the times is as easily eroded as established by allusion.

The will to make secure scriptural allusion must be satisfied within the limits of very brief historical moments or unusually homogeneous periods dominated by a single powerful episteme. Elsewhere, the urge to allude must coexist with a taste for irony, for canonical or foundation texts remain canonical not so long as they enjoy invariant interpretations but by virtue of their capacity to sustain changing interpretations. Allusion, the threshold figure able to assist a reader to cross over from one text and time into another text and another time, is an unstable instrument: its very liminality is as likely to result in imaginative constraint or excess as in imaginative freedom or discovered relevancy.

4 • "The Copious Matter of My Song"

Diane McColley

"Copia" is not popular in modern style; it seems to
assume that readers have infinite leisure. The case
I am going to make for it alleges that it is important in itself
if the language of which it is a feature is also dense and
efficient, charging the reading mind with a proliferating
awareness of connections; and that Milton's copiousness is
not a matter of length, but of many dimensions. The critical
premise of my remarks is that culture, like nature, deserves
ecological respect, as an expanding family and fabric (in the
architectural sense) of interrelations, lest we pull down the
house by demolishing or overexploiting vital parts rather
than justly renovating the shared habitat.

In reaction to the binary schematics of structural and
archetypal criticism, and because of the political aim of de-
mystifying cultural shibboleths, poststructural critics tend
to be suspicious of knowledge imported into the text, even
when the author has brought it to the reader's mind by
allusion, genre, or design. Milton thought of printed writing
as the author's life blood; reading is a sort of transfusion.
The multiple meaningfulness of his work achieves radical

renovation without destruction by cooperating with the reader's naturally, culturally, voluntarily and, some would add, divinely fashioned self to reexamine culture while preserving long-term developments that advance civility. He weaves such a multiplicity of connections into the language of his poems that when he attacks particular flaws in the stuff of civilization he does not conceptually level that civilization to rubble. Or not usually. The nearest he comes is the young Christ's devaluation of Greek and Roman culture in *Paradise Regained*; "*Sion's* songs" are enough. But even that speech is about the copious provision of one tradition at least, and one out of which the speaker's own life would bring a radical and rich new culture that would not repudiate its past.

Paradise Lost is copious in both style and matter, the plenitude of God's works and their works pouring forth in the plenitude of Milton's work. Reformation arts whose topos is Creation, whether in visual images, musical settings, or poems responsive to the creation poetry of Genesis, Job, and the Psalms, restore in some measure a consciousness that I shall only momentarily call by the unbeautiful coinage ecolographic, because it combines awareness of *oikos* (the natural and cosmic household), *logos* (utterance, cause, reason, including *rati* or proportion, hence music), and *grafh* (both drawing and writing). This densely connected way of thinking takes the effects of one's actions on as many beings (including in Milton's case superterrestrial ones) and as many cultural developments (both those worthy of conservation and those in need of iconoclasm and reinvention) as possible into account.

Because it says so many fit things at once, Milton's paradisal diction opposes the "one word, one thing" theory of Adamic language (and, conversely, the modern definition of meaning as residing in difference and hence indeterminable), not by ambiguity or self-cancelling oppositions,[1] but by mutually enhancing resonances, both textual and contextual, that vivify the engaged reader's sense of harmonic relations. Milton incorporates into the language of paradisal speakers, both Edenic and Empyreal, a comprehensive consciousness of creation (natural and cultural) and its moral implications by combining mutually resonating images, sounds, metaphors, and allusions to recreate paradisal consciousness. These connections are not arbitrary or fortuitous, but are generated by ways the universe and the human mind —luminous, limitless, yet intelligible and employable substances that they are—connect to each other. By saying not one word per thing, but several interlocking things at once, Milton puts our faculties to work concordantly, so that we are conscious of the ways the mind, that ocean of all kinds, can contain the creation and remember its interactions in our human callings as caretakers of the natural and cultural life of the planet that sustains us.

"Literary Milton" is also musical Milton, political and social Milton, naturalist and environmentalist Milton, pictorial and architectural Milton (in spite of his blindness and his iconoclasm), theodicial and theophanic Milton, and especially poetical Milton, vitalizer of language, the health and agility of which is essential to the regeneration of nature and the generation of culture. Almost any sustained passage in *Paradise Lost* will contain or suggest several of these kinds of knowledge and use them to illuminate each other. The connections between Milton's poem and the complex Judaic, Greek, Roman, and Christian culture that enters it and that it enters do not render him less original (as originator and as investigator of origins), inventive (as finder and as innovator) or inspired than a non-contextual reader might find him, but part of his innovation is to supply coherence between his work and the work of the culture he renovates by it. I would like to assess two passages, an angelic anthem and a section of Raphael's creation narrative, for ways the tissue of Milton's allusive language—where we see what John Shawcross calls the writer writing[2]—interweaves with the tissues of our minds—the reader reading—and our ethical choices—the just person justicing,[3] the life living.

THE ANGELIC *TE DEUM*: ONOMASTIC MUSIC

"The copious matter of my Song" applies to the whole song of Milton's epic. But in the context of book 3, the phrase is part of the proclamation of the victorious angels in the hymn with which they respond to the Father's acceptance of the Son's offer to die to redeem mankind:

> Hail Son of God, Saviour of Men, thy Name
> Shall be the copious matter of my Song
> Henceforth, and never shall my Harp thy praise
> Forget, nor from thy Father's praise disjoin.
>
> (3.412–14)[4]

What is copious in the view of the angels is not their song but the matter of it, providing eternal *topoi*, constituted by the Son's Name. Compared with the drama and profusion of other passages, the language of the hymn is relatively abstract and serene. This celestial plain style has led to some passive reading. In his learned and eloquent account of celestial messengers, Thomas Greene remarks that in his epic Milton

> had not . . . lost his conservative distrust of language, which had rather been deepening with the years. It affects both that style Milton accommodated to heaven and the other he accommodated to Hell. In heaven it is reflected in the abstract and colorless speeches of God and the decorous choral hymns of the angels which aim at stark simplicity.[5]

Milton's attitude toward the mimesis of heavenly language was not, in my view, distrust. He distrusted the malicious abuse and the pusillanimous misuse of language he represents in hell, but his primary interest was not in discrediting language itself but in regenerating its beauty and utility, and his poems demonstrate abuse, atrophy, and renewal according to the abilities of his characters.

The hymn is addressed to the invisible "Author of all being, Fountain of light"— inaccessible save when "through a cloud / Drawn round about thee like a radiant Shrine, / Dark with excessive bright thy skirts appear, / Yet dazzle heav'n, that Brightest Seraphim . . . with both Wings veil their eyes"— and the Son, "Divine Similitude, / In whose conspicuous count'nance, without cloud / Made visible, th'Almighty Father shines" (3.374–86). The blind poet describes the Father's invisibility in dazzlingly visual lines, raising to the mind's eye, even while they abnegate and supercede, the pictorial history of representations of angels surrounding God's throne,[6] while the Son's conspicuousness to the angels is not visible to us except by remembered pictures or daring acts of imagination. Hence the passage engages our contemplative faculties by overwhelming our perceptual and conceptual ones. The angels then recount the Son's agency in divine acts: the creation of the "Heav'n of Heavens and all the Powers therein," including themselves, and the defeat of the rebel faction. When they come to the immediate topic of their song, the Son becomes more than an agent by his "unexampl'd love." Perceiving the Father inclined to pity sinful Man, he "to appease thy wrath, and end the strife / Of Mercy and Justice in thy face discern'd . . . offer'd himself to die" (406–09). This act of celeritous discernment, compassion, and sacrifice elicits from the angels their remarkable salutation and promise that his Name will provide the matter of their song not only now but "Henceforth."

Considering the vision, drama, and theodicy packed into these lines, they seem, on contemplation, less and less stark and simple. Like *Paradise Regain'd*, they repay meditation. The anthem is even less stark if we remember that it is song and that Milton's anthems are porous to music, as his sun is to light.

Milton's distrust of high-church ritual does not apply in heaven, where "the beauty of holiness" is innocent of snobbery or manipulation and the angels raise their hymns in impromptu jubilation. On the first Sabbath, God does not keep his day of rest "in silence holy":

> the Harp
> Had work and rested not, the solemn Pipe,
> And Dulcimer, all organs of sweet stop,
> All sounds on Fret by String or Golden Wire
> Temper'd soft Tunings, intermixt with Voice
> Choral or unison; of incense Clouds
> Fuming from Golden Censers hid the Mount.[7]
>
> (7.594–600)

When angels sing on earth they employ both solo song and choral voicing for both antiphonal and full choir, as Adam reminds Eve, "Sole, or responsive each to other's note, / Singing thir great Creator: oft in bands / While they keep watch, or nightly rounding walk, / In full harmonic number join'd, thir songs / Divide the night, and lift our thoughts to Heaven" (4.680–88).

Liturgical texts set by sixteenth and seventeenth century composers were sometimes stark enough. The Nicene Creed, though astonishing, is not great poetry, yet musicians express its words in great music. Milton models his redemption hymn on the *Te Deum Laudamus*, a prose poem nearly as matter-of-fact as the creed, but makes it far more poetic than either; and he tells us enough about how the angels perform it to summon remembered experience of musical glories.

Both musical humanism and church doctrine held that the highest art combined music with words, that sung words should be comprehensible, and that music should express rather than obscure them. Neither the requirements of the Florentine Camarata nor the recurrent efforts of reformers, both Catholic and Protestant, confined the inventive energies of composers, however, any more than distrust of language confined Milton's muse. Solo voicing and homophony gained inclusion in sacred music, but few composers abandoned polyphony. Instead of chaining them to a limited style, the insistence on attentiveness to words encouraged stylistic invention; they used both plain and harmonized chant, polyphonic and homophonic harmonies, solo and choral voicing, and verbal and mimetic rhythms to express the text. At the same time, in order to increase intelligibility within polyphony, they reduced overlapping so that the familiar words of psalms and canticles could emerge within polyphonic sections. Taking their warrant from the psalms, composers for churches that retained a formal liturgy, including the Church of England, sometimes added the splendors of instrumental music—in England apparently confined to organs, but in Monteverdi's Italy, Schutz's Saxony, and Milton's heaven all kinds—combined with voices in groups ranging from small ensembles to multiple choirs.

Milton knew the music of the English church at its musical zenith and also the multichoral accompanied polyphony of Venice and Rome.[8] The *stile concertato,* using diverse voices and instruments, and the *stile concertante,* using solo voices within or in alternation with ensemble passages, had more modest native English forms in secular consort music (much of it devotional) and in a style of choral voicing that can be traced back at least to Dunstable and issued in the verse anthems and services of the seventeenth century.[9] This diversity of voicing with frequent emergence of solo voices is important to the imagining of Milton's choral anthems. A choir is also a *polis,* harmony is a metaphor for a just society, and the kind of music Milton describes demonstrates the place of the individual voice in a concenting (that is, harmonious, or *concertante*) commonwealth.

Musical Milton specifies the way the angels sing their anthem:

> thir gold'n Harps they took,
> Harps ever tun'd, that glittering by thir side
> Like Quivers hung, and with Preamble sweet
> Of charming symphony they introduce
> Thir sacred Song, and waken raptures high;
> No voice exempt, no voice but well could join
> Melodious part, such concord is in Heav'n.
>
> (3.365–71)

Literary and musical Milton provides numerous resonances by structuring the anthem after the *Te Deum,* the only nonscriptural canticle in the daily office of the Book of Common Prayer, appointed to be said or sung "After the first lesson . . . in English, daily through the whole year."[10] Milton's choice of this context is appropriate since the canticle sums up the process of salvation which his angels are praising.

The first eleven of the thirty lines of the *Te Deum* praise the Father; the eleventh belongs both to this group and to next three lines, which address Father, Son, and Holy Ghost. The central section of nine lines praises Christ, and the concluding section of eight lines is a prayer for salvation. Milton, too, allots the first eleven lines of his hymn to the

Father. The next eighteen extol the Son and his deeds, but the eighteenth belongs both to this group and the next, in which the "thou" addressed becomes the Father again. The last fifteen praise Father and Son by narrating their cooperation in mercy and acclaiming such "unexampl'd Love," ending with the salute to the "Son of God, Savior of Men" whose "Name / Shall be the copious matter of my Song / Henceforth" and which the angels will never "from thy Father's praise disjoin." This last section, with its easy changing of the addressee of the second person pronoun, illustrates the concluding statement.

The *Te Deum* begins by praising the Father: "We praise thee, O God: we knowledge thee to be the Lord / All the earth doth worship thee, the Father everlasting." Many seventeenth century composers set the first part of the second line on a steady pulse in homophonic harmony for full choir, then shift to polyphonic triple rhythm on "Father," with melismatic extension of "everlasting."[11] Milton's angels also begin by addressing the Father (syntactically echoing the Latin *Te Deum* by beginning with "Thee"), leave "no voice exempt," extend the Father's attributes across three lines, and swing into three beats for the second line: "Thee Father first they sung Omnipotent, / Immutable, Immortal, Infinite, / Eternal King" (3.372–74).

The *Te Deum* continues, "To thee all angels cry aloud: the heavens and all the powers therein," as Milton's angels are doing; he specifically alludes to this line when the angels address the Son: "Hee Heav'n of Heavens and all the powers therin / By thee created, and by thee threw down / Th'aspiring dominions" (3.390–92). These words combine the acknowledgment Satan refuses to make—that the Father created all powers of heaven, including him, by the Son—with the result of that refusal. The next lines of the *Te Deum* allude to Isaiah 6.2–3: "To thee, Cherubim and Seraphin, continually do cry. / Holy, holy, holy, Lord God of Sabaoth. / Heaven and earth are full of the majesty of thy glory," usually set antiphonally because Isaiah says of the seraphim, "one cried unto another." The ensuing lines concern human witnesses not yet born at this point of *Paradise Lost* but foreseen by the Father as those who "shall be restor'd" and live by "My Umpire *Conscience*" (3.288, 195).

The next section of the *Te Deum* begins "Thou art the king of glory, O Christ. / Thou art the everlasting Son of the Father," as the angels' anthem affirms. Milton uses "The King of Glory" in Raphael's hexameron to describe the Father's presence in the creating Son accompanied by the Spirit when Heaven's gates open "to let forth / The King of Glory in his powerful Word / And Spirit coming to create new Worlds" (7.207–09). The source for both Milton and the *Te Deum* is Psalm 24.7–10, memorably set by Handel, "Lift up your heads, O ye gates . . . and the King of Glory shall come in."

The next lines record the actions by which the Son "didst open the kingdom of heaven to all believers," the process Milton's angels are praising although they do not yet know its particulars. They praise what they do know of it, the Son's defeat of "Th'aspiring Dominations" (3.392) and his offer of "himself to die / For man's offense" (3.409). The angels' warm exclamation, with or without ghostly music, is neither stark nor distrustful of language: "O unexampl'd love, / Love nowhere to be found less than Divine!" (410).

The *Te Deum* ends with a brief litany, including the line "And we worship thy name, ever world without end." Milton's angels, too, end by magnifying "thy Name" which will be, day by day, "the copious matter of my Song / Henceforth." The sudden change to the singular "my" has either agitated or pleased critics according to their times and temperaments. John Leonard traces these responses: Richard Bentley, never afraid to tamper, changed the pronouns to the plural; Joseph Addison finds the poet "Directly Mixing Himself with the Heavenly Host"; Alistair Fowler notes that Milton alludes "to his own art, which participates in the concord of the heavenly choir"; and Barbara Lewalski observes a "deliberate ambiguity" between the voice of the narrator and the voices of the angels and remarks that "at this point, the Miltonic Bard suddenly and brilliantly exploits the ambiguity as he associates his own praises with those of the angelic choir, claiming their hymn as 'my song.'"

Leonard cites these observations while discussing this passage as an interruption of Milton's "sense of exclusion from prelapsarian language," but he finds the interruption only temporary.[12]

Milton does not depart from the genre and decorum of the anthem by this shift of pronouns. The *Te Deum* does the same in its final line, changing from "we" and "us" to "in thee have I trusted: let me never be confounded." Nevertheless, composers traditionally mime the experience of not being confounded by taking the choir through a many-voiced canon or fugue. Choral voices often use singular pronouns in liturgical music, since most are settings of scriptural texts or paraphrases of them; many of the Psalms are partly in the first person singular, yet sung in choral polyphony throughout. This practice is often part of, and acknowledged by, the kind of composition, whether verse anthem or polyphony with temporal or harmonic spacing between parts, in which singular voices are discernable within the harmony, as is suitable for a Protestant poet highly conscious of individual election (both choosing and being chosen) concerning participation in the ties or ligaments etymologically metaphorized in the word "religion." We recognize Milton's own voice joining the angels', yet the angels' song is generically uninterrupted as each particular angel within the full-voiced choir hails the Son whose "Name / Shall be the copious matter of my Song."

Since the *name* is the copious matter of the angels' *song*, we might consider ways the names of the Son are sung in sixteenth and seventeenth century music. Music is a cornucopia through which the heavens flow into our souls; add *it* to the names of the Name of names, unifying in one form the *logos* of language and the *logos* of mathematical proportion, and numerous meanings resonate together.

What Name?

As Michael Lieb explains, the writers of the Hebrew Bible do not presume to know the sacred Name of a being above human power to understand. The name they use, with limitations on both writing and pronouncing it, is Jehovah, "I am that I am," which God gives Moses as a means to speak of him and with which the Father endows the Son along with his attributes.[13] In its contracted form of "Jah" in hallelu-jah it is probably the most-sung name in the Jewish and Christian world; and, as Lieb points out, Milton's hymn culminates in a hallelujah.

The other appellations of the Son are many, but the angels do not know the human name that Gabriel will announce to Mary. "Son of God" and "Saviour of Men" are epithets rather than names. Hebrew names contain their own epithets, however, and the Son's future names of Emmanuel (God with Us) and Jesus (Saviour) may be thought to encompass those epithets uttered in heaven in response to the first announcement of his offer. In addition, by alluding to the *Te Deum*, Milton would bring to the minds of his contemporaries a line that received emphatic expressive treatment from composers: "Thou art the king of glory, O Christ." Even though this name (or title and eponym that had come to be used as a name) appears at the beginning of the section on the second person of the Trinity, composers bring the music to a major cadence on that word, and most extend it through repetition, melisma, and striking harmonic changes before the final acclamation of it on a robust homophonic chord. William Byrd in his "Great Service" sets the eight-word sentence for ten-part full choir, giving it seventeen contrapuntal entrances, with repetitions increasing the utterances of "Christ" to twenty-one. Later, in a context of five-part polyphony, Byrd changes to syllabic homophony for appropriately clear articulation on "And we worship thy Name." It would be difficult for a seventeenth century reader of an anthem modelled on the *Te Deum* not to hear that onomastic music when "Name" and "Song" conjoin.

Milton has also chosen among the names of the Son preveniently but only by allusion when the Father says "All knees to thee shall bow, of them that bide / In Heaven, or Earth, or under Earth in Hell" (3.321–22), an allusion to Philippians 2.10: "That at the name of Jesus every knee should bow, of things in heaven, and things in earth, and things under the earth." This "Name" was one of the first words composers set with the kinds of wordpainting and expressiveness associated with the sixteenth century, but adumbrated in the fourteenth in settings of divine names. John Taverner's sixteenth century motet *Mater Christi* (in both Latin and English versions), among other notable treatments, breaks into melisma on *filium* and expresses *Jesu* on long descending chords, like those of the now-familiar "Amen" after hymns, to wordpaint the idea that "at the name of Jesus, every knee shall bow."[14]

A considerable amount of cultural ecology, then, flows into and out of this hymn and particularly this name without whose bearer nothing is produced or redeemed. His name, since he is the Word of words, is copious matter for the arts of angelic and human beings because its bearer speaks into being all living things, by his incarnation joins their lives, and by atonement redeems their specificity so that nothing can be annihilated when "God shall be All in All" (3.341).[15]

RAPHAEL'S CREATION MUSIC

As an example of the way Milton's song incorporates the prolificity of the Word, I would like to turn now to the creation narrative in book 7, in which the Son, "th'Omnific Word," bespeaks the cosmos. As Robert L. Entzminger says, the Book of Nature is "the ongoing articulation of the Word." Mary Ann Radzinowicz observes, "The pleasure Milton proposes by his encyclopedic elaboration of the hexameron consists in detail after detail of natural vitality, grounded in the repeated and persistent identification of God's omnific Word in every act of creation." Michael Lieb quotes John Downame: "the name 'Jehovah' implies a 'Causality' by which God 'is said to *Be*' not only 'because he . . . hath his being of himself' but because '[he] giueth being to all other things'"; Lieb adds, "In this context, one thinks of the Son's act of creating the universe in *Paradise Lost*. In doing so he fulfills a divine decree: 'And thou my Word, begotten Son, by thee / This I perform, speak thou, and be it done'

(7.163–64)."[16] The beings that issue from divine Being are part of the "copious matter" summed up in the Name.

The creation days Raphael recounts to Adam and Eve are filled with "harmonious sound." God's annunciation to the angels that he "will create / Another World" evokes a *Gloria* like the annunciation to the shepherds of the Son's human birth: "Glory they sung to the most High, good will / To future men, and in thir dwellings peace" (7.182–83). When the Creator-Son comes forth in his "Celestial Equipage," "Heavn op'n'd wide / Her ever-during Gates, harmonious sound / On golden Hinges moving"—are the gates made of sound?—"to let forth / The King of Glory in his powerful Word / And Spirit coming to create new Worlds" (7.203–09). The Spirit, rarely mentioned as active before the creation, has come forth to "impregnate the vast abyss" which the "Omnific Word" now calms. The Word's first word is "Silence" (7.216–17).

The compasses with which the Creator literally circumscribes the universe have both literary and pictorial resonances,[17] and the act of circumscription echoes Job: "One foot he centred, and the other turn'd / Round through the vast profundity obscure, / And said, Thus far extend, thus far thy bounds, / This be thy just Circumference, O World" (7.228–31; compare Job 38.11 and Psalms 104.9). To this conception and picture Milton adds prosodic wordpainting, with the centered caesura after "centred," the enjambment at "turn'd / Round," and the series of halts representing the "bounds" in lines 230–31. The authorial Spirit of God then infuses, purges, founds, conglobes, disparts, and spins, and the author concludes with a line, unlike its caesuraed and enjambed predecessors, floating and self-contained: "And Earth self-balanc't on her Center hung."

Looking at one passage from the ensuing particulars of the creation narrative (any passage would do) we may see how literary, musical, pictorial, ecological, political, and theophanic Milton constructs angelic speech. Let us consider (as potentially not very promising) the generation of the fish. According to Raphael—whose epithets include "Divine Interpreter" (7.72)—on the fifth day God said:

> let the Waters generate
> Reptile with Spawn abundant, living Soul:
> And let Fowl fly above the Earth, with wings
> Display'd on the op'n Firmament of Heav'n.
> And God created the great Whales, and each
> Soul living, each that crept, which plenteously
> The waters generated by thir kinds,
> And every Bird of wing after his kind;
> And saw that it was good, and bless'd them, saying,
> Be fruitful, multiply, and in the Seas
> And Lakes and running Streams the waters fill;
> And let the Fowl be multipli'd on the Earth.
>
> (7.387–98)

Much of this passage is paraphrase from Genesis 1.20–22, with additional imagery and specificity.

John Muir, Rachel Carson, Loren Eiseley, and Edward Abbey—even Charles Darwin, omitting the "Forthwith" of 7.999 and allowing some poetic licence with regard to order—would be hard put to disagree with the generative processes Milton attributes to the Creator. God rejoices in the multiplicity of species, pronounces all of them good, gives them the habitats from which (as in both Genesis and Lucretius[18]) they spring, and tells them to increase. In a typically connective piece of imagery, birds "with wings / Display'd on the op'n Firmament of Heav'n" remind us of the second day's creation, the light-filled heavens, the empyreal Heaven, and the earthly perspective from which we, Eve, and Adam, listening, see. Raphael continues:

> Forthwith the Sounds and Seas, each Creek and Bay
> With Fry innumerable swarm, and Shoals
> Of Fish that with thir Fins and shining Scales
> Glide under the green Wave, in Sculls that oft
> Bank in the mid Sea: part single or with mate
> Graze the Seaweed thir pasture, and through Groves
> Of Coral stray, or sporting with quick glance
> Show to the Sun thir wav'd coats dropt with Gold,
> Or in thir Pearly shells at ease, attend
> Moist nutriment, or under Rocks thir food
> In jointed Armor watch: on smooth the seal,
> And bended Dolphins play: part huge of bulk

Wallowing unwieldy, enormous in thir Gait
Tempest the ocean: there Leviathan
Hughest of living Creatures, on the Deep
Stretcht like a Promontory sleeps or swims,
And seems a moving land, and at his Gills
Draws in, and at his Trunk spouts out a Sea.

(7.399–416)

Musical Milton incorporates into his prosody the kinetic, sensuous, and conceptual mimicry of the madrigalists. Most good poets use mimetic sound, whether they are musicians or not, but the intentional joining of "voice and vers" of Renaissance and early baroque composers made both poets and readers especially aware of prosodic opportunities. Raphael's creation poem is a masterpiece of "pictorialism" and other kinds of musical wit, and the creation of the animals is particularly onomatopoetic.

Madrigal composers were apt to ornament words having to do with sight, sound, touch, and motion to alert the senses to the verbal content. Milton/Raphael alerts the senses by using such words even though the words in their contexts do not refer to sense experience; he extracts double meanings from their positions in the passage. Just as musicians called attention to words about sound, Milton calls attention at the beginning of the passage to Raphael's virtuosic display of sounds by the word "Sounds," though it turns out to mean something else. He does a similar trick when he calls attention to sight, in a highly pictorial passage, with "glance/ Show," the quick succession of single syllables and the enjambment also miming both kinds of glancing; with "Graze," having set us up for a tactile image; and, for a kinetic image, with "Sea: part," for the caesura mimes "part" meaning separate, while the sense is "a portion." While alerting both the senses and the wits by these syntactic puns, he displays an array of wordpainting that connects our senses and wits with the design of the creatures and their elements. Alliterations mime the sounds of seas and swishing fish. Kinetic prosody occurs at "Sculls that oft / Bank the mid Sea"—Raphael remarks their amazingly simultaneous turns in the flick of his enjambment—and "on the Deep /

Stretched" stretches across the lines. The pause, or rest, of "at ease, attend" suspends the verse to attend the conclusion in the next line. "Fry innumerable swarm" stirs with fricatives and labials while "Glide under the green Wave" employs a gliding tongue. One can scarcely read "sporting with quick glance" without speeding up, nor "wallowing unwieldy" without slowing down. "And at his Gills / Draws in, and at his Trunk spouts out a Sea" is both kinetically and onomatopoetically imitative.

Like Milton's inset hymns, Raphael's creation poem echoes the Psalms as well as Genesis and Job; and partsinging of Psalms rang in pious households even during the Commonwealth when bare ruined cathedral choirs were silent and parish churches confined to simple tunes. Raphael's images recall for example the sublime nature poem of Psalm 104, mediated through the less sublime though imaginative metrical translation of George Sandys, which was set by Henry Lawes soon after he set the songs in Milton's *Mask at Ludlow*. Milton much refines Sandys's lines on

> The ample Sea; in whose unfathom'd Deep
> Innumerable sorts of Creatures creep:
> Bright-scaled Fishes in her Entrailes glide,
> And high-built Ships upon her bosome ride:
> About whose sides the crooked Dolphin playes,
> And monstrous Whales huge spouts of water raise.[19]

Since Sandys writes decasyllabic couplets, Milton's version could be sung to Lawes's notes as well, with much improvement of Sandys's diction, but considerable loss of Milton's verbal music.

The passage's prosodically musical delights are not just for show. They express Raphael's empathetic response to the creatures, as his language mimes their lives. The same is true of Raphael/ Milton as painter of verbal pictures and as natural historian. He depicts the creation of the animals with an observant eye, attributes virtues and intelligence to them, and takes delighted interest in their plenitude, diversity, and motion. He notices the feeding habits of various fish and whether they stray through coral groves or "sporting with quick glance / Show to the Sun their wav'd coats dropt with Gold" (7.405–06). He knows the underwater habits of shellfish and enjoys the play of seals and "bended dolphins" (7.410). Moving to the creation of the birds, he remarks the hatching, fledging, and vocal clang of shorebirds and the wisdom of geese and prudent cranes. He notes the songs of smaller birds, including Milton's own emblem the "solemn Nightingale" who "all night tun'd her soft layes" (7.435–36), the water birds bathing "Thir downie Brest," the swan who "with Arched neck / Between her white wings mantling proudly, Rowes / Her state with Oarie feet" or towers the sky, the crested crowing cock and the peacock "colour'd with Florid hue / Of Rainbows and Starrie Eyes" (7.445–46). Recounting the sixth day, he notices among the spawn of earth both flocks and herds and singular animals: lion, ounce, leopard, tiger, stag, elephant, hippopotamus, and crocodile (all of whom have multiple emblematic connotations[20]). He focuses on the perfectly formed limbs of insects who "wav'd their limber fans" and decked their liveries "With spots of Gold and Purple, azure and green," worms "streaking the ground with sinuous trace," the communally provident ants who "in small room large heart enclos'd / Pattern of just equity perhaps / Hereafter," the "Femal Bee that feeds her Husband Drone / Deliciously, and builds her waxen Cells / With Honey stor'd," and the subtle serpent "with brazen eyes / And hairie Main terrific, though to thee / Not noxious, but obedient to thy call" (387–498).

Political and moral Milton makes himself evident in this narrative by invoking political virtues like prudence and organizing for mutual aid and including both singularity and commonality. The thread is carried through in the solitary or marital state of fish "part single or with mate" and birds who fly "Part loosely" while "part more wise / In common, ranged in figure wedge thir way . . . with mutual wing / Easing thir flight" (7.403, 425–30). Orderly mutuality is clearly a figure of a well-ordered commonwealth, yet Milton makes room for singularity even while calling mutual help "more wise." Since God created "each / Soul living" even as water or earth "generated" them, each soul is valuable. Applied to human or angelic harmony, where free agents may be singular or mutual as best suits the occasion, this political thread ties to the verse anthem with its voices "Sole, or responsive."

Literary and theodicial Milton raises questions that distrusters of language might see as undermining his theodicy by including "Leviathan," "the wild beast where he wons / In Forest wild," "The River horse and scaly Crocodile," serpents with "Snaky folds" and "brazen Eyes," beasts whose literary connotations resonate with evil and chaos. These references do not subvert Raphael's celebration of God's ingenuity and providence, his all-in-allness, because Raphael's speech assures us that God made nothing evil by calling the serpent "Not noxious"—in contrast to Virgil's *Georgics* where Jove "put fell poison in the serpent's fang" as a deliberate hardship to energize naturally lazy humans[21]— and allying with "play" that Leviathan whom Psalm 104 says God put among the innumerable creatures of "this great and wide sea . . . to play therein." Leviathan in Isaiah 27.1 is the "piercing" and "crooked" serpent whom "God shall punish," but in *Paradise Lost* he is a natural beast "which God of all his works / Created hugest that swim th'Ocean stream" (1.200–02). Although in this simile Milton is indeed comparing Leviathan with Satan, in the alternatives of his epic simile he compares Satan's activities with the rebellion of the Titans, and only his size to "that Sea-Beast Leviathan" (apparently a species of whale or sea-serpent) and exempts him from primordial myths of adversaries to the gods, since this Leviathan is a natural animal "which God . . . created" and on which many a lost seaman anchors and "Moors by his side under the Lee." Of course, the mariner is not secure under this lee, since the whale might suddenly wake and "Tempest the Ocean" when someone fixes an anchor in his rind, and the natural animal thus serves to warn those who think to harbor with Satan. Yet the Leviathan in this simile does not do so; the benighted Pilot "With fixed Anchor in his scaly rind / Moors by his side" while "wished morn delays" (1.206–07). Milton's benignity toward sea mammals is the more striking in comparison with Sylvester's Du Bartas, whose opinion he allusively alters in both this simile and Raphael's description. Du Bartas asks, "Shall I omit the monstrous Whirl-about, / Which in the Sea another Sea doth spout, / Where-with huge Vessels (if they happen nigh)/ Are over-whelm'd and sunken sodainly?"[22]

The "River horse and scaly Crocodile" are the two creations that the voice from the whirlwind in the great theophany to Job delights in at greatest length, not euphemizing their power but stretching human thought to encompass beings beyond its wildest invention.[23] Like Job and the Psalms, Milton acknowledges the energy and wildness, as well as the exemplary prudence or sociability, of God's inventions, not to call the beneficence of creation into question, for no animal is noxious to Adam and Eve while they are in command of themselves, but because God's inventiveness and the dynamic powers of nature are themselves ministrations to human consciousness, producing awesome "others" whether gigantic or minimal that stretch our powers of apprehension and shrink our presumptions.

Pictorial and emblematic Milton links up to illustrations to Genesis and the Psalms, both full of pleasure in God's providence to his creatures including "both small and great beasts" (Psalms 104.25). An engraving of the creation of the reptiles, fish, and birds from a creation series by Nicholaes de Bruyn after Maerten de Vos is typical of northern European seventeenth century creation scenes. Its teeming creatures include great whales and bended dolphins, Leviathan who "spouts out a sea," birds who soar "th'air sublime" or bath "Thir downy Breast" or "on gound / [Walk] firm," and some "ambiguous between Sea and Land" (a day earlier than Milton's amphibians). It cannot include the coral groves, pearly shells, and banking schools that Raphael subaqueously perceives.

Naturalist and literary Milton supplies Raphael with details that show him to be a very observant natural-historian angel indeed: gold glints, pearly shells, jointed armour, movements and habitats observable only under water or high on "Cliffs and Cedar tops," even the air that stirred by migratory birds "floats, as they pass, fann'd with unnumber'd plumes." But

Nicholaes de Bruyn, after Maerten de Vos. *The Creation of the Water Creatures and the Fowl*, from a Genesis Series. Reproduced by permission of the Rijksmuseum-Stichting, Amsterdam.

Raphael has experienced flight both as angel and as bird on his way to tell this very story, when he "Sails . . . with steady wing / Now on the polar winds, then with quick Fan / Winnows the buxom air" and then "within soar / Of Tow'ring Eagles, to all the Fowls he seems / A *Phoenix*, gaz'd by all, as that sole Bird / When to enshrine his reliques in the Sun's / Bright Temple, to Egyptian Thebes he flies"[24] (5.268–74). He has really, not seemingly, practiced being a bird on his way to earth, since once there "He lights, and to his proper shape returns / A Seraph wing'd" (276–77); and who knows whether he has been a fish on some other occasion?

Naturalist Milton has care of the earth and respect for "both small and great beasts" at heart throughout *Paradise Lost* and shares this interest with seventeenth century naturalists and Bible commentators. Walter Blith calls God "the great Husbandman" who "made Man to Husbandize the fruits of the Earth, and dress, and keep them for the use of the whole creation."[25] Edward Topsell writes, "David crieth out, *Quam magnifica sunt opera tua domine, omnia in sapientia fecisti.* The old Manichees among other blasphemies accused the creation of hurtfull, venomous, ravening, and destroying Beasts, affirming them to be made of an evill God . . . because their dulnesse was not kinder to the Lord, (but like cruel and couetous misers, made no account of those beasts, which broght not profit to their purse)." He agrees with Augustine that "the same that appeared vgly to them, was beautifull to [God] . . . as in a great house all things are not for vse, but some for ornament, so is it in the World, the inferiour pallace of God."[26]

Many of the animals that Milton's Raphael mentions by name were recognized by early naturalists, as they have been by twentieth century zoologists and ethologists, as having particularly admirable characteristics, and these have emblematic meanings pertinent to his themes of prudence, social cooperation, and the value of entity. "Bended dolphins" often rescue and guide shipwrecked humans like the poet Arion. Milton invokes them to waft the hapless poet Lycidas.[27] The elephant who "wreath'd / His Lithe Proboscis" to amuse Adam and Eve (4.345–46) belongs to a species long known for temperance, benevolence, sociability, and piety. Caxton reported their greeting salutes in the fifteenth century: "whan they mete and encountre eche other, they bowe their heedes that one to that other lyke as they entresalewed eche other." When hunters trap a sleeping elephant by sawing down the tree it leans on, "ther come many olyfauntes to hym for to helpe hym. And whan they may not redresse and reyse hym, they crye and braye and make a me[r]ueyllous sorowe."[28] Du Bartas thought them the best beast God made, sometimes exceeding humans in prudence yet capable of passionate love.[29] Sir Thomas

Browne discusses animals who bury their dead, mentioning "Elephants, Cranes, the Sepulchrall Cells of Pismires, and practice of Bees, which civill society carrieth out their dead, and hath exequies, if not interments."[30]

Naturalist and literary Milton drew much of his description from the Ur-texts of Genesis, Job, and the Psalms. But his verses also drew on a literary tradition that is classical as well as biblical, kept its course through the Middle Ages and the Renaissance, and produced an outpouring of ecological empathy in the seventeenth century.

Virgil in *Georgicon* 1 gives precedence for empathetic and mimetic description of animal activities, as does Ovid's description in his account of the Flood in *Metamorphoseon* 1 of dolphins grazing their sides on inundated oaks and of the gaits, helplessness, and exhaustion of perishing beasts. Christian texts generally pose the relation of human beings to other animals as one of human responsibility for the animals and animal loyalty to humans. On the sixth day God creates a pair of beings in his own image whose vocation in *Paradise Lost*—and here Milton vastly amplifies his predecessors—includes the care and preservation (dressing and keeping) of an irriguous garden that epitomizes the whole earth, and turns over to them the responsibility for these other "living Souls"—all the *animae*, or animals; these human vicars are to promote by good stewardship of their habitats the increase and multiplicity which God has instituted. They too are to increase and multiply, producing "more hands" for the work of taking care of the natural world. Among medieval treatments, in the *Cursor Mundi* "Fowels of flight, and fish on sand, / All fell down at his foot and hand."[31] In the Towneley *Creation* Adam is God's assistant and intercessor, "keper of more & les, of fowles, and fysh in flood . . . All that is in water or land, / It shall bow vnto thi hand, / and sufferan shall thou be."[32] Among Renaissance writers, Du Bartas also stresses the willingness of the beasts to be ruled by Adam "And com before thee of their own accord,"[33] and Samuel Pordage claims that "each animal / Comes at his beck."[34] Milton's Creator is more considerate, since when he brings the animals to receive their names and pay fealty he tells Adam to "understand the same / Of Fish within thir wat'ry residence, / Not hither summon'd, since they cannot change / Thir Element to draw the thinner Air" (8.345-48).[35]

Adam's monarchy in these analogues is meant to govern willing, even delighted subjects whom he studies, rules, and cares for but does not exploit. Milton attributes this dominion also to Eve.[36] Both are "Lords of all" ("lord" being derived from the Anglo-Saxon "loaf-keeper" or supplier), and the innocent beasts are more "duteous at her call" (9.521) than Circe's bewitched ones because her unfallen virtue wins their trust.

What we now call an earth ethic much concerned seventeenth century writers, many of whom urged temperance and deplored the use of animals for luxuries and self-indulgence. Sir William D'Avenant casts a skeptical eye on Adam's dominion, describing a painting of the Creation in the House of Praise. The animals "play, whilst yet their Tyrant is unmade," but haughty Man terrifies "his Furr'd and Horned Subjects." Beauty, "To cure this Tyrant's sullenness . . . breaks lov'ly forth" in the form of Eve, whose breast is the cradle of quiet love; but Adam's "vain wonder" at her beauty deposes his "feeble sov'raignty." Womanly love might have been "meet help" in preventing human tyranny over other creatures, but Adam's response unmans him.[37] Abraham Cowley especially laments human violence toward song birds, who like other poets get no reward for their music; indeed, "Tis well if they become not prey."[38] Margaret Cavendish condemns the pride of Man who thinks all creatures "made for him, to Tyrannize upon."[39] Thomas Traherne, meditating on Psalm 24.1, remarks that "All Mankind and all the Earth, with all that is therin [are God's] peculiar Treasures. Since therfore we are made in the Image of God, to liv in his Similitud, as they are His, they must be our Treasures. We being Wise and Righteous over all as He is."[40]

Literary Milton has literary company, but he is not literary only by exchanging viewpoints with other writers. He not only joins a choir but composes a new song, welcoming and transforming whatever in genre, style, and echo provides matter for it. His creation narrative is literary because Milton does with language what the "Maker of that maker," as Sidney calls him, does with the matter of chaos, not just ordering but vivifying and diversifying abundant life. The words-made-flesh whose lives his verse describes retain their vitality and particularity as he turns them back into words and so incarnates them in the reading mind.

My theme is *copia*, and I have meant to argue, against critical dismantlers (his language is his prophetic mantle) that Milton's poetry continually unfolds mutually enhancing significances. How can we apply the "one word, one thing" idea to one unnamed name that provides copious matter? A distruster of language as intrinsically misleading (as opposed to a philologist aptly skeptical of its resources for deception) might find here that "absence at the center" that demotes verbal conceptions to manipulative games. My reply is to offer these samples of what the writer writing supplies the reader reading that linguistic atheists may miss and readers aware of liturgy, music, the visual arts, natural and moral philosophy, and literary history may, I hope legitimately, find. The author's signposts, whether by genre, structure, prosody, image, similarity, parallel dissimilarity, or direct allusion, alert us to these connections and so increase our capacity to hold many things together at once in minds that are, after all, designed to make connections and therefore choose courses of action that respect the creatures of God and the humane creations of human art.

5 • Hell, Satan, and the New Politician

Diana Treviño Benet

E ver since Blake suggested that, unknowingly, Milton was of the devil's party, Miltonists have labored to avoid his error by reading *Paradise Lost* with a strong bias against Satan. But our zeal has exceeded Milton's in some respects; specifically, it has misled us in book 2. This essay aims to change the way readers understand Satan and the infernal Council. Given the critical history of this character and scene, the task is not inconsequential. But I bring to the endeavor traces of what John Shawcross calls the "writer writing," materials recovered from the author's local world, and a renewed sense of how such materials can act as limina, thresholds opening into new vistas. "A major detraction from the reader reading what the writer has written . . . is an expectation perhaps derived from another reader's mis-reading, that attention to such limina would avoid."[1] The critical view of Satan and the Council has changed very little since Irene Samuel suggested in 1957 that its "obvious contrasts" with Heaven (in book 3) should guide our reading: "In Milton's Heaven the independent being [the Son, who *"argues"*] speaks his own mind, not what he thinks another would like to hear"; God "does not pretend to seek advice," though he is "the monarch Satan thought to emulate."[2] Following Samuel, readers have not identified the purpose of the scene beyond assuming that Milton meant simply to characterize Satan negatively as a tyrant.

I shall approach the Council and the early Satan by suggesting that the immediate textual context Samuel and most readers assume for the episode is inappropriate. I shall argue that the scene has both spiritual and political significance, and that awareness of the second arises from our understanding of the first. Then I shall introduce a "new" context for the scene, contemporary prose pamphlets featuring councils in Hell. These pamphlets and broadsides give us popular perspectives that illuminate Milton's treatment of politics (celestial and, especially, infernal) and of Satan.

Paradise Lost puts into juxtaposition two kinds of politics and two kinds of rulers. The poem presents the politics of unanimity as well as the politics of opposition. A combative political discourse taught Milton's contemporaries to see Lucifer as a participant in the events and internecine skirmishes dividing England. At the least, Satan had revelations to make about issues, events, and people. Meaning merely to castigate opponents, some pamphleteers added political realism to the popular image of Lucifer, casting him as a challenged leader. This crucial element identifies the prose devils as forebears of Milton's Satan. The pamphlets featuring forerunners of Satan and his Council are important for several reasons but especially because they enable us to see a subtle agonistic pattern in Milton's poem. Like the pamphleteers, Milton put Satan in situations that linked him with a recognizable figure emerging in the contemporary scene: the leader who owes his preeminence entirely to his own capacities, and who must struggle to maintain his position. A more complex figure than an evil tyrant, the able leader of sinful followers is Milton's focal point in his portrayal of the political process as it operates without a hereditary king. Satan, the chief of creatures with motives as questionable as his own, emerges in *Paradise Lost* as a new and fascinating personage: the fallen ruler of fallen creatures—

Satan represents, that is, Milton's portrait of the contemporary politician in action.

ALIENATION AND DEEPER FALLING

The significance of the infernal gathering in book 2 of *Paradise Lost* has been obscured by comparisons with the celestial scene in book 3. A more reasonable comparison would link the Council with the Exaltation of the Son, though there is an important similarity in the scenes from books 2 and 3, the identification of a difficult task for which a central character volunteers. But the difference between the two scenes is greater than the similarity. Basically, we err in comparing a discussion between the Father and the Son to a debate among various characters on a matter of public policy. The Son and the Father are personalities of the godhead, between whom exchanges of whatever nature may be dramatic without being divisive or morally objectionable.[3] The Father acknowledges that the Son, who is his "word," expresses his mind: "All has thou spok'n as my thoughts are" (3.170–71).[4] Moreover, he and the Son discuss the Father's decision regarding the sinners in Hell and on earth. This is not a question to be decided by open discussion. As we shall see, in fact, in the governance of Heaven even matters with communal impact do not proceed by general discussion.

The Council in Hell has spiritual and political dimensions, and once the first are understood, the second come into focus. The emphasis in the orators' speeches suggests that Milton intends more than political observation: the scene defines alienation from God, and it dramatizes a second fall to underscore the justice of God's disposition of the fallen. Satan calls the Council for a particular purpose, but the apostates use the announced agenda to refer again and again to their apprehension of spiritual disunity as existential reality. Satan, who gives "not Heav'n for lost" (2.14), presents Heaven as the desirable territory that victory might yet regain, Hell as the undesirable and temporary region of exile. His drive to maintain authority demands that he grant separation no more than a geographical significance. Moloch, however, speaks of separation more essentially, as exclusion from joy: "What can be worse / Than to dwell here, driv'n out from bliss, condemn'd / In this abhorred deep to utter woe" (85–87). His judgment that expiration would be "happier far / Than miserable to have eternal being" (97–98) indicates a full recognition (though without repentance) of what has been lost.

Belial remarks that disobedience altered the rebels' essence: if they were to fight Heaven, "th'Ethereal Mould / Incapable of stain would soon expel / Her mischief, and purge off the baser fire" (2.139–41). His reference to "Heav'n's highth," from which "All these our motions vain [God] sees and derides" (190–91), transforms the physical distance of Heaven from Hell into the vertical perspective of moral superiority and inferiority. God now looks down on the rebels, their manifest untrustworthiness transforming his omnipotence into a punitive attribute. God could always see all things at one view. But guilt puts the fallen angels in a position to understand the fact in a new, apprehensive way. To Mammon, separation means liberation from an envied sovereign and a strange opportunity to excel:

> Our greatness will appear
> Then most conspicuous, when great things of small,
> Useful of hurtful, prosperous of adverse
> We can create, and in what place soe'er
> Thrive under evil, and work ease out of pain
> Through labor and endurance.
>
> (257–63)

A laborious and painful existence enduring against the hurtful, the adverse, and the evil—Mammon gives a powerful description of the fallen state. Exclusion from joy, a deity perceived as punitive, an inhospitable universe, and never-ending travail are consequences of sin that Hell's inmates first discover.

But Milton leaves it to Beelzebub to explore alienation most cogently.

Thrones and Imperial Powers, off-spring of Heav'n,
Ethereal Virtues; or these Titles now
Must we renounce, and changing style be call'd
Princes of Hell?

(310–13)

Beelzebub asks the question underlying his companions' remarks: by their separation, have the apostates actually severed their link with Heaven and lost the identity conferred by that connection? In the first place, if the rebels must change their "style," they must change their characteristic mode of action. This is obvious. Secondly, if the rebels must change their "style," they must change their honorifics. Their original titles are reminders of their generation and of their dependent, secondary status; "offspring of Heav'n," especially, alludes to their maker and his status above theirs. "Princes of Hell," on the other hand, gives the rebels their own domain in which the Deity does not rank as their superior.

But Beelzebub claims that their identity is not changed. Even their spatial separation from the Father, he points out, still keeps them in relation to him. Beelzebub's view is a corrective to those preceding. God does not mean the rebels to "live exempt / From Heav'n's high jurisdiction" (2.318–19). Nor is separation a condition in which God will permit "His captive multitude" to build a parallel empire:

For he, be sure,
In highth or depth, still first and last will Reign
Sole King, and of his Kingdom lose no part
By our revolt, but over Hell extend
His empire, and with Iron sceptre rule
Us here, as with his Golden those in Heav'n.

(323–28)

Because they are still dependent upon, and defined in relation to, their superior and maker, they are still "offspring of Heav'n." Though Satan may be the rebels' chief and arrogate the trappings of monarchy, God is still their "Sole King," whose governance, power, and justice they cannot evade. They must still serve God, but pain and unwilling servitude now replace bliss and free obedience. Sinfulness, the spiritual condition authored by Satan, is not separation after all. Beelzebub is correct: there can be no true separation from God in Milton's scheme, only alienation from his love and benefits. The Council discloses how abysmally the rebellion failed to remove the fallen angels from God's domain. One of the great ironies of *Paradise Lost* is that sin lands the rebels in the very subjection they feared from the Son's Exaltation.

In addition to describing the fallen condition, the deliberation sketches a second fall. In the apostates' celestial consultation, for the sake of dramatic economy and to stress his initiating role, Satan was the sole spokesman for disobedience. Milton now dramatizes another fall of the apostates to demonstrate that all the rebels were and are responsible, "Authors to themselves in all / Both what they judge and what they choose" (3.122–23). Beelzebub suggests to his fellows that they have forfeited once and for all the ability to choose good or evil action: "What sit we then projecting peace and war? / War hath determin'd us and foil'd with loss / Irreparable" (329–31). As a response to the other orators, he represents as immutable their identity as the "captive multitude" and God's as "the Conqueror" (338). The first speakers had glimmers of themselves as righteous beings and of God as merciful: Moloch remarked, for instance, that, in Hell, "the torturing hour / Calls us to Penance" (91–92); and Belial opined that God, "in time may much remit / His anger" (210–11). He expressed the hope for a future capable of some "change / Worth waiting" (222–23). Mammon imagined that God might relent "And publish Grace to all, on promise made / Of new Subjection" (238–39). The visions of penance, hope, and grace are too potent for Beelzebub to leave before his fellows.

About the actual possibility of reconciliation, the poem is deliberately ambiguous. The Father, in the Exaltation, says that any who disobey will fall "without redemption" (5.615). Still, even in Satan, "conscience wakes despair/ That slumber'd" (4.23–24), and he wonders if there is "no place / Left for Repentance, none for Pardon left?" (4.79–80). We register the seeming inconsistency, but finally it does not matter whether or not the visions of reconciliation are illusory. Milton's ambiguity emphasizes the apostates' obduracy: Moloch judges annihilation preferable to penance (2.95–98), and Mammon rejects the idea of "new subjection" (2.239–49). Milton permits the apostates to entertain the possibility of reconciliation in order to emphasize their free choice of continuing enmity. Speaking of sinners, the Father declares in book 3:

> This my long sufferance and my day of grace
> They who neglect and scorn, shall never taste;
> But hard be hard'n'd, blind be blinded more,
> That they may stumble on, and deeper fall;
> And none but such from mercy I exclude.
>
> (198–202)

In their second fall, Satan and his associates scorn the possibility of grace. Their freedom enables them to "stumble on, and deeper fall." Milton shows that if the apostates are excluded from mercy, their eternity without redemption is just: choosing evil during the Council, they choose again their own exclusion from mercy—and they choose freely, as they are permitted to do by the politics of Hell.

FALLEN AND UNFALLEN POLITICS

Satan was a well-known politician in England long before Milton published *Paradise Lost*. Not surprisingly, public issues that often commingled governmental and church policies generated an intemperate rhetoric. Controversy created "a whole genre that in the period 1642–60 was published again and again to represent one's enemies— Royalist or Roundhead—as associated with the Devil in the councils and plots of Hell."[5] Milton was never a stranger to the impassioned rhetoric of righteousness. But in early 1660, after publishing *The Readie and Easie Way*, willy-nilly he became a member of the devil's party. The position he took about the Parliament identified him to his opponents

as a "Phanatick." The Fanatics were members of the Rump
or those who supported their continuation in Parliament.
Their opponents favored the reinstatement of the members
secluded in 1648, free parliamentary elections, and the restoration of the monarchy.[6] As Fanatics, Milton and his fellows
were accused of being the "Faithfull Servants [of] Lucifer"
and of "Submitting to onely the Government of one Prince,
Beelzebub Emperor of the Infernal Region."[7] Since Milton
was attacked as part of a group, the criticism directed at
him is not important in its particulars; what is important
is the familiarity we can assume he had with the pamphlets
and broadsides locating politicians and policies in Hell.

These prose treatments of infernal councils reveal a
startling perspective on oppositional politics and provide a
glimpse into the popular image of Satan. They vary a great
deal in their formal and literary qualities. Most feature a
degree of action, ranging from characters clapping hands to
a protagonist taking a guided tour of suffering sinners.
Dialogue and dramatic interaction are standard. The more
artistic pamphlets develop character: Satan goes from depres-
sion to equanimity after discussing his problems in *The
Devil in his Dumps*, for example.[8] The pamphlets and broadsides aim variously at social criticism, political commentary
against a particular group, satire of individuals, or attacks
on specific policies. Altogether, they present a Satan im-
mersed in English affairs, governing with the consent of his
earthly servants and with the help of a council. He might
call a parliament or a general assembly for different reasons:
to forge a truce between two of his warring constituencies,
for instance; to plot against an English parliamentary initiative that threatens his power; to encourage his servants
to continue their bad works; or to examine his followers'
records of service on Earth. Variously called Satan, Pluto,
Lucifer, Beelzebub, or the Devil, the infernal governor emerges
as a recognizable politician motivated by the ambitions or
problems of his mortal counterparts. Encouraging, threaten-
ing, and urging his followers by turns, he offers them every
assistance but demands their best service. Pluto is the
"Chaireman" who presides at hearings to examine his

followers, the leader of a political organization with committees and staff who conduct the business of Hell.[9]

This devil-politician is not secularized or morally negligible. In one of the pamphlets, his cabinet council consists of the Seven Deadly Sins, he is said to be greatly proud, and he sketches his history back to the revolt in Heaven. In others, he has the power to send the evil spirits of Nimrod and Machiavelli to the world, or he institutes an anti-ten commandments.[10] Lucifer materializes in the pamphlets and broadsides to declare that the timeless principle of evil moves men on the contemporary political scene.

There is probably no way of gauging the impact of these pamphlets on the local issues they addressed. Overall, however, the continual dramatization of infernal councils encourages the perception of oppositional politics as radical moral struggle. The pamphlets demonize politics and politicians. Whether Satan and his servants are Roundheads, Cavaliers, Brownists, or Fanatics, the infernal councils impose a rigidly bipolar perspective on civil affairs. Policies are not simply mistaken, unpalatable, or impractical when positions on contested issues are equated with moral status. They become the standards rallying the forces of light and darkness, and issues become battles in the universal war.

The disagreement of opponents evinces their moral corruption. Obviously, the demonization of oppositional politics completely disallows dissension, insisting instead on the presumably intuitive recognition of the "good" perspective on any issue. There is no room in this view for honorable difference of opinion or for compromise (good cannot combine with evil, as Belial reminds us in book 2 of *Paradise Lost*). This formulation of opposition implies as ideal a politics of unanimity, in which spiritual uprightness automatically produces a specific frame of mind (though one might object that a "politics of unanimity" is politics no longer). If this sounds familiar, it is of course the situation in Heaven, where a dynamic of unanimity underlies the management of what we might call civil affairs. There, disagreement with the policies of the Father is evidence of moral corruption. As Abdiel reminds Satan in book 5, agreement with the position of the righteous is the only possible defense against the charge of sinfulness. In Heaven, the moral purity of the inhabitants is expressed in their unanimity: the community of spirit holds while they "abide / United as one individual Soul / For ever happy" (5.609–11).

The best illustration of Heaven's governance by unanimity is in the Exaltation of the Son. Because the Father's announcement concerns all the angels this is a more appropriate parallel to the infernal Council than the celestial dialogue of book 3. The Father tells the angelic host that the Son will reign over them, adding: "him who disobeys / Mee disobeys, breaks union, and that day/ [is] Cast out from God and blessed vision" (5.611–13). Demanding total obedience, the Father allows no space for discussion about this hierarchical decision. Nor does Satan think of a verbal challenge to the declaration from on high. Understanding that discussion (or the desire for it) implies a breach of union, he withdraws to gather his strength for a military confrontation. Debate is simply unknown between the Father and the angels. Merit and goodness on the one side and faith on the other join to produce the dynamic of unanimity. The Exaltation shows the chief difference between the governance of Heaven and of Hell: in Heaven the Father's undoubted love and goodness are assumed by the faithful to generate all his decisions and policies; therefore, he elicits their unquestioning and joyful obedience. In Hell, such certainties regarding leader and followers are lost: Satan's merit or preeminence is not a matter of faith and the apostates' acquiescence to his initiatives is doubtful.

Perhaps Satan would like to govern as the Father does in Heaven, by universally acclaimed fiat, but for all that he sits "High on a Throne of Royal State" (2.1), he is not a true king, superior in essence and by merit to his followers— only God can be that in *Paradise Lost*. Satan, immediately after his rebellion, learns that his rule cannot follow the Heavenly model and, altogether, he confronts three challenges in *Paradise Lost*. His fall might be said to create disputation, since it provokes the dissension of Abdiel, arguing against the rebellion of his chief. Subsequently, during the war, Nisroch's dread of pain produces a second, veiled, challenge:

> He who therefore can invent
> With what more forcible we may offend
> Our yet unwounded Enemies, or arm
> Ourselves with like defense, to me deserves
> No less than for deliverance what we owe.
>
> (6.464–68)

Satan counters the threat to his leadership with the invention of gunpowder, though his chagrin is apparent in the "look compos'd" (496) with which he answers Nisroch. The occasion of the third and most extended challenge is the Council in Hell, where the realities of fallen government emerge.

SATAN IN COUNCIL

In a recent edition of Milton, Roy Flannagan advises the reader of *Paradise Lost* about the Council in Hell: "Though his experience in the Parliamentary government must have affected Milton, he seems to have gone to great lengths to keep contemporary politics and English history out of the epic—perhaps to avoid the censorship he might have expected, or to avoid the tediousness of recounting political events." Flannagan's caution may be well taken; it would not seem to be particularly useful to read the scene as a comment on a specific group or parliamentary session.[11] As we shall see, however, a too-broad political reading is not equal to Milton's conception, either. A new interpretive direction is indicated by the genre identified by Kirkconnell, who remarked that "[i]f Milton's 'great consult' were construed politically, it would have plenty of forerunners."[12] The forerunners of Milton's Satan and Council alert us to an agonistic pattern that we might not otherwise notice or appreciate in Satan's government of Hell.

Infernal councils in poetic treatments of the angelic fall were calculated to add princely dignity to Lucifer;[13] but the prose treatments add a measure of political realism to the popular image of Satan. Perhaps what is most intriguing about the Satan of the pamphlets is the frequency with which his leadership is challenged. *The Devil in his Dumps* despairs and seeks advice because he has used up all his "strategems . . . to keep together the pieces of a broken State." He is wary of a too-capable servant: "The old Serpent stood amazed at the transcendent villainy of this whorson [Ignatius Loyola], and to see himself out-done so by such a youngster, was half ashamed; some think jealous and afraid too, least in time he might depose him, and usurp his Kingdom of darkness."[14] In another pamphlet, Sir John Presbyter comes "to demand the sole governance of his infernall Dominions" because Lucifer has "grown careless of his government and . . . made himself unfit to sway the scepter."[15] Lucifer puts the matter before his council for a vote but, finally, the would-be usurper so urges the quality of his evil work in England that Lucifer appoints him his second-in-command. Rebels do not always prevail, however. "Mr. Parliament" asserts his equality to Satan, refusing to obey him: "I can out-doe thee Lucifer my master."[16] But the lesser devils are ordered to seize him.

Of course, such instances of defiance of the devil mean to accuse human politicians of horrendous wickedness. But the plots representing Satan's vulnerability to power plays and rebellions turn him into a figure who becomes at once more comprehensible and more complicated than he could be as a totally powerful and unassailable monarch of evil. This perspective informs Milton's treatment of the early Satan in *Paradise Lost*; ultimately, it endows the Apostate with the peculiarly recognizable qualities of a modern politician. Placing Satan in a dynamic political situation, Milton puts him in a context whose logic we understand and accept. The context requires him to demonstrate his intelligence and subtlety, as well as other abilities and accomplishments that end by making him a worthy adversary. The unstable situations Satan masters show him to be competent and resourceful. He emerges as a new creature: an avatar of the self-made politician achieving prominence in England during the period from 1642–60 when the hereditary ruler of the nation was challenged or absent altogether. But before we can replace the image of Satan as a successful tyrant with a new image of him as an able, if fallen, politician, we must consider the traditional readings of Satan and the infernal Council in *Paradise Lost*.

After Satan has been praised for his intention to travel to the world alone, Milton remarks on the rebels and the Council just concluded:

> for neither do the Spirits damn'd
> Lose all thir virtue; lest bad men should boast
> Thir specious deeds on earth, which glory excites,
> Or close ambition vaulted o'er with zeal.
>
> . . . .
>
> O shame to men! Devil with Devil damn'd
> Firm concord holds, men only disagree
> Of Creatures rational, though under hope
> Of heavenly Grace.
>
> (2.482–85; 496–99)

Insisting on the apostates' moral status, Milton yet remarks favorably on Satan's courage, his followers' gratitude, and the ability of the Council to reach agreement. Every now and then, commentators also acknowledge some relatively positive (or at least neutral) aspects of the parliament: forty years ago, Arnold Stein noted that "hell is formally democratic, [though] the same hierarchy that prevailed in heaven is held to"; a few years ago, Robert Fallon suggested that the Council mirrors worldly government and by no means "a particularly onerous" form of government.[17]

But despite these insights, subsequent readers have been unwilling to give the devils even their limited due. Criticism continues to be levelled at Satan and at the procedures of the Council. M. Christopher Pecheux's views are representative: Satan begins with, though he gradually discards,

> the pretense of democracy. As the archetypal tyrant, he does not intend to use the advice of his followers, but he flatters them by pretending to do so. In this, and in his plan of seducing man by fraud, he has some resemblance to the lying spirit that in Micaiah's vision is used to deceive Ahab.

> In the first council . . . [d]ebate is permitted only on the subject
> of what means to use to regain [Heaven]. Within these limits
> there is, however, freedom of speech. . . . The debate ends,
> however, when the scheme secretly devised by Satan is
> divulged by Beelzebub.[18]

Michael Wilding objects that the Council does not reflect
"an egalitarian society. The majority are excluded and
reduced. . . . There is a show of representation—but, in fact,
only Satan, Moloch, Belial, Mammon, and Beelzebub
speak. . . . they go through the appearance of discussion, but
there is no debate, no discussion." Mary Ann Radzinowicz
adds that Satan's position is "a frozen meritocracy or tyranny," the outcome of his leading the rebels into battle.[19] And
Roy Flannagan comments that Satan "has rigged the debate
to be carried to a conclusion he has planned."[20]

These readings assume that Milton's purpose in the
Council scene is simply to condemn Satan as a tyrant. In
fact, as I have already shown, Milton uses this extended
scene to accomplish several aims, one of which is to define
the fallen condition, another to demonstrate the free will
permitted to the fallen. It will already be apparent that
emphasizing the freedom of the apostates must have an
impact on our view of the political Satan. We can make
him a tyrant only at the expense of the moral responsibility
of his followers. Further, if the rebels were deceived by Satan,
they would be in the same moral position as Eve and Adam.
Satan cannot victimize them without to some extent
mitigating their guilt.

The infernal chief is indisputably a self-directed politician,
but his plan of action evolves gradually and is, in large part,
openly expressed. I shall quote from the poem at length to
establish clearly the relation between Satan's explicit public
statements and Beelzebub's subsequent proposal. In his
conversation with Beelzebub after regaining consciousness
in Hell, he first expresses his "resolve / To wage by force
or guile eternal War" (1.120–21). After more talk, Satan
suggests the possibility that the rebels might "once more
/ With rallied Arms . . . try what may be yet / Regain'd in

Heav'n, or what more lost in Hell" (268–70). With the troops that assemble a short time later, however, his emphasis is different:

> our better part remains
> To work in close design, by fraud or guile
> What force effected not.
>
> . . . .
>
> Space may produce new Worlds; whereof so rife
> There went a fame in Heav'n that he ere long
> Intended to create, and therein plant
> A generation, whom his choice regard
> Should favor equal to the Sons of Heaven:
> Thither, if but to pry, shall be perhaps
> Our first eruption, thither or elsewhere:
>
> . . . .
>
> But these thoughts
> Full Counsel must mature: Peace is despair'd,
> For who can think Submission? War then, War
> Open or understood, must be resolv'd.
>
> (1.645–47, 650–56, 659–62)

The evolution of Satan's thoughts is obvious. He is determined absolutely to continue the conflict with Heaven, but finally recommends working by secrecy, fraud, and indirection—working against God's creatures. "Open" war is mentioned only as the less desirable option. Though he has revealed the course he favors, he suggests that the final decision can be made only in consultation. When the Council gathers, Satan's opening statement specifies their task. "I give not Heav'n for lost" (2.14), he declares; it is up to the counsellors to decide how best "To claim our just inheritance" (38); "Whether of open War or covert guile, / We now debate; who can advise, may speak" (41–42). "Open war" requires no definition, and the general parameters of "covert guile" have already been indicated.

When Beelzebub speaks, the plan he proposes is not substantially different from Satan's. We shall not need, Beelzebub says,

> With dangerous expedition to invade
> Heav'n, whose high walls fear no assault or Siege,

Or ambush from the Deep. What if we find
Some easier enterprise? There is a place
(If ancient and prophetic fame in Heav'n
Err not) another World, the happy seat
Of some new Race call'd Man, about this time
To be created like to us, though less
In power and excellence
　　　　　　. . . .
Thither let us bend all our thoughts, to learn
What creatures there inhabit, of what mould
Or substance, how endu'd, and what thir Power,
And where thir weakness, how attempted best,
By force or subtlety:
　　　　　　. . . .
　　　　　　here perhaps
Some advantageous act may be achiev'd
By sudden onset, either with Hell fire
To waste his whole Creation, or possess
All as our own, and drive as we were driven,
The puny habitants, or if not drive,
Seduce them to our Party, that thir God
May prove thir foe, and with repenting hand
Abolish his own works.

(342–50; 354–58; 362–70)

Satan has already stated his preference for guile and fraud
over war; he has already proposed making the new world
the new battleground; and he has already suggested going
"Thither, if but to pry." That is all that Beelzebub actually
proposes—going "to learn," to spy out the creatures' nature,
their strength and vulnerability. The visions of a world
destroyed or overrun, or of man seduced, are only possibilities contingent upon the yet-to-be-acquired information.
When Milton comments that Beelzebub's plan was "first
devis'd / By Satan, and in part propos'd" (379–80), he means
to credit Satan with the malice underlying the destructive
options. He does not dramatize a conversation in which
Satan shares with Beelzebub the options of destruction,
possession, or seduction; but there is no suggestion that
Satan's plan has been secret in order to deceive anyone
regarding its origin. Deception is neither intended nor
important. It would be necessary only if Satan wanted to

hide his wishes or inclinations, as he plainly does not do. All of the fallen angels hear his preferences. It is also important to stress that Beelzebub's proposal does not embody a specific plan. Proof that the precise nature of Satan's task is indeterminate, unknown even to himself, is the all-knowing Father's statement. He tells the Son that Satan goes "with purpose to assay / If [man] by force he can destroy, or worse, / By some false guile pervert; and shall pervert" (3.90–92).

Though Satan's public statements (quoted above) are attempts to influence the assembly, the counsellors resist him and challenge his ideas. He tries to restrict the matter under discussion: "Whether of open War or covert guile, / We now debate; who can advise, may speak" (2.38–42). One by one, however, the first three speakers ignore their chief's preferences as well as the two options he has declared himself willing to entertain. Moloch, in spite of his leader's partiality for guile, argues for open war. Belial rejects altogether the two alternatives Satan has presented: "War therefore, open or conceal'd, alike / My voice dissuades" (187–88); he proposes that they do nothing. Similarly, Mammon glosses over Satan's alternatives and argues for the creation of a dominion parallel to Heaven: "All things invite / To peaceful Counsels, and the settl'd State / Of order" (278–80). If the Council scene shows Satan's tyranny, it is singularly ineffectual.

Satan neither forces nor deceives the Council into going along with a secret plan devised for the purpose. He carries the day by much more prosaic means. The speeches of Moloch and Belial elicit no demonstration from the group. But when Mammon concludes,

> such murmur fill'd
> Th'Assembly, as when hollow Rocks retain
> The sound of blust'ring winds.
>
> . . . .
> Such applause was heard
> As *Mammon* ended, and his Sentence pleas'd,
> Advising peace.
>
> (2.284–85; 290–92)

Beelzebub rises to counter this popular proposal—the opposite of the policy Satan is known to support. When he finishes outlining his chief's scheme, the general reaction is spontaneous:

> The bold design
> Pleas'd highly those infernal States, and joy
> Sparkl'd in all thir eyes; with full assent
> They vote.
>
> (386–89)

The text is emphatic about the apostates' unqualified approval of Beelzebub's proposal. Undoubtedly, the dispute reveals the speakers' flawed characters, like Mammon's luxuriousness or Belial's sloth, but their faults do not interfere with the freedom they enjoy in debate or with the choice they finally make. That it is a real choice is unquestionable. Milton characterizes their debate as "thir *doubtful* consultations dark" (486, my emphasis): "doubtful" means "involved in doubt or uncertainty; uncertain, undecided. . . . of uncertain issue" (*OED*). The debate represents the apostates' freedom to choose their "own dark designs, / That with reiterated crimes [they] might / Heap on themselves damnation" (1.212–15).

In the Council of book 2, Milton gives us a vision of fallen politics. Satan is a fallen leader, but it does not follow that the political system into which he and his supporters fall is particularly corrupt. The author gives the assembly the dignity of ritual and due process. Heralds blow trumpets "with awful Ceremony" to proclaim the Council (1.753), summoning "From every Band and squared Regiment / By place or choice the worthiest" (758–59). After the official summons is read in Pandemonium, Satan carefully establishes his claim to precedence, introducing the important criterion of merit.

> Mee though just right and the fixt Laws of Heav'n
> Did first create your Leader, next, free choice,
> With what besides, in Counsel or in Fight,
> Hath been achiev'd of merit.
>
> (2.18–21)

Before the revolt, the celestial hierarchy instituted by the Father gave Satan his undisputed place. Since then, however, Satan has been earning the right to lead by serving the interests of the group. We have already mentioned his invention of gunpowder. He refers in the speech above to his performance in the war, and claims to be even yet a "bulwark" protecting his troops against the "Thunderer's aim" (27–29). Eventually, when his plan and Beelzebub's is accepted by majority vote, Satan volunteers for the perilous journey, declaring that it would be unbecoming for him to sit on Hell's throne if he did not attempt "aught propos'd / And judg'd of public moment, in the shape / Of difficulty or danger."

> Wherefore do I assume
> These Royalties, and not refuse to Reign,
> Refusing to accept as great a share
> Of hazard as of honor, due alike
> To him who Reigns, and so much to him due
> Of hazard more, as he above the rest
> High honor'd sits?
>
> (445–56)

Under the new conditions of fallen governance, Satan must win and maintain his position, proving himself over and over again, as he does in the important events of the poem.

Though he emphasizes the service he renders the group and the unenviable distinction as leader of having the "greatest share / Of endless pain" (29–30), Satan cannot take for granted the amenability of his followers. We have already seen the uncertainty of leading by persuasion. Before the debate begins, he makes his opinions known, but does not himself enter into the discussion in which everyone is free to express contrary views. With the help of his lieutenant on the floor, Satan prevails. Even so, he is not confident of the fulfillment of his policy. When Beelzebub announces the need for a volunteer to go in search of the new world, he pauses in "suspense, awaiting who appear'd / To second, or oppose, or undertake / The perilous attempt" (418–20). Someone might still oppose the linchpin of the plan. Satan's followers are fallen, too, after all, and liable to the errors, weaknesses, and unworthy motivations inspiring their chief. Satan assumes their imperfection, addressing their hunger for prominence in his opening statement to the Council as well as in his abrupt termination of its proceedings. He does not want others to "stand / His Rivals, winning cheap the high repute" (471–72) for which he must take an incalculable risk.

Being the governor of the first sinful community, Satan falls into politics and learns it as he goes. Dependent on the support of his followers, he must serve their needs and be seen to do so, though even such a strategy does not necessarily win their compliance. He must persuade the reluctant. The infernal politician knows that he thrives or fails according to the degree that he pleases or outmaneuvers his followers. Satan is the creature of oppositional politics, the leader by wit and merit who survives by his inventiveness, ability, and cunning.

Because the Council in Hell has been read from a simplistic political point of view, its spiritual aspect has been largely ignored. The scene explores a new kind of existence vis-à-vis God, and underscores celestial justice towards the devils by dramatizing a second fall. Recognition of its spiritual burden suggests that the traditional interpretation of the scene is too general, inaccurate, and finally insufficient to Milton's well-drawn portrayal of politics in the fallen sphere. In *Paradise Lost*, Milton juxtaposes two kinds of rulers heading two kinds of political systems. As an unquestionably good and superior being, God is the ideal monarch and the faithful angels the ideal subjects. God's right to govern absolutely and his subjects' joyful and absolute obedience are in perfect equilibrium. The perfection of the politics of unanimity, however, is restricted to Heaven. Satan is the fallen politician governing a fallen populace.

In the years between 1642–60, the effectual or real absence of a king at the head of the English government gave prominence to a new kind of leader, who was first required to achieve and then to maintain his place at the apex of the power structure. Unlike a hereditary monarch, this leader gained his ascendancy by talent, merit, and the support of his followers; he maintained his position, if he did, by the same gifts. During the same time, divisive issues generated an extreme discourse that demonized oppositional politics. Prose pamphlets often featured plots reflecting a heightened awareness of the contention of politics, with participants challenging each other as well as fighting their common enemies. These works depicted the governance of Hell as thoroughly agonistic. The devils of the prose pamphlets raised expectations of the degree of political realism accorded to the literary Satan. Milton's Satan and his Council partake of these parallel historical and literary developments.

The popularity of infernal councils in the pamphlets and broadsides made it likely that Milton's contemporaries would construe the Council scene in book 2 politically, as Milton surely realized. His dramatization of such a scene suggests that, like the authors of the prose pamphlets, he wanted to comment on English politics. Obviously, his own position and the political situation after 1660—not to mention the literary and theological imperatives of *Paradise Lost* itself— constrained him. These difficulties notwithstanding, with his "O shame to men" he positively invites readers to compare infernal and earthly politics. Milton could not risk a high level of specificity. But the very generalness of his images of Satan and of unfallen and fallen politics enables them to reflect a good many figures and political truths as Milton saw them.

Though I have been concerned primarily with the internal affairs of Hell, it is clear that the contrast in *Paradise Lost* between the politics of unanimity and of opposition defines the true monarch. Satan may be a capable leader, but by the poem's standards, he cannot be king. Monarchy is appropriate only, as Abdiel says, "When he who rules is worthiest, and excels / Them whom he governs" (6.177– 78); but the fallen Satan is not the superior of his fallen adherents. Admittedly, a major difference between the Apostate and any monarch who bases his claim on heredity or divine right is Satan's awareness that he must serve the needs of his followers and continually "earn" his position; as we saw, he claims the right of courage and achievement.

But heroic or political virtue cannot constitute moral or essential superiority. The monarchy of Heaven, vested in the Father or the Son, indicts any claimant to kingship whose authority is not grounded in spiritual merit and superiority to those he governs. Thus covertly, Milton criticizes the institution of earthly monarchy and any king who improperly enthrones himself above his equals. Supporters of either Charles (or of both) could have taken no pleasure in the perspective on monarchy in *Paradise Lost*.

Since Satan is a fallen leader as well as a would-be monarch, he offers a paradigm whose light is refracted through various figures. Kings and republican or restoration politicians— indisputably all are fallen creatures pursuing their ends, pure or impure, among fallen people. Through Satan, Milton reveals some of the manifold ironies of fallen leadership: the realities of consensual governance, for example, cast the leader as the servant of his followers. The proud rebel who would not serve the Father or the Son yet must serve those he considers inferiors. To satisfy his desire for preeminence and power, the politician may have to degrade himself and suffer in his own estimation. Satan acknowledges the misery to himself: "But what will not Ambition and Revenge / Descend to? who aspires must down as low / As high he soar'd, obnoxious first or last / To basest things" (9.168–71). The infernal counsellors no less than their chief reflect men who manage public affairs, arguing from personal weakness, so that often pride, cowardice, luxury, or other faults propel state affairs. In spite of this, Milton remarks on the ability of the Council, finally, to reach an agreement serving Hell's best interests (judged by their evil standards). However, the author also stresses the uncertainty of government by persuasion. The opinion of the majority may be swayed in one direction or another, for good or for ill.

Obviously, there is more to say about the Apostate and the Council. Satan will degenerate from the moment when he stands with "transcendant glory rais'd / Above his fellows, with Monarchial pride / Conscious of highest worth" (2.427–29). (Even as the text concedes relative his worth, for instance, the reference to his pride diminishes him, distinguishing him from the one true monarch in *Paradise Lost*.) But in book 2, as the fallen leader of a fallen government, Satan is an accomplished politician, striving to acquire his followers' support, and surviving by the courage, energy, and talent that set him above his fellows. I have been able only to indicate some of the shifts in perspective occasioned by the new context I propose for Hell. But they are enough to dispel the notion that in *Paradise Lost* the fierce polemicist denied his political experience. Whether or not Milton had in mind particular issues, events, or people, in Satan and his Council, he dissects power that is not exercised as a concommitant of perfection: *Paradise Lost* defines politics as the fallen method of conducting the business of the sinful world. Milton also gives us, in Satan, a figure infinitely more engaging and complex than a one-dimensional tyrant. Without endangering himself or marring the integrity of his poem, Milton deflates and in some respects indicts seventeenth century politics and politicians.

6 • "Two of Far Nobler Shape"
Reading the Paradisal Text

Michael Lieb

I

To reencounter what Joseph H. Summers calls "our first vision of perfect man and woman" in the fourth book of *Paradise Lost* is to recognize yet once more the immense range of Milton's artistry, as well as the complexity of his sexual politics.[1] I allude to Summers because his treatment of the depiction of Adam and Eve at this juncture in Milton's epic establishes a point of departure for determining precisely how far criticism has come since the publication of his seminal book *The Muse's Method*, which dates back some thirty years.[2] To remind ourselves of the particulars of the passage in question, I shall begin by quoting the description in full:

> Two of far nobler shape erect and tall,
> Godlike erect, with native Honour clad
> In naked Majestie seemd Lords of all,
> And worthie seemd, for in thir looks Divine
> The image of thir glorious Maker shon,

114

Truth, Wisdom Sanctitude severe and pure,
Severe, but in true filial freedom plac't;
Whence true autoritie in men; though both
Not equal, as thir sex not equal seemd;
For contemplation hee and valour formd,
For softness shee and sweet attractive Grace,
Hee for God only, shee for God in him;
His fair large Front and Eye sublime declar'd
Absolute rule; and Hyacinthin Locks
Round from his parted forelock manly hung
Clustring, but not beneath his shoulders broad:
Shee as a vail down to the slender waste
Her unadorned golden tresses wore
Dissheveld, but in wanton ringlets wav'd
As the Vine curls her tendrils, which impli'd
Subjection, but requir'd with gentle sway,
And by her yeilded, by him best receiv'd,
Yeilded with coy submission, modest pride,
And sweet reluctant amorous delay.

(4.288–311)[3]

The observation that Summers offers on this passage is instructive as much for what it neglects to say as for what it does say. Of this "first vision of perfect man and woman," Summers maintains with full assurance that "here appearance nakedly reflects reality." In that concurrence of appearance and reality, "the inequality of man and woman is imaged as clearly as is their perfection." With our "modern ideas of the equality of the sexes," we impose our own mistaken assumptions upon the passage, an imposition, in effect, that causes us to see problems where there are none and to assert values that Milton did not share. It is all so clear, if only we could see it.[4]

The assumptions reflected in Summers' analysis of the passage appear remarkably and indeed charmingly insular after two decades of criticism in which the feminist movement that has adopted *Paradise Lost* as a *cause célèbre* has effectively demolished any suggestion that the sexual politics implicit in the description of Adam and Eve can be dismissed with the assertion that "here appearance nakedly reflects reality." Such an assertion is simply impossible to make in the highly charged atmosphere of today's critical climate.⁵ In his major statement on the subject, Joseph Wittreich has perhaps said it best. Responding in *Feminist Milton* both to the passage under consideration and to Milton's epic as a whole, Wittreich argues that *Paradise Lost* represents "a field of opposing stresses and signals." Especially in its delineation of the relation between the sexes, the epic is riddled at times with apparent contradictions that are the result of a sophisticated artistry. Viewed in this way, the epic becomes a "strange and slippery text" in which "outward impressions and inward assessments" might not always coincide. Such, argues Wittreich, is particularly the case with the passage cited above.⁶

I remember being present as a guest lecturer and participant at an NEH sponsored Milton Institute at the University of Arizona in July of 1988. During one of the sessions, John T. Shawcross presented his own analysis of the passage in question, and I speak with complete conviction in observing that, as a result of his analysis, any remaining notion of the concurrence of appearance and reality in the description was entirely dispelled. That the inclination to "problematize" the passage has assumed the status of a norm was made clear by William Kerrigan's own astute treatment in his paper "Gender and Confusion in Milton and Everyone Else," that served as the basis of a lively discussion at the Newberry Library Milton Seminar in October of 1990.⁷ Here too the fact of the passage as evidence of Milton's "strange and slippery text," particularly in its portrayal of paradisal sexual politics, was very much at the forefront of the interchange. As ongoing debates concerning the passage have amply demonstrated, then, the "first vision of perfect man and woman" in the fourth book of *Paradise Lost* is delineated in a manner that no one is about to dismiss with remarkably little fuss.

In order to reinforce this sense of the "strange and slippery" nature of the Miltonic text, I propose to extend the debate concerning the passage as the repository of the "opposing stresses and signals" that *Paradise Lost* as a whole encodes. Approaching the passage in this manner will provide a means of coming to terms both with the text itself and with the nature of the complexity that constitutes Milton's poetic artistry. What we are after in such an endeavor finally is a greater understanding of that which is implied by the phrase "literary Milton," an idea founded upon an acknowledgment of the importance of the text as an interpretive field for the establishment of those "limina" or thresholds through which the text itself is defined and understood.[8] As a means of conducting my argument, I shall move intratextually and intertextually, that is, both within the larger framework of Milton's epic and from the perspective of Milton's understanding of that "strange and slippery" text upon which the epic in general and the designated passage in particular are based. I refer to the Bible itself as the richest and most complex repository of "opposing stresses and signals." To move both intratextually and intertextually in this manner is to become aware once again of the extent to which the very notion of textuality reinforces the impulse to read *Paradise Lost* as a work in which such opposing stresses and signals represent the rule, rather than the exception.

From the very outset of an encounter with the passage in question, one must be aware of the circumstances through which the passage itself arises. The passage represents a culminating moment in a series of perceptions through which we are introduced to the Edenic landscape, its characteristics and its inhabitants. It is, of course, the supremest of ironies that those perceptions are delineated through the eyes of Satan, who, having surreptitiously found his way into the paradisal enclosure, views the blissful surroundings beneath him from the vantage point of the Tree of Life as he sits "devising Death/ To them who liv'd" (4.194–208). Before him stretches the Edenic landscape with its glories, including its rivers, hills, valleys, lawns, trees, herbage, flowers, and its animal life. Viewing such glories from his elevated station, Satan sees "undelighted all delight" (4.209–87). As a capstone to this series of seeings, Satan beholds first man and first woman, who, as compared to "all kind/ Of living Creatures new to sight and strange" that Satan witnesses from his vantage point, are "Two of far nobler shape erect and tall." The circumstances encode what Wittreich aptly calls a kind of Chinese box: "Embedded within an extended description of Satan's first view of Eden is a report of his vision of the Garden, and embedded within that vision is Satan's initial perception of Adam and Eve."[9] Text within text and vision within vision: such is the context out of which the passage in question emerges.

Within that context, moreover, the description of first man and first woman is inextricably implicated in the Satanic perspective.[10] In his account of Adam and Eve, the narrator installs himself within that perspective in the very act of extolling the virtues of those he would describe. There is simply no way of avoiding this conclusion. Our first fully delineated sight of Adam and Eve in *Paradise Lost* is one in which the prelapsarian condition is defined by the post-lapsarian consciousness.[11] Nothing can be taken at face value.[12] To suggest here that "appearance nakedly reflects reality" is to overlook the implications of the "strange and slippery" quality of the Miltonic text, one that by its very nature is bound to be distinguished by "opposing stresses and signals." This fact is even further heightened if one takes into account the intratextual forces that come into play in the language through which the description of first man and first woman is construed. This is a language of shifting perspectives, a language of appearance, of seeming. First man and first woman are not named: they appear simply as "shapes" to be discerned by one who views them. "Two of far nobler shape," they exist in contradistinction to other corresponding shapes. As such, they "s*eemd* Lords of all" and "worthie *seemd*." In this language of appearance, their apparent inequality is signaled by a distinction in gender identity: "though both/ Not equal, as thir sex not equal *seemd*" (emphasis mine).[13] The refusal to name as a means of establishing irrefutable identity, coupled with the impo-sition of the language of appearance calls into question any assertion of categorical absolutes.[14]

Not that we are invited to question that their looks are in fact "Divine" or that in those looks "The image of thir glorious Maker shon,/ Truth, Wisdom Sanctitude severe and

pure." It is simply that in the very assertion of such qualities, all pronouncements concerning the relationship of first
man to first woman, of him to her, of shape to shape, based
upon automatic distinctions of gender are immediately
compromised by virtue of the context through which the
vision of the two beings manifests itself. At the very point
that the narrative voice makes such categorical pronouncements as "Whence true autoritie in men" and "Hee for God
only, shee for God in him," the context through which these
pronouncements are uttered obliges us to remember the
extent to which the narrative voice is implicated in the
Satanic perspective out of which the passage itself emerges.
This inextricable linkage of the narrative voice not just to
the postlapsarian but to the Satanic point of view causes
the speech-act to question its own authority, if not its own
intentions. Although such ideas are not unique, they warrant reiteration here. The fact of Milton's "strange and
slippery" text is constantly reasserting itself at the very point
it appears to declare itself as "true." That such is the case
even in the paradisal context in which our first vision of
perfect man and woman makes itself known attests to the
dangers implicit in any attempt to suggest that "here appearance nakedly reflects reality." Given the complexities
of the Miltonic text and the limina that define it, asserting
the concurrence of appearance and reality in the depiction
of first man and first woman is simply untenable.

If this fact is established by the immediate circumstances
(the Chinese box of text embedded within text) that give
rise to the depiction, it is further reinforced by the larger
contexts that both anticipate and define it. I refer to that
earlier narrative in which Satan comes upon two other
(not-so-"noble") shapes, the identity of which the fallen angel
is initially at a loss to ascertain. Those shapes, of course,
are Sin and Death, whose disturbing presence is realized
through a language that fully anticipates and thereby helps
to define the nature of first man and first woman in the
paradisal world:

> Before the Gates there sat
> On either side a formidable *shape*;
> The one *seem'd* Woman to the waste, and fair,
> But ended foul in many a scaly fould. . . .
> The other *shape*,
> If *shape* it might be call'd that *shape* had none
> Distinguishable in member, joynt, or limb,
> Or substance might be call'd that shadow *seem'd*,
> For each *seem'd* either.
>
> (2.648–673; emphasis mine)

In the very act of utterance, the language calls its own delineations into question. Indistinguishability is the one feature that distinguishes: perspective collapses into perspective. Nothing is stable, nothing secure: "each seem'd either." In the portrayal of the two shapes, the language of appearance precludes the determination of identity. Thus installed within the Satanic perspective, one simply cannot get a "fix" on what one beholds. Shifting constantly from shape to shape, that which appears to be so is so only as a result of that which makes it so. The act of beholding determines that which is beheld. Forever bound to the world of appearance, the Satanic mode of perception is one in which a concurrence between "seems" and "is" will never be realized. What is true of perception is no less true of utterance. In its depiction of those "formidable shapes," the narrative voice is inextricably implicated in the illusory world of that which it depicts.

That the portrayal of "Two of far nobler shape" later in the epic by the narrative voice adopts not only the same language of indeterminacy but the same circumstance of witnessing what is beheld through the eyes of Satan imposes upon the interpretive act an almost insurmountable task. As much as one might try, one never will be able to move from "seems" to "is." Each will always seem either. It is comforting to declare absolute contrasts between those "formidable shapes" that Satan beholds in the world of Hell and those "nobler shapes" he later beholds in the world of Eden. The differences that distinguish the two sets of shapes are both obvious and profound in every respect. The first set is the debased product of Satan himself; the second, the product of God. The first set represents a consummate vision of perversion and corruption in all its forms; the second, a consummate vision of sublimity and wholeness in all its forms. The first set is the embodiment of the postlapsarian point of view; the second, the embodiment of the prelapsarian point of view. The first set is the product of the world of Hell; the second, the product of the world of Eden. The purpose of the first set is to subvert and destroy, of the second, to uphold and create. Such contrasts could be extended almost indefinitely.

In the very process of establishing these contrasts, however, we become aware that at some fundamental level the two sets must share a common ground from which each departs. At the source of a contrastive dialectic lies a uniting correspondence. Reinforcing this unitive substratum of shared characteristics is the language of appearance, which underscores the delineation of both sets as the product of the Satanic act of seeing. As much as one might wish to read the paradisal text as that which exists *in vacuo*, in its own enclosure, its own innocence, its own Edenic world of pleasure, perception keeps getting pulled back into the world out of which fallenness arises. One keeps seeing through the eyes of Satan, even in paradise. Although immediately comparing first man and first woman with the paradisal creatures described in the preceding lines, the very phrase "Two of far nobler shape" ultimately extends backward to those "formidable shapes" described two books earlier and to which the comparative phrase is inextricably tied. Shapes "far nobler" than whose? Why, those "formidable shapes" that Satan encounters in the realm of Hell.

To impose a dialectic of contrasts upon these two sets is to unite them all the more. To attempt to extricate oneself from the language of appearance that defines the first set in order to define the second is to implicate oneself all the more in the indeterminacies that define them both. To read the paradisal text is to install oneself within the very perspective that one would transcend. There is no way out of the "strange and slippery" dilemma that Milton's epic imposes. His text will always be a battleground of "opposing stresses and signals" that may on occasion offer the prospect of temporary resolution but that will ultimately confound. The surest way to commit a misreading of the paradisal text is to rest content with the false and dangerous assurance that "here appearance nakedly reflects reality." In the terms that John T. Shawcross has recently posited in his *Intentionality and the New Traditionalism*, such an approach perpetrates an injustice as much upon the "writer writing" as it does upon the "reader reading."[15] In both respects, the text must always be seen as an ever-changing and indeed problematical construct, one that eludes anything like a definitive interpretation.

The passage in which first man and first woman are described is a case in point. Defined intratextually as the product of Satan's act of beholding both within the immediate confines of the Edenic environment and within the larger framework of the landscape of Hell, the passage establishes its own set of limina through which its problematic nature is given full expression. The sexual politics that constitute this nature will forever perplex. "Whence true autoritie in men; though both/ Not equal, as thir sex not equal seemd;/ For contemplation hee and valour formd,/ For softness shee and sweet attractive Grace,/ Hee for God only, shee for God in him." Whose discourse is this? Milton's? The narrator's? Satan's? Is it possible to come at this discourse directly, that is, severed from its own textuality, the circumstances that both frame it and embed it? The intratextual determinants through which the discourse itself is generated preclude such an interpretive act. We keep getting caught up in the "tangles" of the text.

The new Neaera comes equipped with her hairdo as well: at once veiling that which it presumes to disclose, the text, like the first woman it extols, has its tresses too: "Dissheveld, but in wanton ringlets wav'd/ As the Vine curls her tendrils." This may imply subjection for some, but the more it appears to yield, the less it gives; the more we think we have received, the less we possess.[16] No matter how inclined we are to assert "true autoritie" in the interpretive enterprise, all such assertions must be qualified by the complexities (the opposing stresses and signals) that the text encodes. Even with "fair large Front and Eye sublime," we dare not attempt to impose "absolute rule" on this text. To assume we can do so is to risk suffering the demise of one with whom the first man himself is implicitly compared. Lurking behind the figure of the first man with his "Hyacinthin Locks" that "Round from his parted forelock manly hung/ Clustring" is the poor stricken youth whose sad fate is embedded in "that sanguine flower inscribed with woe." "*Ai, Ai,*" we shall cry out: there is no answer here.[17]

The text eludes us. It will not be subjected; it will not yield. "Coy submission, modest pride," "sweet reluctant amorous delay": how these oxymoronic epithets seduce us into believing that power over the text lies within our grasp! The effect is absolutely Satanic, as well it might be, since it is his sensibility that determines the shape of the discourse before us; it is quite literally through his eyes that we see now in the paradisal realm, that we read the paradisal text, as we have seen before in the world of Hell, where we first encountered those formidable shapes ready at once to seduce and accost any who would presume to master them.

Such are the intratextual—what Shawcross would call the "liminal"—determinants of the passage in question. What then of the intertextual determinants? They are limina too. As such, they likewise contribute to the establishment of the literary foundations of the poet's art, its expressive contours, its conduct and negotiations, indeed, its very integrity. Particularly from the interpretive perspective that I am attempting to suggest, the intertextual determinants of the passage find their most immediate and compelling source in Milton's understanding of that most "strange and slippery" of texts, the Bible itself. A profound repository of "opposing stresses and signals" in its own right, the biblical text as a fundamental source of the Miltonic outlook should provide renewed insight into the difficulties that our first vision of perfect man and woman in *Paradise Lost* entails.

II

This is especially true of the sexual politics that the vision implies. The cues are everywhere; indeed, as we have seen, they permeate the very fabric of the passage. We need only be reminded of their presence to become aware of them yet once more. A few phrases will suffice: "in thir looks Divine/ The image of thir glorious Maker shon"; "Whence true autoritie in men; though both/ Not equal, as thir sex not equal seemd"; "Hee for God only, shee for God in him"; "His fair large Front and Eye sublime declar'd/ Absolute rule," and the like. The relationship is aptly emblematized in the length and style of the hair, his hair hanging manly "round from his parted forelock" but "not beneath his shoulders broad"; her hair extending "as a vail down to the slender waste" and in appearance implying the need for "subjection." As the commentators never tire of informing us, the implicit relationship portrayed here is essentially Pauline. In the lines, perhaps within the interstices of the expressive structures, the nuances, the images, lurks the stern figure of St. Paul. It is not absolutely certain whether he is sitting astride the Tree of Life with Satan "devising Death/ To them who liv'd," but he is present nonetheless. Within the context of New Testament doctrine concerning the relationship between male and female, that presence resounds throughout the Pauline epistles. Whether one considers such epistles as those to the Corinthians, the Ephesians, the Colossians, or to Timothy, Pauline and/or pseudo-Pauline teaching establishes a paradigmatic hierarchy between man and woman, one in which male is superior to female and in which the latter is held in subjection to and therefore admonished to obey the former.[18]

The idea is so commonplace as to obviate the need for detailed elaboration here. A few examples should suffice to suggest the terms upon which the Pauline outlook is based. "But I would have you know," Paul declares, "that the head of every man is Christ; and the head of the woman *is* the man; and the head of Christ *is* God." Man, Paul continues, is "the image and glory of God" and woman "the glory of the man. For the man is not of the woman; but the woman of the man" (1 Corinthians 11.7–8). Such sentiments are reflected elsewhere. "Wives, submit yourselves unto your own husbands, as unto the Lord. For the husband is the head of the wife, even as Christ is the head of the church" (Ephesians 5.22–23; cf. Colossians 3.18); and "Let the woman learn in silence with all subjection. But I suffer not a woman to ... usurp authority over the man, but to be in silence. For Adam was first formed, then Eve" (1 Timothy 2.11–14). Such a view finds resonance in 1 Peter, for whom the wife becomes "the weaker vessel" (3.7). In 1 Corinthians, a *locus classicus* for the kind of outlook customarily associated with the teachings that Paul espoused regarding the male-female relationship, the ordinances that underscore the gender hierarchy culminate in a reference to the appropriate length of the hair for man and for woman, respectively: "Doth not even nature itself teach you, that, if a man have long hair, it is a shame unto him? But if a woman have long hair, it is a glory to her: for *her* hair is given her for a covering" (11.14–15).

The Pauline paradigm of the male-female relationship established here is exceedingly complex, and there is not the opportunity to explore the subject in any depth at this juncture.[19] Suffice it to say that Milton made the most of the foregoing passages in his prose works.[20] In *De Doctrina Christiana* (2.15), for example, he grouped them together as proof-texts to address the reciprocal domestic responsibilities pertaining to husband and wife. Having cited these and corresponding proof-texts, he concludes by observing that the principle upon which the ideal relationship between male and female is based can be found in the Genesis account of the creation of man and woman. In this respect, the first three chapters of Genesis are looked upon as the ultimate source of the point of view he is expounding. As might be expected, that point of view is decidedly weighted in favor of male over female. "The very creation of woman implies that this [the subjection of wives to their husbands] should be so, Gen. ii.22: *he made that rib which he had taken from Adam into a woman.* It is wrong," Milton comments, "for one single part of the body—and not one of the most important parts—to disobey the rest of the body and even the head. This, at any rate, is the opinion of God: Gen. iii.16: *he shall rule over you*" (*YP* 6.781–82; *CM* 17.348–53). Transposing what for Milton is the postlapsarian perspective onto the prelapsarian economy, the exegete reformulates the Pauline paradigm in order to establish his own reading of the Genesis account. That reading is one in which the rigid sense of hierarchy imposed upon man and woman as the result of their disobedience justifies an interpretation of the prelapsarian male-female relationship that accords with the idea of male superiority, "absolute rule," to use Milton's phrase.

Milton's own doctrinal assimilation of these biblical prototypes in *De Doctrina Christiana* supports a rigid hierarchical reading of paradisal sexual politics. And this assimilation suggests the extent to which the intertextual limina that define the vision of perfect man and woman in the fourth book of *Paradise Lost* render our understanding of the prelapsarian male-female relationship even more problematical. By imposing the Pauline perspective onto the prelapsarian account, Milton further complicates the terms out of which the account itself arises. Because of the Satanic presence (one might almost suggest complicity) in the creation of the account, the Pauline terms through which the account is articulated are themselves open to interrogation. What Milton asserts doctrinally with so much authority in his theological tract is contextualized poetically in *Paradise Lost* in a manner that highlights the indeterminacy of the terms upon which the vision of perfect man and woman is founded. In that vision, Milton almost appears to be calling into question not only the Pauline paradigm established in the biblical text but his appropriation of the paradigm to support the sexual politics proposed in his theological tract.

If such is the case, the problematical nature of the Pauline presence as subtext of the poetic rendering in Milton's epic manifests itself as a distinguishing feature of his exegetical discourse in the prose. At issue is Milton's analysis of the opening chapters of Genesis in the divorce tracts, principally

Tetrachordon. It is to this tract that we shall now attend. *Tetrachordon* is germane to our discussion because it immediately focuses in Pauline terms the essential texts out of which the passage in question arises. The texts are Genesis 1.27 ("So God created man in his *own* image, in the image of God created he him; male and female created he them") and Genesis 2.18 ("And the Lord God said, *It is* not good that the man should be alone; I will make him an help meet for him"). Both underscore the vision of first man and first woman in the fourth book of *Paradise Lost.* The significance of these texts as a source of Milton's exegetical practices lies in the extent to which they provoke a response in the exegete that is as troublesome as it is fascinating. Such a response at once anticipates and prepares us for the complexities that we have already encountered in the poetic articulations of the epic.

Addressing the first text ("So God created man in his *own* image, in the image of God created he him; male and female created he them"), Milton immediately sets about to devalue the participatory role of woman as a sharer in the *imago Dei.*[21] "It might be doubted why he saith, *in the Image of God created he him,* not them . . .; especially since that Image might be common to them both," for had they both had an equal share in the image of God, the text would have read, "In the image of God created he them." In a marvelous act of female devaluation, St. Paul, Milton suggests, "ends the controversie by explaining that the woman is not primarily and immediately the image of God, but in reference to the man. *The head of the woman,* saith he, I Cor.11. *is the man: he the image and glory of God, she the glory of the man*: he not for her, but she for him. Therefore his precept is, *Wives be subject to your husbands as is fit in the Lord, Coloss.* 3.18. *In every thing, Eph.* 5.24" (*YP* 2.589). It would be reassuring to see this Pauline resolution of the dilemma (or "controversie," to use Milton's word) as decisive both for the immediate concerns of the divorce tract and for the intertextual concerns of the epic. But this is hardly the case.

The reasons for this are not far to seek. We may begin

by touching upon apparent or surface similarities between the Miltonic exegesis and the passage from the epic in question. "He not for her, but she for him," for example, may at first blush recall "Hee for God only, shee for God in him," but the two pronouncements are not really the same; in fact, as articulated, they are quite different. The pronouncement from the tract suggests a narrowing of perspective that results in a reading that would appear, at least initially, to exclude the theology of the *imago Dei* in the construction of the male-female relationship. Although as *imago Dei*, man is obviously "for" God, the way the pronouncement is phrased, such a reading leaves itself open to question. Whomever man is "for," he is certainly not "for" woman. If this is not the purpose of the pronouncement, it is nonetheless its effect. The epic pronouncement, on the other hand, unequivocally reasserts the importance of the *imago Dei* as the *sine qua non* of the ideal male-female relationship. "Hee for God only, shee for God in him" places God at the center of the causal focus in a way that "He not for her, but she for him" does not.

Beyond this, moreover, the assertion that "the woman is not primarily and immediately the image of God" is modified by the assertion in the passage from the epic that "in thir looks Divine/ The image of thir glorious Maker shon," an assertion that emphasizes the importance of a positive participation and reciprocity, not the negative implications of the "not primarily and immediately" attributed to the woman. But even the epic's positive reading of the Pauline paradigm that suggests the presence of imparity in the male-female relationship ("though both/ Not equal, as thir sex not equal seemd") is effectively called into question by the intratextual determinants through which the vision of perfect man and woman emerges. The point here is that if the intratextual determinants complicate our reading of the poetic text, the intertextual determinants reinforce the problematic nature of the process even further.

These problems, moreover, are additionally reinforced by what occurs within the intertext itself, for the exegetical nuances encoded within the divorce tract are themselves constantly subject to qualification and interrogation. Like the epic, the prose tract too is a work in which one discovers "a field of opposing stresses and signals." This becomes apparent in Milton's elaboration upon his own analysis of the Pauline interpretation of Genesis 1.27. Sensing that his analysis might tend to suggest a questionable and unnecessary devaluation of the role of woman, Milton attempts to clarify his position: "Neverthelesse man is not to hold her as a servant, but receives her into a part of that empire which God proclaims him to, though not equally, yet largely, as his own image and glory: for it is no small glory to him, that a creature so like him, should be made subject to him." It is almost as if Milton is attempting to make the most of a bad situation. Moving to the point of suggesting the possibility of a kind of servitude in his citation and interpretation of Pauline precedent ("he not for her, but she for him. Therefore his precept is, *Wives be subject to your husbands as is fit in the Lord, Coloss. 3.18. In every thing, Eph. 5.24"*), he is anxious to qualify what might otherwise be misconstrued. It would be wrong for man to think that woman is to be held as no more than a servant, Milton argues, for she is really much more than that. As one who shares man's "image and glory," woman is received "into a part of that empire which God proclaims him to," although, Milton still qualifies, "not equally."

He has a hard time with this one, for he is immediately prompted to qualify his disclaimer once again: "Not but that particular exceptions may have place, if she exceed her husband in prudence and dexterity, and he contendedly yeeld, for then a superior and more naturall law comes in, that the wise should govern the less wise, whether male or female" (*YP* 2.589). This is really quite remarkable. One wonders what St. Paul would have to say about it. An exegete would be hard put to find *that* one in the Pauline epistles. Reflecting what amounts to his own discomfort with the whole idea of imparity in the construction of a sexual politics based upon Pauline precedent, Milton invents his own "superior and more naturall law" based perhaps upon his own experience, perhaps upon his own deep-seated convictions.

Whatever the source of this "superior and more naturall law," it immediately suggests the extent to which any consideration of the intertextual determinants of the whole notion of sexual politics projected in the poetry must account for the same kind of indeterminacy made evident in the portrayal of first man and first woman as literary constructs. In *Tetrachordon*, Milton may, with all confidence, call upon St. Paul to resolve the "controversie" over gender parity and participation in the *imago Dei*, but one may rest assured that that "controversie" nonetheless rages on unabated, as much in Milton's own psyche as among the feminists in our own time.

If such is true of Milton's interpretation in *Tetrachordon* of Genesis 1.27, it is no less true of his interpretation of the corresponding text, Genesis 2.18. Establishing an exegetical framework for his discourse as a whole, Milton begins by observing that the second chapter of Genesis "is granted to be a commentary on the first." The ostensible function of the second chapter is accordingly that of "clarifying" the first. Of the verses under consideration ("And the Lord God said, *It is* not good that the man should be alone; I will make him an help meet for him"), Milton maintains that they, in turn, are "granted to be an exposition of that former verse, *Male and female created he them.*" Although there are those who, "ingross[ing] to themselves the whole trade of interpreting, will not suffer the cleer text of God to doe the office of explaining it self," Milton will make it all perfectly lucid (*YP* 2.594). In the process, of course, he does nothing more than demonstrate how complex the so-called "cleer text of God" really is. Adopting that text as a commentary upon an earlier text, of which Milton's own text is a commentary upon both, and invoking the biblical text, along with Milton's commentary, as an intertext for disclosing the mysteries of the passage we have been discussing in *Paradise Lost*, we can see just how complex the whole interpretive process becomes. The "cleer text of Milton" is about as clear as the "cleer text of God." To recall and dispute Summers once again, we might say that appearance here as elsewhere *never* "nakedly reflects reality."

That such is particularly true in Genesis 2.18, which Milton takes to be a commentary on Genesis 1.27, is discernible throughout his attempt to come to terms with the meaning of the verses "And the Lord God said, It is not good that the man should be alone; I will make him an help meet for him." As I have already attempted to establish at some length in an earlier study, this is an exceedingly complex text, one that is open to an entire spectrum of interpretations.[22] There is neither the space nor the opportunity to explore these interpretations here. Suffice it to say that despite his claims to be able to demonstrate the lucidity of God's text, Milton himself was entirely aware of the problems attendant upon the text and the readings it elicited. Defining the role of the woman with respect to the man, the phrase "help meet," as Milton acknowledges, is one that is especially problematical.[23] "The originall heer," he says, "is more expressive then other languages word for word can render it." For that reason, Milton invents a whole new text to elucidate it and attributes that text to God: "which God as it were not satisfy'd with the naming of a help, goes on describing another self, a second self, a very self it self" (YP 2.600). God, of course, does no such thing: it is Milton who does so and in the process comes up with an interpretation of an interpretation. This is tantamount to his earlier discovery of "a superior and more natural law" not just to augment but in effect to contravene the biblical law laid down by St. Paul in his interpretation of Genesis 1.27.

Nothing gets clarified; nothing gets settled; everything just gets more complicated. It is out of this complex of exegetical postures and negotiations, this "ingrossing" to oneself of "the whole trade of interpreting" that the "strange and slippery text" of Milton's own epic comes into being. If the passage describing first man and first woman from that epic represents "a field of opposing stresses and signals," it is little wonder. One need only consider the intratextual and intertextual limina that constitute it in order to appreciate just how problematical that passage really is. As a kind of microcosm of the sexual politics reflected in the epic as a whole, this is a passage about which we shall never be empowered to proclaim that "here appearance nakedly reflects reality." As much as we might like to think so, nothing in Milton's epic does that. Particularly in the construction of a sexual politics, this is no "logical epic."[24] As the literary heir of unresolved (and perhaps unre-solvable) conflicts extending back to the biblical text and forward to Milton's own interpretation of those conflicts, *Paradise Lost* encodes within its own fabric a discourse of conflict and indeterminacy that refuses to provide for the imposition of a "final" interpretation. Truth is always "in the making" for Milton, always in process.[25] It is no less so here, in which the limina that constitute his text by their very nature define it problematically. Such is the nature of the passage in question as a reflection of what it means to read the paradisal text.

7 • "Inspir'd with Contradiction"
Mapping Gender Discourses in *Paradise Lost*

Joseph Wittreich

... the "reader's text" is the understanding the reader
derives from reading the text; the "author's text" is
the text the author has provided for the reader to read,
with all its potentialities.... What the author's text
thus emphasizes is the action of writing, the craft that
the writer writing has produced. The text defines continuing authorial presence.

—John T. Shawcross

A writer's response ... often provides a subtext that
either sabotages the surface text's expressed intentions
or escapes them through a language that mystifies what
it cannot bring itself to articulate but still attempts to
register.... In other words, [such writers] ... give the
text a deeper, richer, more complex life than the
sanitized one commonly presented to us.

—Toni Morrison[1]

I n the beginning, the war between the sexes could be fought—and often was fought—from the arsenal of *Paradise Lost*. In the clash of swords, male and female, "Hee for God only, shee for God in him" (4.299) was sometimes deflected by, and other times fell to the ground under the weight of, "O fairest of Creation, last and best / Of all Gods works" (9.896–97). And in this war, where so often the swords were Milton's words, men who spoke from the perspective, and sometimes in the language, of Satan were often disadvantaged, their arguments dismantled, by women who turned other words of Satan as well as those of Adam, Raphael, Michael, or the Son against them. Sufficiently prominent was their argument for Milton as ally and advocate of the female sex that Thomas Newton, in the first variorum edition of *Paradise Lost* (1749), felt obliged to acknowledge of *this* poem, "It has been remark'd that . . . [Milton] seems to court the favor of his female readers very much" even as Newton, again following his consultant Dr. Robert Thyer, poses against *Paradise Lost* the supposed misogyny of *Samson Agonistes*.[2]

Women's appropriation of Milton met inevitably with such efforts at reappropriation—efforts which may reach one culmination in Newton's variorum edition but which in Milton's own century were begun, and practiced paradigmatically, by John Dunton and later John Hopkins. Whatever Milton's disposition in *Paradise Lost*, in *Samson Agonistes*, says Dunton, this poet gives women their true "Picture" in the character of Dalila—and with such accuracy that "they can't deny but 'tis to the Life"; and even *Paradise Lost* is disposed in such a way that, according to Hopkins, women are given minimal access to a poem which, because of their lesser intelligences apparently, they are prone to misunderstand.[3] However much Milton may have distorted the "true" image of woman through an unusually favorable depiction of Eve, or however much women may have contorted that image by their misconstruals of Milton, the masculinist argument is that, returning to the fold of orthodoxy, Milton dealt woman a series of devastating blows not only in *Samson Agonistes* but in the lethal depictions of her in *The History of Britain*.

In the eyes of many, there were, besides, the insistent patriarchy and incipient sexism of the Divorce tracts. If, when he wrote *Paradise Lost*, Milton was an apostate from patriarchy, he remained a man in conflict with himself, eventually mending his ways by emending his arguments into the virulent misogyny of his late publications. That is one—and perhaps now the reigning—perspective on Milton. But such a view should be fronted by another: that as one of the founding texts for the myths of modern culture, *Paradise Lost*, as it reproduces, may also produce ideology; that, as a pivotal literary text of seventeenth century England, it may be in dialogic rather than monologic relation to hermeneutic traditions and thus may be a repository for overlapping, incongruent discourses, as well as a site from which to observe not so much a received myth and dominant ideology as the crevices and contradictions within both. The early myth, strikingly and substantially revised, may thus capitulate to another myth, a new ideology. An enigmatic text especially in its engagements with gender ideologies, *Paradise Lost* here seems to be in league with patriarchy and misogyny and there seems to be at enmity with both.

What is remarkable about this poem, as William Hayley perceived nearly two centuries ago, is that Milton ingeniously adopts, his poem accommodates, "the most opposite interpretations of scripture, as they happened to suit his poetical purposes."[4] In consequence, Milton's poem, instead of formulating transcendental solutions, encapsulates the terms of an historical debate, embodying the sometimes incongruent formations of competing interpretive traditions. *Paradise Lost*, that is, emerges from a controversy over privilege and priority in interpretation (Genesis 1 versus Genesis 2, the Old versus the New Testament, the Hebrew versus the Christian Bible) and issues its own statement concerning that debate. It incorporates rival hermeneutics in a way that highlights their contradictions and interacts with often competing systems of interpretation, implying that, if commentary has had the effect of arresting the play of ambiguities in various scriptural texts, *Paradise Lost*, entering into an oppositional dialectic with hermeneutic traditions, will reanimate such play, thus redeeming the scriptural texts in which such ambiguities operate.

Yet *Paradise Lost* also comprehends more than the contradictions within the Bible—or within and between different hermeneutic traditions accruing to it. Also caught within its embrace are the conflicts of Milton's own day—the dialectics at play within the poet's own culture.[5] What, within this context, becomes the nagging question is whether an author (as Constance Jordan remarks *without* reference to Milton) "is using contradiction for the purpose of establishing irony" or whether the writer "is merely representing uncritically a position characterized by contradiction which becomes ironic retrospectively, by virtue of that contradiction." If the former, Jordan concludes, "one needs to ask: Why is this play? What are the rules of these games? And for what stakes are they being played?"[6] These are the questions my own essay will address.

It does so, moreover, in the full realization that *Paradise Lost* is about the losing of paradise and the realities of fallen existence where words are deceptive, where harsh contention and fierce dispute are the order of the day. From the dialectics of this debate, Milton may wrest a higher truth; yet he also stands free of the illusion that the new truth is the whole truth. Rather, like what it supersedes, the new truth is partial, limited, relative, contingent, while perhaps bearing a clearer, ampler imprint of the original truth. *Paradise Lost* is mapped by—and a mapping of—debates between the sexes in the seventeenth century. Seated within the poem are a full array of gender discourses (patriarchal, misogynous, and feminist) that Milton's century produced, the inflections of which, if not their broad outline, are distinctly Milton's own. Because Milton brings so many different gender discourses within the reach of *Paradise Lost*, representing each in delicate nuance, he may be said to embody another more complete, even if still *in*complete, version of the truth concerning the relationship between the sexes—a truth that still eludes full embodiment.

Start with the obvious: not the interpretation by St. Paul but the rendering of the Creation story in the book of Genesis furnishes the principal subtext for the representations of Adam and Eve in books 4 and 5, and later in books 7 and 8, and accounts for the shifting movements in each of these books. Milton here implies that received interpretation should give way to reinterpretation; that, while fallen consciousness may achieve interpretive breakthroughs, it remains forever vulnerable to conflicting and conflicted perspectives, sometimes embracing partial truth as if it were the totality and other times giving parity to variant interpretations, then using them for polemical convenience rather than as a ground for intellectual commitment and approval.

Behind the representations of Adam and Eve (in books 4, 5, 7, and 8) are three fragments of the Genesis text, which address first inferentially, then explicitly, the matter of divine resemblance—whether it is shared equally by Adam and Eve or in differing degrees; indeed, whether Eve participates in the divine image at all. The Genesis sequence, orchestrated as a movement of mind and an evolution of consciousness, plotting the movements of and shifts in an ideology as it travels through history,[7] swerves from inference to inference to bold assertion, thus affording a rhetorical pattern that can be replicated within the increasingly spacious ruminations and reflections of *Paradise Lost*. The Genesis sequence, like that in Milton's poem, is sometimes misrepresented as a movement in which the originating thesis is overthrown by its antithesis when, in fact, the antithesis is overthrown by return to, and confirmation of, the initial thesis; by the swerve from dialectically patterned inferences into plain declaration. In *Paradise Lost* sequentiality makes lessons out of the Genesis fragments, the different stages of the myth they inscribe, wherein the senses, closed by the Fall, are subsequently cleared and human consciousness, occluded, eventually is opened again.

The competing perspectives of Genesis 1 and 2 are well-known and now well-worn by citation. The related text from Genesis 5, on the contrary, is often slighted by omission. Yet the three fragments, part of one realized vision, are interdependent in their concerns but also mutually reflective, corrective, and illuminating. In the "P" (or Priestly) account, we read:

> And God said, Let the waters bring forth abundantly the moving creatures that hath life. . . .
> And God created great whales, and every living creature that moveth. . . .
> And God said, Let the earth bring forth the living creature after his kind, cattle, and creeping thing, and beast of the earth. . . .
> And God said, Let us make man in our image, after our likeness: and let them have dominion over . . . the earth.
> So God created man in his *own* image, in the image God created he him; male and female created he them.
> And God blessed them, and God said unto them, Be fruitful and multiply, and replenish the earth, and subdue it: and have dominion over . . . the earth.
>
> (1.20–28)

In the "J" (or Yahwist) account, which is thought to predate the preceding one by at least several centuries, we are told alternatively:

> And the LORD God formed man *of* the dust of the ground, and breathed into his nostrils the breath of life; and man became a living soul.
> And the LORD God planted a garden . . . ; and there he put the man whom he had formed.
> And out of the ground made the LORD God to grow every tree . . . : the tree of life . . . , and the tree of the knowledge of good and evil. . . .
> And the LORD God said, *It is* not good that the man should be alone; I will make him a help meet for him.
> And out of the ground the LORD God formed every beast of the field, and every fowl of the air; and brought *them* unto Adam to see what he would call them: and whatsoever Adam called every living creature, that was the name thereof.
> And Adam gave names to all . . . ; but for Adam there was not found an help meet for him.
> And the LORD God caused a deep sleep to fall upon Adam, and he slept: and he took one of his ribs, and closed up the flesh instead thereof;

And the rib, which the LORD God had taken from man,
made he a woman and brought her unto the man.

And Adam said, This *is* now bone of my bones, and flesh
of my flesh: she shall be called Woman, because she was
taken out of Man.

Therefore shall a man leave his father and his mother, and
shall cleave unto his wife: and they shall be one flesh.

(2.7–9, 18–24)

The discrepancies between the two accounts are obvious:
in the former telling male and female are conterminous with
one another, both aspects of generic Man with both presumably sharing in God's "image" and "likeness," both together
being given dominion over the world: let *them* rule. In the
latter account, however, man (gender-specific man) is the
first created; he is made from the dust of the ground, she
from one of his ribs, and to him alone is given the interdiction against eating from the tree of knowledge. So that
man will not be alone the beasts of the field and the fowls
of the air are created, with Adam empowered to name them.
Only then is Woman created—as an afterthought and supplement to Creation. Nothing is said of *this* creation (male or
female) participating in the divine image although, when it
is assumed as Milton himself did in *Tetrachordon*, that the
second account fills in the silences, repairs the omissions
in the first, that rather than being antithetical to the first
it is an elaboration and interpretation—when this view is
assumed it is often presumed that man, not woman, is created
in the image and likeness or, alternatively, that man pos-
sesses the image and woman a *mere* likeness. The second
account can then be harmonized with the first through ret-
rospective interpretation accompanied by the argument,
which Milton himself once made, that the slippery use of
pronouns ("he him . . . he them") in Genesis 1 signals sexual
difference and inequality.[8] Even when disparity and difference are discerned in the two accounts, they are often
harmonized in the understanding that equality is a condition
of prelapsarian, inequality the curse of postlapsarian existence, with the curse belonging to the woman. In either case,
interpretation is usually by inference, according to how things

seem, with Genesis 1 often emerging as a reflection of the world before the Fall and Genesis 2 as a revelation of fallen existence.

Not until Genesis 5 do we meet with the plain but, given the persistence of the pronouns ("he him . . . he them"), still seemingly equivocal declaration:

> This *is* the book of the generations of Adam. In the day that God created man, in the likeness of God made he him;
> Male and female created he them; and blessed them and called their name Adam, in the day when they were created.
> And Adam lived an hundred and thirty years, and begat a son in his own likeness, after his image. . . .
> . . . and he begat sons and daughters:
> And all the days that Adam lived were nine hundred and twelve years: and he died.
>
> (5.1–5)

From what has become the feminist perspective, which views Genesis 1 and 2 as competing texts, Genesis 5 effectively and emphatically gives authority to Genesis 1 by underlining Adam as generic Man (Adam is *their* name), by eliminating the ambiguity of image/ likeness with respect to *their* creation (they are created in the *likeness* of God, both in his *image*), and by then allowing them to reproduce their own image in their creations. The principle implicit in Genesis 5 is that every new stage of creation replicates the image of its immediate creator: Adam and Eve of God; the sons and daughters of Adam and Eve, their image. But from what is now the masculinist perspective on these texts, Genesis 5 simply extends the patriarchy of Genesis 2 by its slippery use of pronouns, by sliding away from the generic toward gender-specific Adam, and by memorializing his death without mentioning hers.

What have become gender-marked interpretations were in Milton's day interpretations often determined by politics and ideology: left/right, liberal/conservative, Puritan/Royalist. That there are sometimes differences between perspectives advanced in Milton's prose writings and those assumed within his poems becomes evident when we notice that in both books 4 and 7, in the latter instance through God's very words, Milton eliminates the ambiguities inherent in pronouns but also in the terms "image" and "likeness." *They* are created in God's image, in *them* is divine resemblance. Indeed, Milton moves here and in books 8 and 11 to silence negative interpretations resting on inference: for instance, that Adam but not Eve is privy to the interdiction, that this fact signals God's valuing of man over woman; or that dominion and rule belong to him because he, not she, is empowered with language, thought, intellect, and poetry.

Instead of bending Genesis 1 to fit with Genesis 2 (as Milton does in *Tetrachordon*), Adam's first speech in *Paradise Lost* revises Genesis 2 so that it accords with Genesis 1: *they* are "rais'd . . . from the dust" (4.416) and *together* asked "to keep / This one, this easie charge . . . / . . . not to taste that onely Tree / Of Knowledge" (4.420–24). Apparently, Eve has heard the interdiction from God himself, hence can quote his very words (9.661–63). Presumably *they* are "Charg'd not to touch the interdicted Tree" (7.46). Thus Eve tells Satan:

> But of this Tree *we* may not taste or touch;
> God so commanded, and left that Command
> Sole Daughter of his voice. . . .
>
> (9.651–53; my emphasis)

The narrative voice concurs:

> . . . *they* knew, and ought t' have still remember'd
> The high Injunction not to taste that Fruit. . . .
>
> (10.12–13; my emphasis)

Complementing Adam's account of naming the animals, moreover, is Eve's aside in which she claims to have named the flowers (11.273–77). Milton's point is made insistently: not just fallen but unfallen humanity, not just humankind but angels make wrong inferences and can be foiled by a false surmise, many of which *Paradise Lost* purports to expose. Satan's deception of Uriel in book 3 is typical of such instances—of the many interpretive hazards—in Milton's poem.

Milton's representation of Adam and Eve when taken whole, instead of read piecemeal, points toward an interpretation the opposite of the one usually presumed. The effect of Milton's authorial maneuverings is to problematize both Scripture and its interpretive traditions, as well as Milton's poem. What we can say—now only provisionally and perhaps never with full certainty —is that Milton means to remind us that his entire poem is the product of a fallen, though not necessarily false, consciousness; that what always seems to falsify consciousness, especially fallen consciousness, is its propensity for taking the part for the whole, an improved interpretation (Copernicus's over Ptolemy's, let us say) for the final truth. Indeed, this centering of cosmological theory and dispute in *Paradise Lost* is one of many conspicuous signals that this poem is about what it relates: competing interpretations, the status that should be accorded each of them, their respective truth-claims and truth-values. *Paradise Lost* is a poem in which a sun-centered cosmology upholds a Christocentric (son-centered) theology—is a poem that out of such interdependency creates what one theologian will call a "science of salvation" wherein Jesus, as both "the true center of the world" and "the sun of our souls," subtends a heliocentric astronomy and a theocentric religion.[9] Milton's exceptional education included, as Toni Morrison says of William Dunbar, "the latest thought on theology and science" with a poem like *Paradise Lost* representing Milton's effort, again like Dunbar's, to make theology and science "mutually accountable, to make one support the other."[10]

Milton's foregrounding of contending cosmological theories is, in fact, doubly interesting inasmuch as this discourse is wedged between two competing Genesis accounts of Creation in what (if now two books) were in the first edition of *Paradise Lost* one book, and in such a way that the lesson drawn from cosmological discourse may be applied to the Creation myth and its interpretive traditions: competing interpretations complicate truth in such a way as to illustrate the deconstructionist proposition (even as they reject its underlying philosophical skepticism) that "there is a way of thinking about truth which is more adventurous, risky. At that point, truth, which is without end, abyssal, is the very movement of the drift. There is a way of thinking about truth which is not reassuring, . . . bring[ing] us into a discourse about the truth of truth . . . ; the field is open"[11]— perhaps more in matters of cosmology than in human affairs. In *Paradise Lost*, the one discourse sits in irresolution while the other moves toward resolution.

Books 7 and 8 are a lesson in how "truth" in *Paradise Lost* is processive, in how "resolution" is achieved through gradually unfolding revelation. In Milton's poem no less than in its sourcebook, different accounts of Creation complete but also compete with one another; and the point is driven home by the further analogy that what comes first in chronological sequence both in the Bible and in Milton's poem, through narrative scrambling, actually appears last. Thus Jonathan Richardson and his son accurately remark, in annotating book 8.478, that "Here is the First of Eve's History, which is Compleated by what she says to *Adam;* 4.449. & c. and by what follows; 5.481."[12] Completed yes, but also complicated. And the complications invariably derive from Milton's artistic strategy, so ably described by Richard Corum, of "writing all these narratives simultaneously" and of writing them in such a way that he "leave[s] out not only large segments of each of them but also temporal, spatial, and generic markers which would allow us to separate them into distinct stories."[13] That is, what may seem separate, discreet panels of narrative continually elide with one another and thus become interdependent elements in interpretation. Still, if some narrative panels conciliate, others collide: for example, the accounts of Creation by Uriel and Raphael exhibit concord whereas those by Raphael and Adam are at odds. In the process, *Paradise Lost* demonstrates repeatedly that what may seem like mere repetitions or redundancies inherited from the scriptural accounts of Creation are, rather, the areas of contention through which the problems in a myth are gathered into focus and from which that myth takes its deepest meanings.

For a poet who can imagine a "bottomless deep" (as Milton

does in *Paradise Regained* 1.361), the very notions of "truth" and "resolution" are likely to be problematical. A poem that everywhere champions moral and political freedom emblematizes both, if we can borrow Stanley Rosen's reasoning, in "the freedom to choose or to reject the Copernican revolution," a main consequence of which, as Milton seems to have understood, was "to transform science into a *fiction* in the literal sense: something not simply arranged but *formed* by human intelligence" whose "truth" therefore is contingent, perspectival. A poem inset with analogies, and in its middle repeatedly testing the divine analogy—whether things on earth correspond with things as they are in heaven—*Paradise Lost* focuses this matter in books 7 and 8 by running scientific debate between discrepant accounts of Creation, thus analogizing science and religion, and thereupon collapsing both into fictions, as if to make the point that cosmological theory is, as Rosen says of another intellectual revolution, "a radicalized version of the theological problem of the proliferation of sects"; as if to say, as Rosen does, that "whereas there may be one comprehensive truth, there is no single *interpretation* of the truth."[14]

The radical implications of such a view—that truth is processive, hence always partial—are objectified in cosmological debate but also dramatized within Scripture by the warring hermeneutics encamped around Genesis 1 and 2 and within *Paradise Lost* by the competing versions of Creation proffered by Raphael and Adam. Interestingly, those implications show up only to be suppressed in early commentary on *Paradise Lost*. In a poem that hides so much contemporary history within its master-myth, it is remarkable, only because such instances are so rare, that conspicuous allusions to Galileo and Copernicus should balance one another in the two halves of Milton's epic. It is also ironic that two figures experiencing and thus emblematizing censorship should then become occasions for a censorship of sorts within critical commentary. The irony is compounded when we remember that, in the prologue to book 7, Milton comes closest to openly addressing his own fears of censorship — "fall'n on evil dayes, / . . . and evil tongues;/ In darkness, and with dangers compast round" (25–27), even as he now identifies his muse as "Urania" (1) who had given her name to a work by Lady Mary Wroth that had recently been caught up in a scandal of censorship.[15]

Patrick Hume's annotation is curt: *"Copernicus* his Opinion, tho first broach'd by *Pythagoras* and *Aristarchus."*[16] Jonathan Richardson and his son are more expansive, but then their elaboration is all the more curious because it is situated within the context of an open acknowledgment that Milton labors under the "Secret History" of censorship. Indeed, their elaboration is doubly curious inasmuch as it forces the Richardsons to surrender one of their principal critical strategies, that of eradicating contradictions on the surface of Milton's poem by privileging the voice of this or that speaker therein, Raphael's over Adam's let us say. In order to keep *Paradise Lost* remote from its contemporary scene, from any notion of progressive truth or philosophical irresolution, the Richardsons declare flatly that Milton's poem is geocentric even if this theory is voiced by Adam and later Satan while its heliocentric counterpart is formulated by Raphael. The Richardsons are emphatic: Raphael, despite the fact that he is the mouthpiece for Copernican theory, is an ancient not a modern and certainly no Sir Isaac Newton. That, they say, "would have been Ridiculous": what is new in cosmology, though not forgotten in Milton's poem, "could not be a part of its System."[17] The argument here is so tendentious that it constitutes a tear in the text of the commentary and is, one supposes, intended to hide something: not just that Milton's system is conflicted, not just its philosophic irresolution, but the very uses to which Milton puts such knowledge by deploying a theory of science to gloss the Creation story of religion, even to subtend the poem's Christocentric theology, and to mediate, at the same time, another problem of the "modern" world, the relationship between the sexes.

It is sufficiently odd that Milton makes no mention of Tycho Brahe, indeed it is so odd, that one wonders if it is not just this mediatorial role, assumed by Brahe in the world of science, that Milton here assumes in matters of religion where he must mediate between two conflicting Genesis accounts, the second probably preceding the first in order of time.[18] One wonders, too, if Brahe does not provide Milton with the hidden logic by which he will eventually privilege Genesis 1 over 2. Brahe had been used to maintain the validity of both Ptolemaic and Copernican theory by arguing that the former pertains to the world before the Fall, the latter to the world afterwards. The same sort of logic had been used by biblical commentators to ratify the competing accounts of Creation in Genesis: Genesis 1, coming first in the order of narrative but last in the order of time, depicts the equality of the sexes before the Fall but lost when Paradise is lost; and Genesis 2, the subjection of woman that pertains to fallen existence.

Milton's accommodation of the two texts is altogether more slippery and, with reference to each text, is perspectival: how things were and how they should have been, how things now are and how they will be—or ought to be. Genesis 1, encapsulating an idealism, envisions a mutuality of the sexes under the paternal rule of God; and Genesis 2, how they were owing to Adam's psychology and Satan's pathology. Genesis 2 reflects the unequal relationship of the sexes, woman under man's subjection, that has pertained in fallen history and Genesis 1, the realized equality of the sexes just before the expulsion from the Garden and the equality to be achieved before the Kingdom of God can commence in history.

Milton's compromise solution, that is, can best be understood in analogy with that of Brahe: both change the state of knowledge and alter interpretation by posing problems that, challenging conventional solutions (sometimes only obliquely), effect a break with tradition. Milton's commitment to ongoing revelation makes space for mutating thought and evolving explanations—for the correction of error through the refinement of observation. In his mapping of gender discourses, Milton the theorist seems always to outrun and overrule the traditions, and traditional explanations, he contemplates, in the process appropriating innovations (not always his own) and through them casting such discourses into a distinctly modern form. Milton does not claim to have presented through his concatenated discourses *the* truth but does imply that, because they are more reliable, his observations, along with the interpretations founded upon them, provide readier access to the complete truth.

Competing accounts of Creation (and of much else) in *Paradise Lost* are thus indicators of different stages and states of consciousness—unfallen and fallen, villainous and visionary. It matters that in book 4 Adam intuits the Genesis 1 account which later, in discursive argument, gets displaced by his own distorting elaboration of Genesis 2. This displacement occurs, a new fiction is created, in just that moment when it behooves Adam to be self-serving. Correspondingly, it matters, again in book 4, that Satan stumbles into "the truth" of the Genesis 1 account but, more usually, occupies the interpretive space and spouts the interpretive commonplaces of Genesis 2: that Adam is "rais'd / From dust" (9.177–78) and that Eve is the lesser, Adam the "higher" intelligence and "Heroic" figure (9.483, 485). Or to be more delicate still: Milton revises existing explanations, both of cosmology and creation, while holding all such speculation within the realm of hypothesis, thus keeping certain forms of truth tentative. In this poem, with its plentitude of speculation and so replete with theorization, Milton fixes limits on both as he allows for, even urges, concern over conditions and degrees not in other worlds but in this one. The appropriate end of Adam's questioning (and of ours), as he himself perceives, is not a searching of God's "secrets," but acquest of knowledge: "the more / To magnifie his works, the more we know" (7.95–97). Where there is—or should be—rejoicing on Adam's part is in *this* world, *this* paradise, and in his fair *Eve*.

Some contradictions may achieve resolution in *Paradise Lost*, but not all do, as is befitting a poetic universe that is large, that contains multitudes; that through contradictions subverts all claims to dogmatic certitude both in religion and science; that, as in *De Doctrina Christiana*, values ongoing revelation and multiple possible interpretations over one that is certifiably correct. Books 7 and 8 treat contending scientific theories, conflicting religious myths as fictions to contemplate and, if not certifying this rather than that one, nevertheless privilege one over another; and what often gets privileged in this poem are those revelations that come later, if not in order of narrative, certainly in order of time. Contradictions and inconsistencies may effect alarming dislocation in theological but not in poetic systems where the possibilities are completely open, where an utterance may be true or false relatively. The Richardsons understood that "Milton is Writing a Poem, not a System of Divinity or Philosophy," but also expected an analogous consistency in Milton's poetical system, the very sort of consistency from which, alas, the poet was now breaking free.[19] What the Richardsons do not understand, as Terry Eagleton informs us in a more generalized context, is that in a poem like *Paradise Lost* "coherence . . . [may be] nothing less than systematic contradiction."[20]

The account of Creation in book 7 leaves the impression that Raphael is an eyewitness, here relating to Adam what Raphael heard God say and watched Him do. Book 8 revises this impression—"I that Day was absent . . . / Bound on a voyage uncouth . . . / Farr on excursion toward the Gates of Hell" (229–31)—as Raphael confides that God has indeed bestowed gifts upon mankind, the chief of which is His own image: God "pour'd / Inward and outward both, his image fair" (220–21). That is, as the Richardsons were probably the first to point out, this admission in book 8 makes clear that Raphael's earlier account derives from "Hear-say, or Inspiration," presumably the latter as Adam insinuates.[21] The balancing of their separate stories, Raphael's at the end of book 7 and Adam's near the end of book 8, pits divine revelation against human interpretation: Raphael's inspired story ("with Grace Divine / Imbu'd" [8.215–16]) against Adam's human dialect, which here articulates a story hard —perhaps impossible—for man to tell since "who himself beginning knew?" (251). Having mediated God's account of Creation, His story, Raphael now hears from Adam man's story: "now hear mee relate / My Storie, which perhaps thou hast not heard" (204–205). "Divine instructer," "Divine interpreter," "Divine / Hystorian" (5.546, 7.72, 8.6–7), Raphael listens as Adam poses his against God's story, some words of which are attributed to God himself.

In the process, woman who was created with the man (according to Raphael), is now, as Margaret Homans observes, "recreated, by Adam's imagination, as a derivative of the man."[22] *Paradise Lost* may not evade the patriarchal and often times misogynous notion that the female contributes the matter, the male the form and spirit, of Creation; but—and indeed this perspective falls outside the boundaries of Homans' feminist reading—Milton's use of such commonplaces becomes sufficiently slippery in this poem that by the time Adam relates his version of the story, and then once we witness his response to Eve's Creation, the patriarchal underpinnings of the Genesis 2 account are eroded through inversion as Adam, now contributing the matter for Eve's Creation, in his initial response to her, implies that she, not he, is the perfect form and spirit, the sum and quintessence of Creation. Through this pairing of Raphael's and Adam's Creation stories, while simultaneously aligning the former with Genesis 1, the latter with Genesis 2, Milton implies a movement from God's word to Adam's fictions and on then to culture's mythic fabrications. If there is privileging in Milton's poem, it is a privileging of Genesis 1 over Genesis 2,[23] of angelic over human report. Generally in agreement with one another, the supplementary and corroborating accounts by Uriel and Raphael relate to one another as report to revelation. Uriel witnesses what Raphael knows only by hearsay—or through revelation: "I saw when at his Word the formless Mass, / This worlds material mould, came to a heap" (3.708–09).

Written in an interrogative mode, books 7 and 8, organized around Adam's own interrogations, thrust important interpretive questions at the reader: who is the reliable narrator, translator, mediator of God's word? is the fact that Adam's (and later Satan's) view of cosmology is Ptolemaic and Raphael's Copernican a hint? is the fact that one cosmology is earth-centered (or as Satan expounds it, man-centered) and the other sun- or (as Raphael relates it) Son-centered a further clue? What, if anything, are we to make of the correspondence between God's physical universe (which is sun-centered) and Milton's poetic universe (which is son-centered)? And how does the perception that Raphael's story, broadly speaking, accords with Genesis 1 and Adam's with Genesis 2 affect the veracity and value of their separate narratives or, alternatively, of the different scriptural subtexts informing their narratives? Both Raphael's and Adam's accounts entail supplementation; but whereas Raphael's supplement is scriptural (the few splicings from Genesis 2 are God's word), Adam's is experiential. The authority is Adam's word—or Eve's, whose earlier words are here abridged and sometimes censored, or briefly God's "reported" words contradicting what otherwise He says in the poem.

The different accounts of Creation according to Raphael and Adam foreground questions of authoritative voice and privileged text, but also focus the problem exhibited by Adam whether he is defining his place in the cosmos or his relationship to Eve: he is prone to all sorts of contrivances in order "To save appearances" (8.82), with the consequence that he fails repeatedly to value rightly. Their separate narratives are an example of what Mieke Bal calls "a fracturing interpretation, an interpretation that will bring out into the open the contradictions within a text attributable to a gendered plurality of voices or focalizations."[24] Indeed, their respective narratives are evidence of Milton's moving toward such fracturing interpretation, which, focusing contradictions, capitalizes on coexisting meanings but which also, by reversing the customary privileging of Genesis 2 over 1, has the effect of opening up instead of closing down interpretive possibilities.

The sixth day of Creation yet remains, says Raphael: "There wanted yet the Master work, the end / Of all yet don" (7.505–06) whose correspondence will be with Heaven and not, as Satan had hoped, with Hell. In words reminiscent of the narrator's description of Adam in book 4, Raphael describes this new creation as "not prone / . . . but endu'd / With Sanctitie of Reason" that he "might erect / His Stature, and upright with Front serene / Govern the rest . . . and from thence / Magnanimous to correspond with Heav'n" (506–11). Yet if the reference here seems to be to gender-specific man, the male portion of Creation, through the intervention of God's voice, this false surmise is checked with God addressing the Son and, in His plain-talk, stripping away all ambiguity from Genesis 1:

> Let us make now Man in our image, Man
> In our similitude, and let them rule.
>
> (519–20)

By God's account as mediated by Raphael, generic man named Adam is now created:

> ... in his own Image hee
> Created thee, in the Image of God
> Express ...
> Male he created thee, but thy consort
> Female for Race; then bless'd Mankind, and said,
> Be fruitful, multiplie, and fill the Earth,
> Subdue it, and throughout Dominion hold. ...
> Here finish'd hee, and all that he had made
> View'd, and behold all was entirely good. ...
>
> (526–32, 548–49)

Rather as Genesis 5 reconfirms the perspective of Genesis 1, in song the angels reiterate that generic Man ("men") is now "Created in his Image, there to dwell / ... and in reward to rule" (625, 627–28).

It is right that we recognize in this account of Creation "the inextricably plotted relations of the 'P' and 'J' accounts"; that in "this splicing ... two heterogeneous accounts [become] a single one that is both intellectually and aesthetically coherent," though not necessarily (as this critic thinks) "ideologically" troubling,[25] especially from a feminist perspective. Man, generic man, is made in God's "own image" and given "rule" over the rest of creation. The animals are created first with emmet and bee singled out as "Pattern[s] of just equalitie" and emblems of "Commonaltie," mutuality (7.487, 489). If there is any rupture in Milton's text at this point, it is created by the emblematic movement from emmet to bee—with the bee, as Thomas Newton was quick to recognize, being actually an image of *"Feminine Monarchie."*[26] Then, in the order of creation, comes Man: they are given dominion over the rest of creation, as well as the interdiction concerning the tree of knowledge. That is, the chief appropriation from Genesis 2, the interdiction, is resituated in order to dispose of the argument for the inequality of the sexes that, as situated in Genesis 2, it was commonly used to uphold: man, gender-specific man, is created, then the animals; man is empowered to name them and thereupon given the interdiction.

Man is empowered with language, thought, intellect—that is why the interdiction is given to him, not Eve, who only later is created. To revise the sequence is to revise this argument. To resituate the interdiction episode within the context of Genesis 1—"Here finish'd hee, and all that he had made / View'd, and behold all was entirely good" (7.548–49)—is to displace an argument for inequality with one for equality. Raphael's account of Creation accentuates men/ *them.* Alternatively, Adam's account emphasizes *I* and *my*: "My Tongue obey'd and readily could name / What e'er I saw" (8.272–73); "I nam'd them, as they pass'd, and understood / Thir Nature, with such knowledge God endu'd / My sudden apprehension" (352–54). In a modest parenthesis, we learn from Eve that, similarly gifted, she named the flowers (11.273–77). There is "radical privileging"[27] here: Raphael's voice, God's words, over Adam's voice and human articulations. Only in the upside-down world of fallen human consciousness does man's word take precedence over God's, Milton seems to be saying in this poem where there is a carefully orchestrated hierarchy of voices, where God's plot does not always agree with man's stories and where those stories are themselves riddled with contradictions.

To turn from Genesis 1 to Genesis 2, from Raphael's voice to Adam's, is to turn from fact to fiction—to a fiction so self-aggrandizing that Adam loses stature, not Eve. That Adam's story is here viewed as a fiction is made evident by three details: he has God denying the equality of His Son that elsewhere God and the angels assert; he edits Eve's earlier account of Creation, and censors it, in a way that advantages the self by diminishing the other. He does this, in part, by claiming that the interdiction is given to him before Eve's Creation whereas the rest of the poem implies that both are made privy to the interdiction by God himself (see 4.426–27, 5.51–52, 7.45–47, 9.651–53, 751–54, 863–64).

Sometimes the narrator's (as distinct from Milton's) voice, but more often Adam's, is responsible for bleaching Eve's history. That is, Adam hears Raphael's story (Genesis 1) and uses it in the same way he uses Ptolemaic theory: to center himself, to exalt his own position in Creation. Eve may have stooped to her own self-image when she awakened from creation; but Adam, by his own account, "Strait toward Heav'n my wondring Eyes I turnd" (8.257), then "My self . . . perus'd, and Limb by Limb / Survey'd" (267–68). Thereupon Adam is approached by "methought, of shape Divine" (295) and is raised over "Fields and Waters" (301), then led up "A woodie Mountain" (303) where he sees fruit laden trees "Tempting . . . in me sudden appetite / To pluck and eat" (308–09). Adam's dream is an oracle of temptation: his own and later Jesus's on the mountain.

It is also an example of the unusually thick layering, as well as steady convergence, of multiple interpretive traditions within *Paradise Lost*, these lines recalling the Boehmean claim that *"Adam* was (before his *Eve*) *forty dayes* in Paradise, in the Temptation," along with the fact that the second Adam goes into the wilderness for forty days, and there stands in *"Adams* stead before the Devill and Gods Anger" but also concludes his *forty houres . . .* in the Grave . . . [by awakening] *Adam* out of his sleep."[28] In *Paradise Lost*, when Adam awakens, he falls submissive before the "Presence Divine" from which he hears, in accordance with Genesis 2, the "rigid interdiction," then is given *with his race* rule over creation—the birds and beasts whom he proceeds to name. Yet Adam's first impressions are of their inferiority. With them he can have no society such as exists in heaven: "Among unequals what societie / Can sort, what harmonie or true delight?" (8.383–84). For the first time— and in contradiction of everything we have heard previously (from God, from the angels)—we hear, by Adam's report of God-talk, that "none I know / Second to me or like, equal much less" (406–07; cf. 3.306–07). Adam then reports God's perfection and man's imperfection: "in unitie defective" (425). Allowing that He has been trying Adam who is "My image" (441), God creates Eve and leads her to Adam: "Grace was in all her steps, Heav'n in her Eye, / In every gesture dignitie and love" (488–89). Adam is now in possession of the fairest of all God's gifts, which is grace, he learned earlier, but which here he objectifies as Eve: "my Bone, . . . my Flesh, my Self / . . . one Flesh, one Heart, one Soul" (495–99). Adam does not say so, but here he seems precariously close to thinking that Eve who is created from him is created by him, hence naturally inferior to him according to the logic that the creator is superior to, and thus rules, his or her creation. Repeatedly, as Diane McColley observes, "Adam is . . . inclined to arrogance about his dominion," yet an arrogance that by the end of book 8 is tamed.[29]

Eve, in her version of this part of the story, now turns from Adam but is brought back by his pleading. But Adam here censors her account in a way that promotes self over other and that suggests submission is woman's natural condition. However, like Satan's in book 4, Adam's perspective now shifts: Eve who had seemed inferior now seems superior. And Adam proceeds to accuse God of taking "More then enough," of having "bestow'd [on Eve] / Too much of Ornament" (8.537–38). She is too elaborate in "outward shew" and less exact in "inward Faculties"; she is "th' inferiour," Adam concludes, "resembling less / His Image who made both, and less expressing / The character of that Dominion giv'n / O're other Creatures" (538–45). Adam's account here does not match well with Raphael's in book 7. In book 4, Satan had checked his own faulty perception; here, in an enormously complicated and confusing speech, Raphael corrects Adam's: Eve is created for Adam's love, "Not . . . Subjection" and, as Raphael reminds him, in her wisdom has seen "when thou art seen least wise" (561–78).[30] Adam gets it right at last as he acknowledges "Those thousand decencies that daily flow / From all her words and actions mixt with Love / . . . which declare unfeign'd / Union of Mind, or in us both one Soul" (601–04).

With these words, Adam acknowledges their interdependence—their equivalence and equality. Various images of Eve have floated through his mind; and he is free, as he displays here, to choose and approve the best:

> I to thee disclose
> What inward thence I feel, not therefore foild,
> Who meet with various objects, from the sense
> Variously representing; yet still free
> Approve the best, and follow what I approve.
>
> (8.607–11)

What Adam has chosen—and here approves—is made abundantly evident when, in book 9, he says that by Eve, owing to her "influence," he is given "Access in every Vertue" and simultaneously, when in her presence, is made "More wise, more watchful, stronger . . ." (309–11). Satan's exaltation of Eve over Adam as the higher spiritual principle and superior intelligence may smack of gnosticism (yet another heresy he embraces within Milton's poem). On the other hand, "there is nothing peculiarly 'gnostic' in an exegetical tradition," such as is here invoked, that acknowledges Eve "to be a principle of Wisdom and spiritual enlightenment for humanity. This view," as Pheme Perkins proposes, "may go back to the origin of the Genesis material itself" and has the effect, finally, of corroborating Eve and Adam as co-images of deity.[31]

We know from Milton's Commonplace Book, from *De Doctrina Christiana* and other of his prose works, that Scripture and its warring hermeneutics had always been Milton's workshop. We learn from *Paradise Lost* the secret concatenations and the consequences thereof: that poetry may revise the interpretive traditions it encodes, that rather than corroborating it may challenge received opinion. Interpretive commonplaces are not explained, but explained away, by a poem that is itself (in the version we all read) a second edition and that in its last books portrays Eve as herself a second edition. In Milton's poem, Eve comes to be centered in human history, whereupon patriarchy subsides and misogyny is pressed beyond the borders of the text. Both are parts of the history Milton's poem reflects, but only *parts*; and each is situated in such a way as to mark a phase in the history of consciousness which, as depicted in the sequence of books, is linear and progressive. The Genesis subtext has the effect of locating *Paradise Lost* in a moment of history, of changing consciousness, but also of implying an analogy between mythic (past) and actual (present) history. A new consciousness is here being forged on the anvil of past history, with this new Miltonic formation lending credence to the claim of the (probably) pseudonymous Esther Sowernam: "The feminine sex is exceedingly honoured by poets in their writings."[32]

In the last decades of the seventeenth century, such credit is given increasingly to Milton, presumably because *Paradise Lost* contained what, from the point of view of some women, was "a successful persuasion"[33]—one that negotiated its way around (sometimes nullifying) respected human authorities and one that, simultaneously, recuperated divine authority by enlisting the Bible as a sanction for sexual equality and women's rights. In this way, *Paradise Lost* achieved the status of a secular scripture, quite literally so when one remembers the extent to which Matthew Poole's followers drew upon Milton in annotating Genesis, and felt comfortable doing so, precisely because Milton's "persuasion" relied upon the successful accommodation of a variety of authoritative traditions (Hebrew and Christian) and different interpretive voices (patristic as well as rabbinical, Catholic as well as Protestant, humanist as well as Puritan).[34]

Paradise Lost summons diverse traditions but is slave to none. Its transactions with biblical texts are all the more intricate because they proceed by now expanding, now abridging their sources, thereby exposing some suppressions in earlier commentary, disclosing what previously had gone unseen, thus unreported, while also exonerating what often seemed to be the most intractable and even regressive of scriptural texts. In the process, Milton's source-books are problematized but so, too, are his own poems—so much so that Harold Bloom's exasperated response to them would seem to be the best description we have of the current posture of Milton's fit audience:

> ... I'm increasingly uncertain, with Milton in particular, as to whether we have a way of talking about what it is that Milton is actually doing in *Paradise Lost*. I reject completely the orthodox accounts.... To call him a Christian poet is, I think, to beg the question in the extreme.[35]

One way, certainly, of charting shifts in discourses concerning the sexes in the seventeenth century is to recall that this century, which began with a female arraignment of Joseph Swetnam the woman-hater, ends with some women embracing Milton as an ally and advocate, while their male counterparts protest (often approvingly) that Milton is another hater of women, outdoing Swetnam apparently and even, they will eventually argue, Euripedes.[36] What Milton's male and female readerships *together* can teach us is that this poet interleaves *Paradise Lost* with a variety of gender discourses. This poem maps patriarchal, misogynous, and feminist discourses within a cacophony of competing but not equally authoritative voices, each of which marks a different state—and stage—of consciousness. The problem inherent in such a strategy, as perceived by Joan Kelly, is that "many of the male authors who defend women persuasively set forth the misogynous as well as the pro-woman side of the debate, which makes their concern for women seem at least as literary in origin as it may be heartfelt"[37] and which allows for their position, therefore, to be easily misunderstood.

Milton *is* such an author who, in his deployment of such strategies though, is more wily than most: he writes on various sides of a debate wherein, characteristically, women write on but one (though not always the same) side of the debate. In consequence, rather than instantiating an ideology, *Paradise Lost* serves as an ideological index, indicating when *and how* misogynous attitudes are formed, as well as how patriarchal systems are established and why they still prevail. Still, by virtue of his inclusion of the feminist side of this debate and through the support he gives it, especially in the concluding books of *Paradise Lost*, Milton transforms what might have been a set of different, competing positions into a conceptual vision wherein subordination leads to domination and both to female—and sometimes male—victimization. Milton's poem, then, does more than simply array different gender discourses: it pits them against one another in such a way as to set this entire poem in an oppositional relationship with the dominant culture and displays through that poem an unwillingness simply to endorse the accepted cultural attitudes. If there is risk to such a strategy, it may best be formulated in the paradox that systems devised for overthrowing a partial truth, while themselves not the whole truth, are too often embraced as if they were. Milton's poetic purpose is not to create a new system but to deliver us from existing ones.

By challenging certain authorities it invokes, as well as many of the traditions it inscribes, *Paradise Lost* emboldens its readership to look at both Milton and his age anew: *from the vantage point of women*. From this enabling perspective, we are encouraged to date the Renaissance for women to the age of Milton and, perhaps even more precisely, to the decade of *Paradise Lost*, which, if it does not itself bring gender consciousness to a crisis, suggests that gender consciousness already is in a state of crisis; that the battle of the sexes is, in actuality, a contest over gender wherein the crucial issues concern how women are represented and how they are perceived. Nor should it be forgotten that in *Paradise Lost* not only wisdom but truth is gendered female. Is this *his* song—or *hers*? Is the song falsehood—or truth? What "if all be mine, / Not *Hers*" (9.46–47; my emphasis), Milton asks plaintively.

It has been said that "To shift the perspective, to adjust the vantage point, creates new contours, possibilities, and realities. To look at the Renaissance from the perspective of women explode[s] all previous understanding about women in history."[38] It remains to be said, however, that this altering

eye, as it fixes attention on Milton's poetry, is just as apt
to revise—perhaps even shatter—received opinion concerning Milton's attitude toward women: their place in his poetry
no less than their role in history. A compensatory and, as
such, an emancipatory history, *Paradise Lost* is a poem that,
returning to origins and thus to woman's history at its
inception, both figures a broader conception of humanity
and a more generous view of woman, resisting the narrow,
often confining, gender prescriptions of its day and that also,
through such resistance, fosters the development of female
consciousness, furthers woman's struggle, in the very decade
when, by some accounts, feminism is born. Not John Milton
but interpreters and translators like John Hopkins, through
their misreadings and sometimes contorted renderings, are
responsible for deepening, as well as advancing, misogyny
in the seventeenth century.

If Milton's task was to begin the invention of her-story
that had been blotted from the historical record, our task
now involves "uninventing"[39] the poet of our literary histories—those telling us that "the Milton who composed
Paradise Lost was an angry and embittered man who . . . had
become, theoretically at least, a polygamist and at times a
misogynist. . . . And so Milton sets out to show that man's
chief enemies had from the first been two—the devil and
woman, Satan and Eve."[40] Not only male literary historians
of an earlier generation but female novelists (and some critics)
of the current generation are creators of such fictions and
subscribers to these sentiments. In the voice of Deborah
Milton, Eve Figes inveighs against a father who denies "the
dowry" of learning to his daughters, believing, "in his deepest
heart," that women are unredeemed, unredeemable; servants
to others, not speakers of their own minds. Deborah's
imagined words need to be turned against their imaginer:
"there's none so blind as they who will not see."[41]

We need no more blind guides. Like *her* story, Milton's
needs to be excavated from history and told anew. This
rescue will involve the separation of Milton's voice from
that of his characters, even from that of his sometimes Pauline
narrator, as well as the recognition of disjunction between

his consciousness and theirs, including Eve's initial self-perceptions and including, once again, the consciousness of the narrator however alert and educable that narrator sometimes proves to be. In this rewriting of history, Milton emerges as a controlling and enlightened consciousness, assuming the same sort of relationship to his characters (especially the narrator and unfallen Eve) as Zora Neale Hurston's Moses assumes with regard to his wife Zipporah:

> Moses [here, for the sake of my argument, read Milton] was stubborn on that point. He had no wish to impose his will on others and he said so every time the subject arose. So she [i. e., Zipporah, like most of Milton's characters including the narrator and Eve] looked towards what had been in men's relations to each other, and he faced towards what was to be, and a whole world stood between their two horizons.[42]

Produced by a culture whose limitations its bursts and boundaries it extends, *Paradise Lost* derives its singularity from Milton's writing his "way through the death of one historical moment and the birth of another." And, as Nancy Armstrong and Leonard Tennenhouse go on to suggest, because writing *Paradise Lost* (at least partly) and then publishing it during a period of censorship, and thus affronting patriarchy and misogyny obliquely, Milton accomplishes changes in attitude (rather as Foucault is credited with doing) "through small revisions, new connections, filaments of explanation broken off and rearticulated." In these ways, Milton challenges attitudes he is sometimes thought to champion and revises value systems he is accused of merely reproducing. Through a poetics of disclosure and an aesthetics of indirection, Milton begins shaking to dust the most oppressive forms of religion and politics, including sexual politics.[43]

8 • Intention and Its Limits in *Paradise Lost*
The Case of Bellerophon

Stephen M. Fallon

B ellerophon appears twice in Milton's works, near the
beginning of the writer's career and near the end. The
order of Bellerophon's appearances reflects the shape of his
story, and more intriguingly the lineaments of Milton's own.
We find Bellerophon in the Sixth Prolusion in triumph, where
as part of an elaborate and facetious compliment to Milton's
auditors he slays the Chimaera. We leave him, in the invocation to book 7 of *Paradise Lost*, wandering on the Aleian
Field, a self-cautionary simile for the audacious poet. He is
yoked in that invocation with a more familiar figure, Orpheus,
whose evolving significance for Milton is unavoidable. Unlike
Orpheus, Bellerophon is easy to miss, but we do so at a cost.
In the Bellerophon allusion we will witness the precision
and control of Milton the craftsperson, but we will witness
also the process by which this careful control is undermined
and overwhelmed. The sparsity of Milton's allusions to
Bellerophon compared with the profusion of Orpheus' appearances itself can tell us something important about Milton;

it may be easier to contemplate the external threat of being savaged by an ignorant audience than the internal threat of foolish presumption.

I

As book 7 begins, and as Milton is about to turn from heaven to earth, his narrator addresses Urania:

> Up led by thee
> Into the Heav'n of Heav'ns I have presum'd,
> An Earthly Guest, and drawn Empyreal Air,
> Thy temp'ring; with like safety guided down
> Return me to my Native Element:
> Lest from this flying Steed unrein'd, (as once
> *Bellerophon*, though from a lower Clime)
> Dismounted, on th'*Aleian* Field I fall
> Erroneous there to wander and forlorn.
>
> (7.12–20)[1]

The general sense here is clear: writing of heaven, Milton has courted presumption. Even without a gloss, the reader sees in the Bellerophon myth a family resemblance to the familiar myths of Phaeton and Icarus. Editors' glosses establish more fully the aptness of the allusion: the name for the "Aleian" plain of Lycia comes from the Greek word for "wandering," and Bellerophon like Milton spent his final years blind.

To pursue the strands of the Bellerophon myth beyond the common glosses is to glimpse something of the depth of Milton's conscious control of his poem.[2] Homer's digression on Bellerophon in the *Iliad* (6.155–210) incorporates several aspects of the myth useful to Milton. In Homer the hero falls out with his patron King Proetus of Argos, whose wife Anteia charged Bellerophon with attempted seduction after he rejected her advances. Proetus, loath to kill his guest, sends him with a coded message to Anteia's father, King Iobates of Lycia. Sharing Proetus' scruple against murdering a guest, Iobates orders Bellerophon to complete several tasks, each designed to end in his death. Against all odds, however,

Bellerophon kills the Chimaera, defeats the Solymians and the Amazons, and, finally, dispatches a select band of Iobates' soldiers lying in ambush for him. At this point Iobates relents and presents Bellerophon with his daughter in marriage. Some time later, perhaps grieving for the death of two children, Bellerophon leaves his home to wander disconsolately on the Aleian plain.

Two elements from this Homeric account stand out as relevant to Milton's allusion, the false accusation against Bellerophon's chastity and the superhuman nature of his victories, particularly over the Chimaera. These elements are if anything more pronounced in other versions of the myth. Hesiod is the first to place Bellerophon on the back of the supernatural winged Pegasus, a story repeated with variations by Pindar, Apollodorus, and Pausanias.[3] In Pindar's version, Pallas Athena gives Bellerophon the golden bridle with which he subdues Pegasus. Plutarch highlights Bellerophon's extraordinary modesty and chastity. In the *Moralia*'s elaboration of the story of the attempted ambush, Plutarch has Bellerophon ask Poseidon to flood the Xanthian plain behind him as he advances on Iobates' palace. Desperate to stop Bellerophon, the Xanthian women raise their skirts above their waists and run toward him, offering their bodies if he will stop: "And now, when the men . . . laboring to put a stop to Bellerophon, availed nothing at all, the women plucking up their petticoats met him full butt; upon which confounded with shame he turned back again and the flood, as they say, returned with him."[4] In retelling the story of Anteia's false accusations, Horace refers to "chaste Bellerophon [*casto Bellerophontae*]."[5]

In Pindar's Seventh Isthmian Ode, we first hear of the incident at the heart of Milton's Bellerophon allusion, the presumptuous flight to Olympus: "Pegasos, / the winged, cast down / Bellerophon, his master, when he strove to reach / the houses of the sky and the fellowship / Of Zeus."[6] In Pindar, Bellerophon falls to his death. Conflating the versions of Homer and Pindar, mythographers would have Bellerophon survive his fall in order to wander on the Aleian plain until his death.[7]

As this survey suggests, Milton inherited the Bellerophon myth in significantly different versions; the plasticity of the myth makes it extraordinarily useful to Milton. In all versions Bellerophon is aided by supernatural powers. In several versions, most notably that of Apollodorus, the story ends triumphantly, with Bellerophon's marriage to Iobates' daughter and prospects for a long and happy life. The version with the happy ending finds its way into the *Ovide moralisé*, where Bellerophon is credited with strength, wisdom, and kindness (as well as beauty).[8] Bellerophon's chastity is thrown into relief by Anteia's false accusation and embodied in his reaction to the genital display of the Xanthian women. On the other hand, Bellerophon becomes a figure of foolishness and immaturity in the disproportionate grief marking the end of Homer's version (a sense picked up in Cicero's *Tusculan Disputations* 3.63) and in his ill-fated attempt to fly to Olympus. The many resonances of the Bellerophon myth, left unmentioned in the brief allusion in the invocation to book 7, are left to do their work upon the fit audience, still unearthing after three centuries the clues buried in the text. The clues point toward the manner in which the Bellerophon allusion continues a self-referential dialogue that Milton had been having with himself and with his readers for many years.

II

Throughout his literary career Milton found or invented occasion to speak about himself. As Milton suggests in the preface to the second book of *The Reason of Church-Government*, the function of the autobiographical writings is to establish his authority, an authority often in danger of being overwhelmed by his chosen tasks: the young layperson takes on the bishops; the newly married man takes on Matthew 5.32 on divorce; the mortal poet presumes to speak of "things invisible to mortal sight." As he matures, Milton perceives clearly and intimately the dangers of overreaching, of speaking of what he cannot or should not know. To sustain himself, Milton cultivates a prophetic persona and attempts to demonstrate his worthiness for that role through a defense of his own life and character, a defense heavily dependent on his chastity. In invoking Bellerophon, then, Milton points to a hero who is empowered by the virtue upon which Milton had grounded his special status as select spokesperson of God, and at the same time to an overreacher who had fallen through presumption of intimacy with the divine. Bellerophon embodies Milton's conception of his potential for great achievement and great error.

In his "Vacation Exercise" poem, the young Milton hopes that his "mind may soar / Above the wheeling poles, and at Heav'n's door / Look in, and see each blissful Deity" (33–35). Absent from this appropriately airy poem is the shadow of danger that fleetingly crosses "*In obitum praesulis Eliensis,*" written two years before in 1626. Here Milton has Nicholas Felton describe a chariot ride to the heavens reminiscent of Elijah's; unlike the Milton of the "Vacation Exercise," Felton cannot tell what he sees: "But here I fall silent, for who that is begotten of a mortal father can tell the delights of that place? [*Sed hic tacebo, nam quis effari queat / Oriundus humano patre / Amoenitates illius loci?*]" (65–67). The special mark of divine favor sets Felton apart; it would be indecorous to share divine secrets or for those still on earth to presume to speak them.

There are ways other than celestial ascent to see the secrets of the divine and to be numbered, in the words of *The Reason of Church-Government*, among God's "selected heralds,"[9] and here also trepidation is wise. In the "Nativity Ode," Milton's speaker hopes to reach the Christ child before the Magi, to "Have . . . the honor first, thy Lord to greet" (26). In what may be an implicit acknowledgment of the overreaching of the opening, Milton ends the poem with the speaker's shedding his assertive identity and merging into the group in a remarkably un-Miltonic moment of self deprecation: "Time is our tedious Song should here have ending" (239).[10] Stanley Fish traces a similar trajectory from assertive identity toward anonymity in "Lycidas."[11]

In the polemical prose Milton is not as coy. Milton grasps

the prophetic mantle with both hands in *Of Reformation,* apocalyptically denouncing his episcopal enemies. In the stinging peroration he shares with Christ the role of separating sheep from goats. The singular and prophetic stance is explicit in *The Reason of Church-Government,* where Milton pointedly compares himself with Jeremiah (*CP* 1.803). Echoing the prayer, modelled on Isaiah 6, at the confident beginning of the "Nativity Ode" that his voice will be "From out his secret Altar toucht with hallow'd fire" (28), Milton relies in *The Reason of Church-Government* on the "eternall Spirit who can enrich with all utterance and knowledge, and sends out his Seraphim with the hallow'd fire of his Altar to touch and purify the lips of whom he pleases" (*CP* 1.820–21). If he shares the scruples against pride and vainglory enacted in the transformation of voice in the "Nativity Ode," they come out only indirectly and implicitly, for example in the contrast between the aspiring pyramidal shape of prelacy and the more modest globes and cubes of the presbyters (*CP* 1.790).[12] A detractor might ask Milton if his own claims for prophetic status do not place him at the top of an aspiring pyramid rather than within a modest cube. To assign opponents to hell can be a kind of overreaching, as can the claim to be a new Jeremiah or Isaiah.

As I noted above, Milton seems to ground his serene confidence in, or even complacency about, his special status in that other quality signified by Bellerophon, chastity. Milton had defended the Lady of Christ's chastity in the Sixth Prolusion; by the time of *Comus* chastity is defending the Lady. In the antiprelatical tracts Milton, a young and relatively obscure man, relies on the ethical proof to justify his temerity in taking on men such as Joseph Hall and James Ussher, who are older, more credentialed, and ostensibly wiser. Heroic personal and literary chastity is at the center of Milton's deployment of the ethical proof. He gains warrant to speak against the prelates in *The Reason of Church-Government* because he writes godly poetry, not the "corruption and bane" that "our youth and gentry . . . suck in dayly from the writings and interludes of libidinous and ignorant Poetasters" (*CP* 1.818). In *An Apology for Smectymnuus,* Milton hopes to join Dante and Petrarch,

who "display[ed] sublime and pure thoughts, without transgression" (*CP* 1.890). Milton rejects the charge that he has
frequented bordellos, pledging himself, in a notable chiasmus,
to defend "the honour and chastity of Virgin or Matron"
(*CP* 1.891).

The painful initial failure of Milton's marriage with Mary
Powell shook Milton's serene and naive confidence in his
special prophetic election. Whether or not he ever pledged
himself to celibacy, Milton now looked to a life of married
chastity.[13] As Annabel Patterson has eloquently demonstrated, *The Doctrine and Discipline of Divorce* is punctu-
ated by episodes of veiled autobiography, veiled to some
extent from Milton himself, which record the author's distress
and doubts.[14] In third-person accounts, Milton presents the
plight of the chaste young man who, through laudable lack
of amorous experience, chooses an unfitting spouse unwisely
(*CP* 2.249–50). The text records new tensions in Milton's
thinking about chastity. On the one hand, sexual desire can
be controlled and even extinguished: "As for that other
burning, which is but as it were the venom of a lusty and
over-abounding concoction, strict life and labour with the
abatement of a full diet may keep that low and obedient
anough" (*CP* 2.251). On the other hand, the virtuous man
trapped in an unhappy marriage may be forced "to piece up
his lost contentment by visiting the Stews, or stepping to
his neighbours bed, which is the common shift in this
misfortune, or els by suffering his usefull life to wast away
and be lost under a secret affliction of an *unconscionable
size to humane strength*" (*CP* 2.247; my emphasis).

As hidden biography and reflections on the limits of human
endurance converge, the familiar Miltonic claims for heroic
virtue and its concomitant special prophetic status become
tenuous. To the extent that we find in the *Doctrine and
Discipline* a Milton reacting with pain and outrage to his
disappointment in marriage, that is, a Milton feeling "the
spurre of self-concernment" (*CP* 2.226), the more startling
will we find his distinction between the heroic virtue of
the few and the weakness of the mass of men that makes
the remedy of divorce indispensable:

> When he perceives the just expectance of his mind defeated,
> he will begin even against Law to cast about where he may
> find his satisfaction more compleat, unlesse he be a thing
> heroically vertuous, and that are not the common lump of
> men for whom chiefly the Laws ought to be made, though
> not to their sins, yet to their unsinning weaknesses, it being
> above their strength to endure the lonely estate, which while
> they shun'd they are fal'n into. (*CP* 2.253–54)

There is an implicit fall here from the special and exalted
prophetic status propped up by the ethical proofs of the
antiprelatical tracts. And Milton falls farther a moment later.
The man trapped in an unhappy marriage,

> though he be almost the strongest Christian, he will be ready
> to *dispair* in vertue, and *mutine against divine providence*; . . .
> therefore when human frailty surcharg'd, is at such a losse,
> charity ought to venture much, and use bold physick, lest
> an over-tost faith endanger to shipwrack. (*CP* 2.254; my
> emphasis)

If Milton in earlier works had claimed to be an heroically
virtuous and specially elect Christian, now through the
obscuring veils of third-person autobiography he slips a notch
to "almost the strongest Christian" (or several notches to
join "the common lump of men") and contemplates in
prospect a precipitous and fatal descent into despair. He who
had been assured of special favor as a teacher of believers
now seems uncertain even of the salvation promised to the
humblest believer.

The confrontation with weakness in the *Doctrine and
Discipline* leaves its mark in anxiety and defensiveness, in
circumlocutions and qualifications.[15] The implications for
earlier prophetic claims are betrayed in a strangely paradoxical moment when the *Doctrine and Discipline* rewrites *The
Reason of Church-Government*. Acknowledging in the earlier
work that his argument against bishops will be unpalatable
to some, Milton compares himself with John in Revelation,
who ate the book of divine wisdom: "though it were sweet
in his mouth, and in the learning, it was bitter in his belly;
bitter in the denouncing" (*CP* 1.803). In the *Doctrine and*

Discipline, Milton reverses direction. Wondering why custom is foolishly but generally taken as the "best instructor," he speculates that it is

> because her method is so glib and easie, in some manner like to that vision of *Ezekiel,* rowling up her sudden book of implicit knowledge, for him that will, take and swallow down at pleasure; which proving but of bad nourishment in the concoction, as it was heedlesse in the devouring, puffs up unhealthily, a certaine big face of pretended learning. . . . (*CP* 1.222–23)

The passage from Revelation (10.9) alluded to in *The Reason of Church-Government* itself alludes to this episode in Ezekiel (3.1–3), but in the divorce tract Milton rereads the biblical type. Merritt Hughes notes bemusedly, "The roll symbolizes the prophet's message, and Milton's use of it here hardly harmonizes with its Biblical context."[16] The startling reversal participates in the same general process of displacement as the hidden autobiography. Milton cannot directly acknowledge to himself or to us his falling off from the standards of heroic virtue, so he ascribes that falling off to an unspecified third person; Milton cannot acknowledge the implications of this falling off for his prophetic vocation, so he undermines by use in a dubious analogy the very biblical model of that calling that he had earlier invoked.

III

Paradise Lost is informed by the prophetic confidence of the antiprelatical works, but it is tinctured by the anxiety and the awareness of the possibility of error, alienation, and transgression that haunts the *Doctrine and Discipline.* The allusion to Bellerophon is apt not only to the visits to heaven, but to the entirety of an epic that "intends to soar / Above th'*Aonian* Mount" (1.14–15). Though mindful that the darkness within must be illumined, the voice of the first invocation is calm and confident. If there is a foreboding of falling off from flight, it is in the evocation of the Grand

Parents and the Serpent that immediately follows. Milton's epic narrator will continue to soar while others fall. The invocation to the third book is more nuanced in this respect. "Hail holy Light,.... / May I express thee unblam'd?" (3.1–3). Louis Martz finds in this passage the "modesty and humility of th[e] bard's approach to the divine."[17] But one could turn this around. The poet is singing of God and will continue to do so, and the invocation might well record the anxiety of the poet who is the opposite of humble and modest, the poet who realizes the gravity of his prophetic claim and the implications if he is in error. He seeks to domesticate the danger of the vertical movement to Heaven, a movement figured later in the Bellerophon allusion, by juxtaposing it with the danger he has just eluded when he "Escap't the *Stygian* Pool" (3.14), an escape made possible, ironically, by his singing "With other notes than to th'*Orphean* Lyre" (3.17).

It is at this point in the invocation that Milton refers first to his blindness. In the *Second Defense* he had answered the charge that his blindness was a divine punishment by claiming that it placed him in the line of prophets (*CP* 4.584). Here in book 3 of *Paradise Lost* the appearance of blindness shortly after the question of whether his narrative and prayer can be "unblamed" raises again the question of punishment. The anguished description of blindness is followed by a confident reassertion of poetic power, "Yet not the more / Cease I to wander where the Muses haunt," and a moment later of prophetic power, "So were I equall'd with them in renown, / Blind *Thamyris* and blind *Mæonides*, / And *Tiresias* and *Phineus* Prophets old." But at this point, when the agony of blindness seems to have been laid to rest, it returns in a recoil of pathos and bitterness: "not to me returns / Day, or the sweet approach of Ev'n or Morn." While the invocation ends with the reiterated claim of the divine gift of internal vision, the double recoil on blindness opens the way for a third or fourth, destabilizing the invocation's apparent resolution.

IV

In Milton, then, an early, uncomplicated, and naive confidence in divine election to prophetic status, an election validated in large part by chastity, is followed by a complex self-conception that by turns maintains the confident claim to prophetic status and entertains doubts and misgivings potentially damaging to that claim. The narrator in *Paradise Lost* embodies this complex self-conception, and the Bellerophon allusion in the invocation to book 7 encodes it.[18]

Milton begins by placing himself in the position of Bellerophon just before his fall; with the help of his Muse Urania, "above th'*Olympian* Hill I soar, / Above the flight of *Pegasean* wing" (7.3–4). Without the protection of the divine muse, Milton has less between him and the earth than did the presumptuous Bellerophon. The equipoise of confidence and anxiety is captured in a paradoxical claim:

> Up led by thee
> Into the Heav'n of Heav'ns I have *presum'd*,
> An Earthly *Guest*, and drawn Empyreal Air,
> Thy temp'ring; with like safety guided down
> Return me to my Native Element.
>
> (7.12–16; my emphasis)

Milton is a guest who has presumed, one who has crashed a party to which he has been invited. If he is still one of the "selected heralds" of God, he is safe, but "if all be mine, / Not Hers who brings it nightly to my Ear" (9.46–47), he is in grave danger.[19]

The Bellerophon allusion serves to inoculate Milton from the threatened danger. As I noted in the beginning, this is true both in a general sense, for Bellerophon shares with Icarus and Phaeton the dubious distinction of presumptuous flight, and also in a particular sense, for Bellerophon was viewed as Milton wished to be viewed, as a hero of wisdom and chastity. If Bellerophon gains supernatural powers through heroic chastity, then his career parallels Milton's. Milton can be saved from Bellerophon's subsequent foolish presumptuousness by the inspiration of the true muse.

The closeness of the parallels between the cases of Bellerophon and Milton testifies to the subtle control that Milton exerts over his poem. It is particularly intriguing to consider the question of control at this point of the poem, when Milton is wrestling with the specter of overreaching and presumption. Has he ventured beyond mortal limits, and will his poem as a result enact the literary and spiritual equivalents of free fall? The Bellerophon allusion, with its nuanced and masterly precision, represents a gesture toward the exorcism of the demon of presumption. By recognizing the error of Bellerophon, the hero who most closely prefigures his position, Milton will be able to avoid it. His assertion of control, as opposed to the free fall of Bellerophon, is authenticated by the careful control demonstrated in the allusion.

Milton is now able to breathe a sigh of relief:

> Half yet remains unsung, but narrower bound
> Within the visible Diurnal Sphere;
> Standing on Earth, not rapt above the Pole,
> More safe I Sing with mortal voice, unchang'd
> To hoarse or mute.
>
> (7.21–25)

But, like the relief from blindness in the invocation to book 3, the relief from a sense of danger is short-lived. For it is precisely at this point, when Milton has erected a pale around himself as a protection from danger, that danger floods back into the poem. His voice is unchanged,

> though fall'n on evil days
> On evil days though fall'n, and evil tongues;
> In darkness, and with dangers compast round,
> And solitude.
>
> (7.25–28)

Michael Lieb has written perceptively of the anxiety in these lines: "In an epic about the devastating effects of the Fall, [Milton] finds that he himself is 'fall'n' on evil days that encompass him on all sides."[20] The depth of anxiety here is difficult to overstate, given that Milton chooses language to describe himself that echoes language with which he had had Sin describe herself earlier in the epic. Sin has been assigned the role of portress of hell, made

> To sit in hateful Office here confin'd,
> Inhabitant of Heav'n, and heav'nly-born,
> Here in perpetual agony and pain,
> With terrors and with clamors compasst round
> Of mine own brood, that on my bowels feed.
>
> (2.859–63)

It is a small step from "With terrors and with clamors compast round" to "In darkness, and with dangers compast round." And with this short step we turn the corner to find that the language, Milton's language, is working in spite of rather than for the author. Here it seems that Milton is not in control of the subtle dialogue across half of his epic; it would be more than surprising if he were intentionally to have put himself in the place of Sin.

With this in mind, one might notice in the Bellerophon allusion language associated with Satan and the fallen angels. The author fears for the moment lest "on th'*Aleian* Field I fall / Erroneous there to wander and forlorn" (7.19–20). After his fall Satan turns to Beelzebub with a question, "Seest thou yon dreary Plain, forlorn and wild?" (1.180). The exploring devils of book 2 are described as "roving on / In confus'd march forlorn" (2.614–15). If the Bellerophon allusion had succeeded in quieting the narrator's anxiety more completely, these echoes might pass without comment, for Milton would have separated himself finally from Satanic overreaching. But the echoing of Sin's words in the narrator's own blurs that separation and awakes the ominous echoes in the allusion.

Anxiety and a hint of transgression return at the end of the invocation, in the familiar allusion to Orpheus:

> But drive far off the barbarous dissonance
> Of *Bacchus* and his Revellers, the Race
> Of that wild Rout that tore the *Thracian* Bard
> In *Rhodope*, where the Woods and Rocks had Ears
> To rapture, till the savage clamor drown'd

> Both Harp and Voice; nor could the Muse defend
> Her Son. So fail not thou, who thee implores:
> For thou art Heavn'ly, shcc an empty dream.
>
> (7.32–39)

Richard DuRocher finds in this allusion simultaneous confidence in inspiration and anxiety about reception.[21] Perhaps he is right, but I have traced up to this point substantial anxiety about inspiration. There are different opinions in the tradition concerning the reason for Orpheus' dismemberment by the Bacchantes. While some credited Orpheus with chastity for spurning the Bacchantes,[22] Ovid implies that Orpheus angered the Bacchantes by his practice and advocacy of sodomy.[23] Some viewed Orpheus' spurning of the women as a refusal to honor the god Dionysius. These interpretations mark the Orpheus allusion with some of the internal anxiety that we noted in the Bellerophon allusion. And one might recall behind this reading of Orpheus the fate of Pentheus in Euripides' *Bacchae*, who is torn apart by the Bacchantes both for refusing to honor the god and proximately for his unhealthy sexual curiosity and voyeurism as he approaches the Dionysian rites.

A structural parallel connects the invocations in books 3 and 7. The relation between the Orpheus and Bellerophon allusions reenacts that between the two anguished cries of the blind speaker.[24] The recoil or return, from blindness to blindness and now from Bellerophon to Orpheus, can point as easily toward an unceasing oscillation between despair and confidence as it can to the final laying to rest of doubt. If a second reassurance is needed, why not a third, fourth, fifth, and so on indefinitely?

A similar paradoxically double significance marks the lines that immediately follow the Bellerophon allusion:

> Half yet remains unsung, but narrower bound
> Within the visible Diurnal Sphere;
> Standing on Earth, not rapt above the Pole,
> More safe I Sing with mortal voice, unchang'd
> To hoarse or mute, though fall'n on evil days.
>
> (7.21–25)

The poet stands on earth, upon secure ground, but he is "narrower bound." It may seem more comforting to be "not rapt above the Pole," but rapture can be of at least two kinds, the mental imbalance associated with presumptuous flight or the divine madness of inspiration anatomized in Plato's *Phaedrus*. And the comparative "more safe" is particularly slippery; it can mean simply a confident assertion of greater security, or it can, like many comparative adjectives, be weaker than a simple one. On the one hand the narrator asserts that he is more safe than he was in previous books, on the other the nice calculation of degrees of safety unsettles the security of unqualified safety. The ambiguity is compounded when he adds that the safety depends on his singing "with mortal voice," which is both a voice that prudently recognizes its limits and a voice that participates in frailty and error. Safety is purchased by the fallen state, and a prudent respect for the danger of soaring is purchased by a loss of rapture. The ambiguity of the passage is heightened at the enjambment in "unchang'd / To hoarse or mute." Read without a break, the phrase suggests that the voice has not faltered or wavered despite adversity, but if we pause for the brief moment we hear that the the narrator speaks "with mortal voice, unchang'd." The model of inspiration offered by the poem, and by Milton throughout his career, is of a mortal voice transformed by divine favor and election.

In this essay, I have been offering the invocation of book 7, and particularly the Bellerophon allusion, as an example of the operation of what John Shawcross has called the "author's text" and as an example of the disruption of that operation. Shawcross distinguishes between "text," "reader's text," and "author's text": the " 'text' . . . is the specific words as they appear on the page; the 'reader's text' is the understanding the reader derives from that text; the 'author's text' is the text the author has provided for the reader to read, with all its potentialities."[25] The distinction between the "text" and the "author's text" for Shawcross is often a matter of the intertextual "clues" to meaning left in the text by the author to direct the process of reading (12–13). These clues carry and reveal the author's "intention," and attention to these clues should lead a reader "to examine the poem differently from the way that reader would deal with it as disembodied text" (10). Enough of the Bellerophon story is explicit in Milton's text for the reader to "understand" the passage. But, the argument would go, Milton has left the fit reader, or Shawcross's "knowing reader" (10), clues in the form of the unmentioned episodes of the Bellerophon myth to allow for a deeper, more complex, and less arbitrary and disembodied reading of the text. Bellerophon is more like Milton than we realize at first, and the more we learn the more we see the uncanny precision of the device by which Milton seeks to exorcize the specter of presumption.

But, as I have argued, precisely at this moment of exquisite control, meanings apparently unintended by the author flood back into the text. They return in the form of resonances within the text between language with which Milton describes infernal characters and language with which he describes himself. In this sense, to take Blake out of context, Milton was "of the Devils party without knowing it." To read these resonances as intentional would be to neglect Milton's history of self-representation; in a lifelong project of ethical proof, Milton establishes himself as a prophet inspired by God as a reward for personal merit and shields himself from his own doubts about his fitness. And thus it is left to the "reader's text" to point to a meaning that is no part of the writer's intention, and that indeed runs counter to the writer's intention.

V

There is a fleeting moment in the Sixth Prolusion, the one other work in which Milton mentions Bellerophon, that gestures poignantly toward the drama to be played out in the later Milton:

> You see, O my hearers, how far I have been rapt [*me raptat*] and carried away by my excessively violent desire and yearning to please you. Actually it comes over me quite suddenly, that I have been swept away by a desire that is

unholy [*Sacrilegium*] and yet, if the thing be possible, is also pious and righteous [*piam, & honestum*].[26]

Milton is rapt here by a desire to please his audience; his tone is light and humorous. Later, when he claims in all seriousness to be rapt by divine inspiration, he will face in deadly earnest the fine line between the pious and the sacrilegious.

To conclude this essay, I will invoke a pregnant case of intertextuality interesting in part for its exploration of this fine line, Andrew Marvell's reading of Milton in "On Mr. Milton's *Paradise Lost*." The commendatory poem has been printed just before the epic in most editions since the second in 1674, and thus it has had the privilege of introducing the poem that it follows. The poem is equal to the position; it displaces onto itself and reenacts the drama of inspiration and presumption at the heart of *Paradise Lost*. In bowing to the sublime authority of the epic, Marvell's poem is a record of a reading that follows Milton's intention. At the same time, its self-questioning imitates the doubts and misgivings that threaten to overwhelm the "author's text" of *Paradise Lost*. Moreover, in the tentativeness and repeated qualifications of his commendation, Marvell raises more directly the question of the degree of mastery asserted by the author over the text.

Confronted with the "great Argument," Marvell fears that Milton "would ruine (for I saw him strong) / The sacred Truths to Fable and old Song."[27] In the second verse paragraph, Marvell comes to terms with Milton's ambition:

> Yet as I read, soon growing less severe,
> I liked his Project, the success did fear;
> Through that wide Field how he his way should find
> O'er which lame Faith leads Understanding blind.
>
> (11–14)

Line twelve holds a fine ambiguity. Marvell's primary sense is that, having come to approve Milton's plan, he now feared that he would not be able to fulfill it. But a residue of the mistrust of the plan itself remains in the language ("the success did fear"). The language suggests that Marvell fears both that Milton would not successfully embody his project and that he would. As Marvell continues to reflect on the audacious enterprise in the following couplet, he takes an image from Milton's book, specifically from the Bellerophon allusion. Marvell's "wide Field" responds to Milton's "Aleian" one; Marvell fears that Milton will end up like the author's own Bellerophon, wandering blind on a trackless field.[28]

In the middle section of the poem, Marvell complicates his reflections on Milton's audacity by evoking his own audacity in questioning a poem that he has come to view as inspired.[29] With this displacement, Milton rises above reproach: "And things divine thou treatst of in such state / As them preserves, and thee, inviolate" (33–34). If Milton had to suppress fears that he had violated divine mysteries, Marvell places Milton, now paled around by commas, among those divine things worthy of defense against violation. In a fine and unintended irony, Marvell seems to endorse also the chastity that Milton once relied upon for his prophetic vision.

The final verse paragraph of Marvell's poem might seem anticlimactic. A poem that began with a consideration of sacred truths ends with a weighing of Milton's decision to abandon rhyme. Yet here, while speaking of an apparently trivial matter,[30] Marvell continues and brings to fruition his reflections on one of the creative paradoxes of *Paradise Lost*. He notes parenthetically, "I too transported by the Mode offend, / And while I meant to Praise thee must Commend." Marvell began his poem with misgivings about Milton's; now, in an ironic tautology generated by witty self-deprecation of his own rhyming, he chides himself for praising or promoting when he meant to be praising. It is as if, in the presence of Milton, praise is not praise enough. And Marvell's offense is tied to his (ironic) transportation, to Marvell's being taken out of himself, to his being, as Milton would say, "rapt."

Thus Marvell, even when speaking of rhyme, is engaged in witty but intimate dialogue with the inspired poet of *Paradise Lost*. He reads, displaces to himself, adjusts for book is over he will begin to interpret the judgment on the serpent as the promise that releases him from that law. If Adam's despair is an unbearable burden to him, his cruelty to Eve just after the soliloquy is painful for the reader. The pressure to dissolve the present situtation increases, and the reader's desire for resolution meshes with Adam's longing for release from the law. The *protevangelium* promises that resolution and that abrogation. But at a price.

Adam under the law can never satisfy God's rigor. He may intend "to resign and render back/ All [he] receiv'd" (749–50); but God and his Son know that he is bankrupt: "Atonement for himself or offering meet,/ Indebted and undone, hath none to bring" (3.234–35). Only Christ, infinite contracted to finite, obedient and capable of enduring punishment, fulfills both parts of legal justification:

> 1. Of *Obedience*, when all such things are done, as the Law commandeth. . . . He that does so is a just man.
> 2. Of *Punishment* or *Satisfaction*, when the breach of the Law is satisfied by enduring the utmost of such penalties, as the rigour of the Law required. For not only he who doth what the Law commandeth: but even he also that suffereth all such punishments, as the Law-giver in justice can inflict for the breach of the Law, is to bee accounted a just man, and reckoned after such satisfaction made, as no transgressor of the Law.[22]

Christ's satisfaction through torture and death ("on mee let thine anger fall" [3.237]) does not improve human nature, which is degraded after the Fall by Pauline anthropological dualism. Following the Torah of paradise, which was a way of life rather than merely an externally imposed code of restrictions, Adam described himself to Raphael as "free [to]/ Approve the best, and follow what I approve" (8.610–11). In his soliloquy, anticipating Kant's antiparadisaic admonition against any rationalistic system of thought that issues in the pursuit of an ideal, Adam is the crooked timber from which no straight thing could ever be made:

> But from me what can proceed,
> But all corrupt, both Mind and Will deprav'd,

genre, and rewrites Milton's subtle language of inspiration and transgression. And in the witty self-accusations of his own poem, Marvell hints at the anxious self-representation of Milton in *Paradise Lost*. This anxious self-representation takes the form of an oscillation between confidence and anxiety, which, I have argued, receives concentrated expression in the invocation to book 7. One pole of this oscillation is revealed by the "author's text," and the other pole is constructed by the reader who perceives what Milton attempts, with only partial success, to suppress.[31]

9 • The Law in Adam's Soliloquy

Jason P. Rosenblatt

I f Adam, in his long soliloquy (*Paradise Lost* 10.720–844), feels he is more miserable than he knows, at least we readers can find in Pauline theology the doctrine we need to keep pace with his experience. The soliloquy occurs in the interval of a double take, after the Son has pronounced sentence on the serpent but before Adam has interpreted that sentence correctly as an evangelical promise. This interval belongs to the state of misery that follows innocence and precedes grace. Adam's opening antitheses, "O miserable of happy," "Accurst of blessed,"[1] suggest that a glance at his former happy, blessed state will help us to measure his losses.

We can begin to understand the polity of that earlier state by turning to the famous paragraph in Milton's *De doctrina Christiana* that lists the many sins contained in Adam's first act of disobedience: faithlessness, ingratitude, greed, uxoriousness, theft, murder, etc. Milton concludes that paragraph with a scriptural verse: "*whoever keeps the whole law, and yet offends in one point, is guilty of all.*"[2] The Miltonic bard in the Edenic books of *Paradise Lost* exploits the obverse of this statement. If the Mosaic law is a single entity, then Adam and Eve in Eden keep the entire law by keeping one law, obeying the terms of the single prohibition. The Mosaic law in Eden is originally benign. It coexists with natural law, just as Raphael's revelations of scripture coexist with the revelations of the book of nature. But after the Fall, Milton turns away from the Torah to meditate upon Romans and specifically upon the Pauline theme, begun in Galatians, that faith and law are contradictory. Though the law, good and holy, comes from God, it was never intended to last forever; rather, it was a temporary measure, valid only until the coming of Christ. Paul's own life story dramatizes the passing from Pharisaism to Christianity.[3] And Milton's own life could serve as another example, since he had passed from Hebraic religious sympathy in the tracts of 1643–1645 to the peremptory rejection of even the moral law in the Pauline chapters of *De doctrina Christiana*. The law of paradise contains the entire Mosaic law, and the mortal sin original transgresses it. It would be futile to maintain our first parents in a dispensation already violated in paradise and thus manifestly inadequate in the face of postlapsarian reality. So the Son appears as "mild Judge and Intercessor both" (10.96) even before the expulsion from the garden, at once fulfilling the benign law of paradise as judge and signalling a new dispensation as intercessor. Adam in his agony remains unaware of this mildness and of the supreme sacrifice it anticipates ("It is Christ that died . . . who is even at the right hand of God, who also maketh intercession for us" [Romans 8.34]).

Under the Torah of prelapsarian paradise, existing before and apart from the New Testament, Adam needs no mediatorial prophet, priest, and king, for he is himself good, holy, and just. The prohibition, "This one, this easy charge" (4.421), is all the law that Adam must follow. In his confidence, Adam can scarcely credit Raphael's conditional formulation "*if ye be found/ Obedient*" (5.513–14). He assures the angel: "we never shall forget to love/ Our maker, and obey him whose command/ Single, is yet so just" (5.550–52).

The conditional nature of the promises of the law is a

commonplace. Here is Gulielmus Bucanus on the difference between the law and the gospel:

> They differ in the forme or difference of the promises: for the promises in the law of eternal life & temporall benefits are conditional. That is they require the condition of perfect fulfilling the law, as a cause, as for example, *If thou do these things thou shalt live in them*, where the particle, If, for because, expresseth the cause, for our obedience is required in the law as a cause. But the promises of the gospel are free, & are not given because of fulfilling the law, but freely for Christs sake.[4]

The verse Bucanus interprets here is Leviticus 18.5, one of many verses in the Torah that resemble the original prohibition by attaching a condition of obedience to the promise of life. It is not surprising to find Milton, in *De doctrina Christiana*, speaking generally of the Mosaic law in terms that remind us of the interdiction: "THE MOSAIC LAW . . . HELD OUT A PROMISE OF LIFE FOR THE OBEDIENT AND A CURSE FOR THE DISOBEDIENT" (*YP* 6.517). What is surprising is to find Milton interpreting this particular verse in ways so utterly incompatible that one could be an analogue of Edenic polity, the other of the state of misery.

The Edenic analogue is found in *Tetrachordon*, one of the half-dozen prose tracts written between 1643 and 1645 that assert faith in human beings as agents capable of exercising choice to improve their condition. The Mosaic law of divorce (Deuteromony 24.1–4) offers escape from tyrannical custom, which would place an intolerable marriage above charity. This Mosaic law "is perfect, not liable to additions or diminutions" (*YP* 2.640). Indeed, "*Moses* every where commends his lawes, preferrs them before all of other nations, and warrants them to be the way of life and safety to all that walke therein, *Levit.* 18" (*YP* 2.654). Although Milton concedes that Christ has fulfilled and thus abrogated the ceremonial law, he argues that the moral and judicial laws have not been superseded.

Years later, in *De doctrina Christiana*, Milton's antithetical interpretation of this verse reflects a changed conception of the law and of human nature. Here Milton argues against those conservative Reformers who hold that only the ceremonial law has been abrogated:

> ... the law of which it is written, "the man that doeth them shall live in them," Lev. xviii.5. Gal.iii.12 and, "cursed is every one that continueth not in all things which are written in the book of the law to do them," Deut. xxvii.26. Gal. iii.10. was the whole law. From "the curse of" this "law Christ hath redeemed us," v.13. inasmuch as we were unable to fulfill it ourselves. Now to fulfill the ceremonial law could not have been a matter of difficulty; it must therefore have been the entire Mosaic law from which Christ delivered us. . . . [I]f therefore he abrogated the whole, no part of it can be now binding upon us.[5]

Leviticus 18.5, associated in *Tetrachordon* with life, has now become the agent of a curse. In this excerpt, Milton juxtaposes proof-texts from the Torah with those from the Pauline epistles. In fact, Milton's unorthodox dogma regarding the abrogation of the whole Mosaic law, including the decalogue, derives largely from this radically Pauline conception of the law as a single, indissoluble entity. Like Paul, an ex-Pharisee and of the strictest school, Milton argues that to violate one commandment is to break the law. And also like Paul he now insists on either obedience to all the commandments or on life by faith. He concludes: "Faith, not law, is our rule" (*YP* 6.536). Adam before the Fall was a perfect man obeying a single perfect law. After the Fall, he is under a curse, an imperfect man under a law whose perfection mocks him. The poet begins to exploit the ironic possibilities of a conception of the law as a single entity just after the Fall, when Adam anticipates the decalogue: "if such pleasure be/ In things to us forbidden, it might be wish'd,/ For this one Tree had been forbidden ten" (9.1024–26). Tertullian asserts the decalogic nature of the Edenic prohibition:

> ... in the beginning of the world [God] gave to Adam himself and Eve a law, that they were not to eat of the fruit of the tree planted in the midst of paradise; but that, if they did contrariwise, by death they were to die. Which law had

continued enough for them, had it been kept. For in this
law given to Adam we recognise in embryo all the precepts
which afterwards sprouted forth when given through Moses;
that is, Thou shalt love the lord thy God. . . . Thou shalt
love thy neighbour as thyself; Thou shalt not kill; Thou
shalt not commit adultery; Thou shalt not steal; False witness
thou shalt not utter; Honour thy father and mother; and
That which is another's shalt thou not covet. For the primordial law was given to Adam and Eve in paradise, as the
womb of all the precepts of God.[6]

For Milton, as for other Renaissance systematic theologians,
the white light of the original prohibition has been broken
up into countless refractive prohibitions of every color, a
spectrum of offenses.

Turning to the soliloquy in book 10, we find Adam lying
under the weight of this Pauline conception of the law. Once
Adam violates it, the law becomes *"a prison that shutteth
up, the yoake of bondage, the power or force of sinne, the
operation of wrath and of death, . . . the ministerie of death
and condemnation, the killing letter."*[7] Read in the context
of Protestant commonplaces concerning the Mosaic law,
virtually all of them deriving from Paul, the soliloquy becomes
at once more ironic and more poignant.

Adam begins:

> O miserable of happy! is this the end
> Of this new glorious World, and mee so late
> The Glory of that Glory, who now become
> Accurst of blessed, hide me from the face
> Of God, whom to behold was then my highth
> Of happiness: yet well, if here would end
> The misery, I deserv'd it, and would bear
> My own deservings.

> (10. 720–27)

Adam, who replays Satan's "Me miserable!" (4.73), has already
undergone a form of that death threatened in the interdiction. John Wollebius makes this point explicit in the first
rule of his chapter on misery: "God comprehended all mans
misery under the name of death. Gen. 2.17."[8] Unsurprisingly,
the four degrees of death he outlines resemble Milton's in

De doctrina Christiana. The worst form of death is spiritual death, whereby the sinners are "forever excluded from the fellowship of God, and of the blessed. *Matth.* 25.41. Go from me ye cursed."[9] A comparison of Adam's plight with the state of spiritual death may seem exaggerated, until we recall God's dialogues with the Son in books 3 and 11. There we learn that without the free operation of grace (3.174–75)—without God's "motions" (11.91)—Adam would be "quite . . . lost" (3.173).

The soliloquy reminds us that God has not yet activated the machinery of grace. The various polarities Adam amasses here—misery and happiness (10. 720), curses and blessings (723), life and death (729, 731)—are brought into focus by a law that promises life but threatens death: "O voice once heard/ Delightfully, *Increase and multiply,*/ Now death to hear!" (729–31). God's primal blessing of humankind with fertility in Genesis 1.28, recounted first by Raphael (7.531–34) and then even more exuberantly by Adam (8.338–41), contains one imperative that stresses human kinship with the other animals through sexuality ("Increase and multiply") and another that stresses human superiority over them ("master . . . and rule"). Milton cites this blessing and commandment as proof that the "providence of God . . . which relates to [man's] prelapsarian state is that by which God placed man in the garden of Eden and supplied him with every good thing necessary for a happy life. . . . Gen. i.28" (*YP* 6.351). Adam's peremptory devaluation of the Torah's first law derives from Romans 7.10: "the very commandment which promised life proved to be death to me." Adam and Eve, now "manifold in sin" (10.16), will multiply curses and evil by multiplying progeny: "for what can I increase/ Or multiply but curses on my head?" (731–32). Adam and Paul identify the Mosaic law, God's "voice once heard / Delightfully," with death and a curse. In one of *De doctrina Christiana*'s most thoroughly Pauline chapters (1.26), Milton cites Romans 7.7–13 as proof that the Mosaic law is an instrument through which humankind recognizes its depravity (*YP* 6.518).

Paradise Lost as well as the history of interpretation suggest that proliferation can indeed be a curse. The original blessing of procreation could be both particular and universal, since unfallen Adam and Eve were the world's total human population. The Fall and the subsequent expulsion from paradise dissociate particularity from universality and thus create competition for privilege. The primordial blessing of Genesis 1.28 has been invoked to enforce value systems that deal explicitly in preference and implicitly in rejection. Human dominion over the animals becomes a metaphor of Israel's relation to the other nations of the world or of Christianity's dominion over Judaism. God's first, expansive blessing of humankind becomes, over the centuries, contested territory that opposing cultures struggle to appropriate. What was originally a blessing whose recipients were neither Jewish nor of the same gender becomes in rabbinic tradition a law applying only to free Jewish males. The oldest patristic reference to Genesis 1.28, in the *Epistle of Barnabas*, employs the verse polemically, so that the primordial blessing is addressed by God to his son Jesus, and it bespeaks the triumph of the church. For some Christian interpreters, the verse typifies the old law of the Jews, now obsolete. The world is already sufficiently populated, the parousia is imminent, and procreation ranks noticeably below the ideal of celibacy. In a soliloquy that devalues life, law, and progeny, Adam cites a verse so thoroughly emptied of its original universality that a countertext eventually had to be found to authorize the settlement of the macrocosm by all the nations of the earth: "[God] did not create it a chaos, he formed it to be inhabited" (Isaiah 45.18).[10]

Bereft of grace or the language of grace, Adam's soliloquy represents a law that works wrath in a language unremittingly legalistic. To end his misery Adam would die, thus returning the gift of life he has received:

> if here would end
> The misery, I deserv'd it, and would bear
> My own deservings.

> (725–27)

it were but right
And equal to reduce me to my dust,
Desirous to resign, and render back
All I receiv'd, unable to perform
Thy terms too hard.

(747–51)

The terms of the one easy prohibition have become too hard to perform, like the Mosaic law described by the angel Michael: the ceremonial law cannot appease, "nor Man the moral part/ Perform, and not performing cannot live" (12.298–99). The law which was easy is now impossible, and Adam cannot render back what he received because he is now utterly bankrupt.

Here is Bucanus trying to reconcile two apparently contradictory statements attributed to Jerome: "Cursed is hee who saith that God commanded impossible things: and cursed is he who saith, the law is possible":

> They are to be reconciled by a distinction of times and subjects. God did not commaund impossible things, namely, to our first parents before the fall, neither also to the regenerate, unto whom the Law is possible by grace. . . . But the Law is impossible, namely, to a man in this corrupt nature, in his owne strength and actions, and the Scripture feareth not to say concerning the observation of the Law, that it is, a yoak, which neither the Apostles, nor they which beleeved, neither the primitive Church, nor the fathers could beare.[11]

Before the Fall, then, Adam can easily fulfill the law on its own terms. After his justification, which imputes his sin to Christ and Christ's righteousness to him, he can fulfill it by believing in Christ. In what we but not Adam can recognize as the interval, Adam lies under the curse of a law that he was once able to perform through his own obedience. He and Eve are the only people both capable and incapable of performing the law. For the Reformers at least, God does not change the rules in the middle of the game. The game remains perfect, but not the player, who injures himself. Bucanus provides a less anachronistic context, using

Adam's own legalistic terms, but with a certain ruthless efficiency:

> *Is God therefore unjust, because he requireth these things of us which we cannot doe?* Farre be it we should say so, for he asketh againe of us that which is his owne, and which before hee had given us: for hee gave to our first parents in their creation a power, and ability to performe the Law. Even as if one should lend any man money, and the debter should by his negligence and fault spend or lose it, and is no more able to pay, notwithstanding the creditor can not bee proved to deale unjustly, if he demaund the lent money of him & his heires.[12]

By interpreting the Law's efficacy in different ways before and after the Fall, Milton can present as logically separate ideas that in the New Testament sometimes coexist uneasily. Luke in Acts dismisses the Torah on the not wholly compatible grounds of its misuse by the Jews and of the impossibility of performing it.[13] By placing the Law in paradise, however, Milton can suggest that Adam misuses it when he chooses to fall and that he is unable to perform it once he has fallen.

Though Adam at first articulates the assumption that his death can render back to God all he has received, he also from the first senses an even darker misery that would ensue should God call in his debts. Adam's fear that suffering can be protracted beyond the grave is too terrible to be expressed or even perceived all at once. It first approaches him dimly and from afar, in the complaint that his posterity will curse him: "for what can I increase/ Or multiply, but curses on my head?" (732). At this point, in a tone querulous rather than tragic, Adam recognizes that living infamy can be worse than death. The uneasy feeling that continuity is a curse grows slowly in the soliloquy, in phrases like "lasting woes" (742), "the sense of endless woes" (754), and "deathless pain" (775). Adam uses these phrases in a general way to increase the pathos of his current situation. The specific terror of their most literal meaning has not yet manifested itself.

Similarly undeveloped at this point is the split between

divine and natural law, a topic not apparently related to perpetual torment. Adam contrasts the cause of his progeny's birth with that of his own:

> him not thy election,
> But Natural necessity begot.
> God made thee of choice his own, and of his own
> To serve him.
>
> (764–67)

The laws of nature lie behind the birth of a child, and these may not accord with a parent's choice: the existence of childless couples, unhappy parents, and unwanted children tells us that election does not always determine birth. How different from pro-choice paradise, where birth is a matter of election, in Eve's case by Adam as well as by God. And God the Father's relationship with Adam before the Fall is like his relationship with the Son. According to Milton, the Son "is called God's own Son simply because he had no other Father but God, and this is why he himself said that God was his Father. . . . This particular Father begot his Son not from any natural necessity but of his own free will: a method more excellent and more in keeping with paternal dignity, especially as this Father is God" (*YP* 6.208–09). In paradise, where "God and Nature bid the same" (6.176), the terms of the interdiction and of nature's law were entirely compatible, a point Raphael emphasized near the end of his visit (8.561). The disjunction began after Eve tasted the forbidden fruit, when Adam chose to disobey the divine law for the sake of the natural: "I feel/ The Link of Nature draw me" (9.913–14).

The key but problematic source of the rupture between nature and election is Galatians 4.22–30, the allegory of Hagar and Sarah, Ishmael and Isaac, Sinai and Jerusalem, which reverses the iron law of primogeniture and asserts the primacy of the new. Paul contrasts Hagar the slavewoman and her son Ishmael, who was born in the course of nature, with Sarah the freewoman and her son Isaac, who was born as the result of election: "But he who was of the bondwoman was born after the flesh; but he of the free woman was by

promise" (4.23). The two women—related as carnal to
spiritual—and their two sons provide a lineage for the two
peoples, the Jews and the Christians. They tell in a figure
of the rejection of the Jews and the election of the Christians
in their place, and Milton cites them frequently in the Pauline
chapters of *De doctrina* to underscore the differences between the two covenants (*YP* 6.499, 522, 527, 530, 592, 605).
Adam reaches back beyond Hagar and Sarah to paradise,
where election precedes natural necessity. By asserting the
primacy of the original, he inadvertently and momentarily
restores the balance upset by Paul.

The sudden fusion of two topics kept carefully separate—
the duration of suffering and the split between the laws of
God and Nature—detonates in Adam's imagination the
mechanism of terror that was carefully set ticking early in
the soliloquy. Nature offers rest, while the thunder of the
law evokes the dreadful Sinai theophany:

> How gladly would I meet
> Mortality my sentence, and be Earth
> Insensible, how glad would lay me down
> As in my Mother's lap! There I should rest
> And sleep secure; *his dreadful voice no more*
> *Would thunder in my ears,* no fear of worse
> To mee and to my offspring would torment me
> With cruel expectation.
>
> (775–82; my emphasis)

Adam, like a pagan brought up on naturalism, wants to rest,
but God's thunder will not let him. In *De doctrina Christiana*,
Milton defines rest specifically as escape from the Mosaic
law: "rest, that is, from the curse of the law. Hence the
agitation in Paul's mind while he was under the curse of
the law. . . ." (*YP* 6.519).

Adam's mortalism, a comfort when he considers the
alternative, derives from his interpretation of natural law:

> though the Lord of all be infinite,
> Is his wrath also? be it, Man is not so,
> But mortal doom'd. How can he exercise
> Wrath without end on Man whom Death must end?

Can he make deathless Death?

(794–98)

> Will he draw out,
> For anger's sake, finite to infinite
> In punisht Man, to satisfy his rigor
> Satisfi'd never; that were to extend
> His Sentence beyond dust and Nature's Law,
> By which all Causes else according still
> To the reception of thir matter act,
> Not to th' extent of thir own Sphere.

(801–08)

Adam relies on his body's frailty to thwart God's wrath. He finds consolation in natural law: since, according to this law, causes operate, not in proportion to their own power, but in proportion to the capacity of the object they work upon,[14] finite Adam will not suffer infinitely though he deserves eternal damnation. But Adam has transgressed a commandment divine rather than natural. He intends three questions to sound rhetorical, and they do, but they are not. The questions are posed in a way that suggests they will not take yes for an answer, but they do. Is God's wrath infinite? The immediate reply, "be it," concedes that it is. The infinite wrath of the Old Law was a commonplace among the Reformers. When Milton opposes the covenant of grace to the Mosaic law, he quotes Romans 4.15 ("The law worketh wrath" [*YP* 6.518, 523, 528, 533]); and in *Paradise Lost*, wrath is used as a virtual synonym of law ("over wrath grace shall abound," 12.478). Can God make deathless Death? He can according to the terms of a Mosaic law that operates absolutely as Paul believes it does, independent of human ability to perform it. Bucanus's legal metaphor now becomes ominous: even if the debtor is bankrupt, "the creditor can not bee proved to deale unjustly, if he demaund the lent money of him & his heires."[15]

John Marbeck's formulation is more direct: "it is impossible for a man to fulfill the lawe of his owne strength and power, seeing that we are by birth and nature, the heires of eternall damnation."[16] As Peter Bulkeley notes, "The covenant stands fast, but we have not stood fast in the covenant, but it is now become impossible to us, that we are unable to fulfill it, as the Apostle speaks, Rom. 8.3. Yea, it is the unchangeableness and stability of this covenant, which condemns all the world of sinful and ungodly men."[17] Fallen Adam's position under the law most closely resembles that of the Jews, who were given oracles, scriptures, and promises. God's faithfulness in making the promises is not invalidated by the failure of the Jews to keep their part of the covenant (Romans 3.2–4; 10–11). Calvin endlessly pursues the relentlessness of the law for those who do not accept Christ's grace:

> Doth the impossibilitie of dooing it, discharge us of our service which wee be bound to doe unto God? No. For the evil commeth of ourselves. . . . It is no marvel then, that God in his lawe shoulde have no regard to mans abilitie or unabilitie, but rather to the dutie which we owe him, or that he shoulde require the right that belongeth to him . . . . If wee had continued in our integritie, and not beene perverted and corrupted through sinne, then should we have beene able to have discharged all that God requireth of us in his lawe. That is certaine.[18]

The impossibility of performing the Mosaic law, then, is no objection to it, and Adam now sees himself paying through eternity a debt of suffering to a God of infinite wrath. This is worse than the "debt immense" of which Satan complains, "So burthensome still paying, still to owe" (4.52–53). Even the Son's "immortal love/ To mortal men" (3.267–68) turns sinister in the soliloquy, proving as it does that God can after all exert immortal force on a mortal object.

It is clear that the Miltonic bard carries the Mosaic law back to Eden, identifying it with the first prohibition, and later, after the Fall, exploiting its power to evoke the terror of eternal condemnation. Adam faces directly the claustrophobic terror of unextinguished sinful consciousness:

> endless misery
> From this day onward, which I feel begun
> Both in me, and without me, and so last
> To perpetuity: Ay me, that fear
> Comes thund'ring back with dreadful revolution

On my defenseless head; both Death and I
Am found Eternal, and incorporate both.

(810–16)

The returning thunder that follows Adam's confrontation
of his worst fear is the thunder of Sinai, which Hebrews
12.18–21 describes as unendurable, a symbol of the Mosaic
law. Adam and death are incorporate and eternal, and we
remember Paul on sin and the Law: "O wretched man that
I am! who shall deliver me from the body of this death?"
(Romans 7.24). Milton cites this verse in *De doctrina
Christiana*, in the chapter on the Fall, where he connects
the sin of our first parents with the body of death under
the Law:

> Evil concupiscence is that of which our original parents were
> first guilty, and which they transmitted to their posterity,
> as sharers in the primary transgression, in the shape of an
> innate propensity to sin. This is called in Scripture "the old
> man," and "the body of sin" . . . "the body of death" . . . "the
> law of sin and of death." (*CM* 15.193; compare *YP* 6.389)

The law of God, which Adam disjoined from natural law
when he chose to fall, now exacts vengeance on him by
cancelling even the small comfort of dissolution afforded by
natural law.

Adam's entire soliloquy is a product of the Reformation.
The speculations of Adam unparadised are not "by the mere
light of nature"; and his "intimation of unimmortality" is
positively welcome compared with its alternative, intermi-
nable sinful consciousness beyond the grave.[19] David Pareus
describes the tribunal where God's justice prosecutes:

> Before [God's] tribunal we all stood guiltie of eternal death
> through sin: Gods revenging justice stood against us, requir-
> ing, that we should suffer temporal and eternal punishments,
> For what was committed by us against his infinite majesty:
> *For it is the judgement of God that they who commit such
> things are worthie of death* [Rom. 1:32]. Against us stood
> the law of God pronouncing cursings against the trans-
> gressours thereof: Our own evil conscience also, arguing and
> convincing us of eternall guiltinesse.[20]

In Milton's first outline for a tragedy on the theme of paradise lost, Moses and Justice are the first two "Persons"; in the second plan, Moses is the prologue, followed immediately by Justice and Mercie, who debate "what should become of man if he fall"; and in the continuous scenario "Adam unparadiz'd," where Milton moves toward the actual method of the epic, Adam "is stubborn in his offence Justice appeares reason[s] with him convinces him. . . ."[21] Before Adam in the great epic relents and despairs, convicted of sin, he complains to God: "inexplicable/ Thy Justice seems" (754–55). At that invocatory moment, Adam's conscience begins to speak to him in the second person ("thou," "thee," and "thy" appearing eleven times in ll.757–70). Adam has internalized the character Justice as a Mosaic superego:

> God made thee of choice his own, and of his own
> To serve him, thy reward was of his grace,
> Thy punishment then justly is at his Will.
> Be it so, for I submit, his doom is fair.
>
> (766–69)

Adam will escape from God's infinite wrath in the implications of a phrase that terrifies him: will God "draw out/ . . . finite to infinite/ . . . to satisfy his rigor/ Satisfi'd never"? (801–04). "Rigor/Satisfi'd" suggests "rigid satisfaction" (3.212), God's term for the necessary atonement in which infinite becomes finite. The Son of God offers to save Adam, thus satisfying a concept of justice that Paul and his Protestant interpreters would regard as inalienably Old Testament in character. The Son's faith stands in marked contrast to Adam's despair:

> Though now to Death I yield, and am his due
> All that of me can die, yet that debt paid,
> Thou wilt not leave me in the loathsome grave
> His prey, nor suffer my unspotted Soul
> For ever with corruption there to dwell.
>
> (3.245–49)

Adam, unaware of his allusion to Christ's atonement, ends the soliloquy convicted under the law, but before the

Not to do only, but to will the same
With me?

(824–27; my emphasis)

Adam is the unclean fountain, the bitter root, the wild vine, the *"evill tree* [that] *cannot bring forth good fruite."*[23] He has meditated on Romans 7.14–25: "for what I would, that do I not; but what I hate, that do I" (15); "For the good that I would, I do not: but the evil which I would not, that I do" (19). Adam's self-assessment depends entirely on Paul's description of the Mosaic law as a code of restrictions that resembles Roman law rather than Torah. Human beings cannot obey that law because their physical bodies contain another law, which forces them to act against their will and prevents them from doing the good that is required by the Mosaic law. The anthropological dualism of a good soul in a weak, evil body can lead to a Marcion-like theological dualism that separates the bad creator-God of the Old Testament from the good redeemer-God found primarily in the Pauline epistles. As E. P. Sanders has noted, "anthropological dualism . . . denies a cardinal theological belief of Judaism: that God created the world and pronounced it good (Genesis 1.31)."[24]

Book 10 presents the epic's most grimly methodical devaluation of the laws of Moses and of nature (651–715), whose "growing miseries" (715) put Adam immediately in mind of his own misery. Philo comments on the biblical curses delivered against the transgressors of the Mosaic law (Deuteronomy 28.15–68): "The story of Thyestes will be child's play compared with the monstrous calamities which those times of terror will bring about."[25] And the Miltonic bard describes the terrible alterations in nature that are the consequences of disobedience: "At that tasted Fruit/ The Sun, as from Thyestean Banquet, turn'd/ His course intended" (687–89). The passionate hostility directed against the laws of nature and of Moses to which Milton had appealed in the divorce tracts—laws that emphasized the human capacity for achievement—may represent the cynicism and disappointment of a disillusioned idealist. The ruining of paradise is also a compulsive, systematic spoiling of Israel, which had been Milton's model for England. Just as human-kind can no longer find redemption even in the moral law, so can it find no saving knowledge in the laws of external nature: neither the signs of the Jews nor the wisdom of the Greeks but only Christ crucified (1 Corinthians 1.20–25; Romans 1.16–17). We must be dead to one law and blind to the other.

Adam reprises his soliloquy later in the book, when Eve proposes suicide as a form of celibacy, to stop the production of children destined to feed death:

> doubt not but God
> Hath wiselier arm'd his vengeful ire than so
> To be forestall'd; much more I fear lest Death
> So snatcht will not exempt us from the pain
> We are by doom to pay; rather such acts
> Of contumacy will provoke the Highest
> *To make death in us live.*
>
> (1022–028; my emphasis)

Adam in this state of wrath solves the problem by carefully reinterpreting Genesis 3.15, understanding for the first time its promise of redemption. His reprise of God's primal blessing of humankind with fertility dramatizes the thinness of a Pauline conception of Torah [26] Evoked before the Fall, Genesis 1.28 emphasized the mutual benefits of a covenantal rela-tionship between humankind and the animals brought by God "to receive/ From thee thir Names, and pay thee fealty" (8.344). Fallen Adam now reinterprets Genesis 1.28 as a promise of vengeance against the devil: "to crush his head/ Would be revenge indeed; which will be lost/ By death brought on ourselves, or childless days/ Resolv'd, as thou proposest" (10.1035–38).

The shift in equilibrium suffered by the entire epic as a result of the Fall includes a shift from a comprehensive to a monolithic interpretation of the law. After the Fall, Milton's radical Paulinism revises and reduces the Hebraic view of the law in paradise, thus making the gospel an inevitability. The sudden disappearance from the epic of the positive Mosaic law and its unacknowledged replacement by a law identical in name but diminished in character parallels another disappearance familiar to Miltonists. According to A. J. A. Waldock, the glorious Satan of books 1 and 2 of the epic threatens Milton's overall scheme, and he is therefore replaced by a less dangerous character: "The Satan of the address to the Sun is not a development from the old, he is not a changed Satan, he is a *new* Satan."[27] The alleged degeneration of the law (to paraphrase Waldock on Satan) is actually of the nature of an assertion that certain changes occur. The changes do not generate themselves from within: they are imposed from without. The Mosaic law does not degenerate: it is degraded. According to a Reformation commonplace, the law places us "under the power of the divel . . . [and] in the lawe we finde death, damnation and wrath, moreover the curse and vengeance of God upon us."[28] More pertinently, Paul in Romans 7 regards Sin as a quasi-demonic power that makes use of the divine commandment to further its own ends: "sin, taking occasion by the commandment, wrought in me all manner of concupiscence" (7.5). Paul occasionally blurs distinctions between the content of the law and the effect of the law, between a law that reveals sin and a law that arouses sin. For Paul, the Mosaic law and Satan would have more in common than their degradation.

Waldock regards the technique of degradation as a form of literary cheating, a sign of authorial nervousness when threatened with loss of control. Adam in his soliloquy wishes that he were "Earth/ Insensible" (776–77), for oblivion would provide escape from God's wrath: "his dreadful voice no more/ Would Thunder in my ears" (779–80). But God has never thundered in his ears. The harshest sound Adam has ever heard is the Son's mild voice of judgment (10.96). Adam is here identifying the prohibition with the negative Mosaic law—specifically, with the Israelites' experience at Sinai as interpreted in the New Testament:

> God from the Mount of *Sinai*, whose gray top
> Shall tremble, he descending, will himself
> In Thunder, Lightning and loud Trumpet's sound

Ordain them Laws.

. . . .

But the voice of God
To mortal ear is dreadful.

(12.227–30; 235–36)

> For ye are not come unto the mount that might not be
> touched, and that burned with fire, nor unto blackness, and
> darkness, and tempest, and the sound of a trumpet, and the
> voice of words; which *voice* they that heard entreated that
> the word should not be spoken to them any more: for they
> could not endure that which was commanded . . . but ye are
> come unto Mount Zion . . . and to Jesus the mediator of the
> new covenant. . . . (Hebrews 12.18–20, 22–24)

The benign law whose ease of fulfillment Adam had often
acknowledged has suddenly become terrible. Is this changed
characterization of the law a sign enabling us to interpret
Adam's argument as self-serving, ungrateful, conveniently
forgetful?[29] Or is it an example of Milton's degrading the
law after the Fall, making it a mere foil to the gospel, under-
scoring the consolation of *felix culpa* by pretending that this
inferior law operated in paradise from the beginning? The
latter seems a likely explanation of another example: the
Son's otherwise puzzlingly peremptory dismissal of paradise,
its dispensation, and its works (11.22–36). Once the law has
been reduced sufficiently, it can be dismissed without regret.
The Son speaks of the dispensation of paradise as if it had
always been merely the Mosaic law as understood from
within a Pauline realm of discourse.

The redemption dimly foreseen at the end of book 10
comes at a heavy price: the torture and death of Christ; an
anthropological dualism that devalues human nature and
denies the goodness of the created order; the degradation of
the Mosaic law; a thin and factitious sense of history that
does not merely replace and blot out the past but actively
misrepresents it; and the squeezing of the dense poetry of
prelapsarian paradise into a thin line of doctrine.

Despite its extreme Paulinism, Adam's soliloquy cannot
suppress entirely the evocation of Milton's Hebraic paradise.

The element of supersession in Pauline typology emphasizes
the contrast between weak Old Testament types and their
strong New Testament antitype. Paul's incursions against
his own past require "forgetting what lies behind and straining forward to what lies ahead" (Philippians 3.13). But even
the internalized voice of Justice, using the language of Calvin
to contrast life before and after the Fall, reminds Adam of
an original grace that does not require the death of the
redeemer: "thy reward was of his *grace*,/ Thy punishment
then *justly* is at his Will" (10.767–68; my emphasis). Adam's
soliloquy inadvertently reverses the dynamics of supersession by asserting the priority and authority of paradise: the
covenant of grace precedes the covenant of works. Paul saw
the events of the Hebrew Bible as "written down for our
instruction, upon whom the end of the ages has come" (1
Corinthians 10.11).[30] But *Paradise Lost* is a radically nos-
talgic work that looks back to election in paradise preceding
natural necessity in the fallen world. In the Edenic books
of the great epic, Torah is the antitype that precedes the
law, and Genesis 1.28 celebrates fertility and amplitude rather
than vengeance. Satan, preferring paradise over heaven,
parodies the aggressively antithetical impulse of the typolo-
gist: "For what God after better worse would build?" (9.102).

Early in the soliloquy, Adam anticipates his children's
curses:

> Who of all Ages to succeed, but feeling
> The evil on him brought by me, will curse
> My Head: Ill fare our Ancestor impure,
> For this we may thank *Adam*; but his thanks
> Shall be the execration.
>
> (733–37)

Adam's bitter question is unanswerable within Milton's
Pauline Christian tradition, where only Christ the second
Adam can reverse the sin of the first Adam that has spread
to all of his children. The *Zohar* has an answer which,
appropriately, lacks resolution, balancing Father Adam's
perpetual anxiety about original sin against his assurance
that he is not responsible for it:

When a human being is about to depart from life, Adam, the first man, appears to him and asks him why and in what state he leaves the world. The man says, "Woe to you that because of you I have to die." To which Adam replies, "My son, I transgressed one commandment and was punished for so doing; see how many commandments of your Master, negative and positive, you have transgressed. . . ." Adam appears to every man at the moment of his departure from life to testify that he is dying on account of his own sins and not the sin of Adam.[31]

10 • Milton and the Hartlib Circle
Educational Projects and Epic *Paideia*

Barbara K. Lewalski

M ilton's own testimony makes clear that he wrote his tractate *Of Education* (June, 1644) in response to the "earnest entreaties" of Samuel Hartlib, to elaborate ideas Milton had expressed to him during their several "incidentall discourses" on that topic.[1] Set forth as a letter "To Master *Samuel Hartlib*," it begins by praising the emigre scholar from Elbing as "a person sent hither by some good providence from a farre country to be the occasion and the incitement of great good to this Iland"—an opinion shared, Milton notes, by "men of most approved wisdom, and some of highest authority among us" (YP 2.363). Like Hartlib, but with even more urgency, Milton insisted that educational reform and the dissemination of knowledge are vital to a reformed commonwealth—"for the want whereof this nation perishes" (363). But in his prose tracts and especially his great epics, Milton conceived of education and learning in his own terms, which are in dialogue with, but not, I think, in close agreement with, the projects of the Hartlib Circle.

Despite casual connections and gestures of respect on both sides, Milton was not part of the Hartlib Circle, which included, at or near its center, the Moravian scholar J. A. Comenius, the Scots proponent of Protestant unity John Dury, Joachim Hubner of Cleves, Theodore Haak, John Pell, John Hall, Robert Boyle, Benjamin Worsley, William Petty, John Sandler, Sir Cheney Culpepper and several others. Their interconnections and activities have been analyzed in major studies by G. H. Turnbull, Charles Webster, and many scholars involved in publishing the Hartlib papers.[2] Milton probably knew Hartlib by 1643 but there is no evidence that he met Comenius when that scholar visited England from September, 1641 to June 1642.[3] Also, though Milton addressed his treatise on education to Hartlib, he took some care to associate it with ancient classical and humanist programs and to dissociate it from the Comenian texts that were seminal for the Hartlib Circle's educational schemes: "To search what many modern *Janua's* and *Didactics* more then ever I shall read, have projected, my inclination leads me not" (2.365–66). By the time Milton wrote *Of Education*, Comenius's much discussed and widely used reformist manual on teaching Latin, *Janua linguarum reserata*, had reached its sixth English edition. That Milton, a prodigiously learned practising schoolmaster, was entirely innocent of the Comenian texts and educational theories strains credulity. Ernest Sirluck suggests, plausibly, that the disclaimer is disingenuous, affording Milton an excuse, in courtesy to Hartlib, not to spell out his own serious criticisms of the Comenian educational program.[4]

For their part, the Hartlib Circle evidently did not count Milton one of their number, though they showed interest in his work and kept up some casual contact with him. *Of Education* was published anonymously, without a prefatory commendation from Hartlib such as is found in most works on education sponsored by him. But Hartlib did distribute it to members of his Circle, eliciting a mixed response: Dury termed it "brief and general"; Hall thought it excellent and desired Milton's acquaintance; Culpepper found in it "good sprinklings" but not "descending enough into particulars."[5] Later, Hartlib included Milton's name as one of ten members of a Council for Schooling he proposed to the Commonwealth government, possibly in 1650.[6] Also, the Hartlib Circle took note of some Miltonic works in progress, apropos of their concern to compile information about all kinds of scholarly projects. Haak told Hartlib in 1648 that "Milton is not only writing a Univ. History of Engl. but also an Epitome of all Purchas Volumes."[7] Milton published his incomplete *History of Britain* in 1670; the Purchas project, if there was one, has its only trace in the posthumously published *History of Moscovia* (1682), based on travellers' accounts in Purchas and Hakluyt. In the 1650's John Dury, then on the Continent, wrote several letters to Hartlib,[8] with information to be passed on to Milton regarding Salmasius and Alexander More, the satiric targets of Milton's Latin *Defenses*. Dury clearly knew something of the matter and tactics of Milton's *Defensio Secunda* before its publication in May 1654. His April letters to Hartlib warn that Milton was likely wrong in attributing the *Regii Sanguinis Clamor* to Alexander More; Dury's information was accurate, though Milton either disbelieved or chose to ignore it. After the publication of the *Defensio Secunda*, Dury's letters offered Milton some support by reporting More's unsavory reputation both in the Hague and Geneva.[9]

The Hartlib Circle's educational programs and projects, based on the theories and texts of Comenius, form a link between Bacon and the Royal Society. The reformers differed as to particulars but shared several fundamental ideas: the conviction that educational reform is "the Maine Foundation of a Reformed Commonwealth";[10] disgust for the logic chopping, metaphysical subtleties, and rhetorical emphases of the *trivium* as currently taught in schools and universities; a Baconian emphasis on "useful" knowledge—languages not for themselves but for the knowledge in them, and the "scientific" study of things rather than words, nature rather than books. They believed in state-supported elementary schools for all classes and both sexes; in a comprehensive system of articulated schools from infancy through the university; and in a Baconian progression from subject matter grounded upon the senses to abstract subjects discernible by reason, with dialectic and rhetoric at the culmination of the course (rather than at the beginning, as was common practice). Like Bacon also they had an abiding faith in method—in the true and proper method for educating the young, and in elaborate systems for promoting, collecting, disseminating, and judging scholarly projects and discoveries throughout Britain and all Europe.

Comenius's best known educational works were those Milton so cavalierly dismissed. The *Janua Linguarum Reserata* (1631), an immensely popular Latin grammar based on 1000 sentences about several classes of phenomena— nature, art, trade, fire, gardening, arithmetic, diseases, angels, etc.—purported to offer "real knowledge" in the language rather than the Latin classics.[11] The *Didactica Magna*, published in Amsterdam in 1657 but summarized earlier in several works,[12] proposed a perfect and pleasurable method of education applicable to and intended for all—boys and girls, the able and the dull, all social ranks. After the "Mother School," which begins in the cradle and emphasizes sensory learning, would come three levels of free, state supported schools. The Vernacular Schools for ages six to twelve would offer education to all in the mother tongue—writing, arithmetic, the scriptures, history, cosmography, the mechanical arts, and (later) modern languages—so that "artisans, rustics, porters, and even women" will possess "the material for thinking, choosing, following, and doing good things."[13] Latin Schools for ages twelve to eighteen, theoretically open to all but clearly designed for the male gentry and nobility, would teach, in sequence, Latin grammar, natural philosophy, mathematics, moral philosophy and politics, dialectic and rhetoric; history and geography would be studied throughout the course, and Greek and Hebrew in succession. The University (entered by public examination) would train leaders in church and state—lawyers, clergy, physicians, and scholars in various subjects. At all levels and in all subjects students would learn where possible by direct observation of things, by experience, and by dialogic interchange; their books would be chiefly epitomes, compilations, or encyclopedias.

It is Comenius's Latin School (chiefly for upper class boys) that invites some comparison with the academies projected by Milton in *Of Education*. In the *Great Didactic* Comenius declares that the function of the Latin school is "to give a more thorough education to those who aspire higher than the workshop";[14] it is clear, however, that after lower-class boys complete the genuinely democratic Vernacular Schools, Comenius expects most of them to go to farms, trades, or workshops. Also, further education for some women would apparently take place privately or in special women's schools. Comenius argues that there is no reason to exclude women from the pursuit of knowledge "whether in Latin or in their mother-tongue," noting that they are "endowed with equal sharpness of mind and capacity for knowledge" and are often called to be rulers, counsellors to kings, or even prophets. But he retreats from the implications of this opinion, insisting that their chief education will be in things befitting the sex, "all that enables her to look after her household and to promote the welfare of her husband and her family."[15]

English versions of the Comenian program, chiefly by Dury and Hartlib, diluted its universalist aspects by fitting it even more firmly to the class structure. Hartlib's profound concern with poor relief led him to propose workhouses for poor children to teach them basic literacy as well as a useful trade.[16] Dury's educational treatises (usually with prefaces by Hartlib) propose several kinds of schools under the supervision of state overseers: 1. Common schools with much the same curriculum as Comenius's Vernacular Schools, but explicitly for *commoners* of both sexes, to prepare them for "publick usefulnesse."[17] 2. Vulgar or Mechanical Schools to fit men for husbandry, navigation, mining, surveying, architecture, painting, etc. 3. Noble Schools for "the Nobilitie, Gentrie, and the better sort of Citizens, which are fit to bee made to bear offices in the Common-wealth."[18] In the Noble Schools boys from ages eight to thirteen would study the subjects of the common school as well as *Januas* for Latin,

Greek, and Hebrew; at ages thirteen to nineteen they would study useful arts and sciences (including medicine and law) according to a graduated reading program.[19] Noble Schools for girls would chiefly teach them to be "good and careful houswives . . . understanding in all things belonging to the care of a Family," but those "found capable of Tongues and Sciences" would be "assisted towards the improvement of their intellectual abilities," though always with reference to what will "perfect them in Graces and the knowledge of Christ."[20] There would be special colleges to train ministers and teachers, and others to foster scientific experiments and inventions. University professors would devote themselves to new research and publication, to "add unto the Common stock of humane knowledge."[21]

Comenius's crowning project was Pansophia, a Grand Encyclopedia of all useful knowledge to be culled out from the useless residue by collaborating scholars, and published in all languages. The Hartlib Circle also proliferated schemes for the promotion, dissemination, and compilation of knowledge. But these projects often had the stated design of promoting intellectual uniformity. Besides his grand pansophic encyclopedia, Comenius proposed in 1642 the creation of a Universal College of ministers and laymen to unify religious knowledge and thereby end dissent.[22] And he proposed at first to eliminate the false pagan classics from his school curriculum, though he recanted that position later.[23] Hartlib, in his utopia *Macaria* (1641), imagined a society with "no diversity of opinion": once a year all would be allowed to dispute freely on any subject before the Grand Council, after which those opinions that win general assent would be declared true, and proponents of new opinions at other times would be executed.[24] In his *Reformed Librarie Keeper* (1650) Dury, then Librarian of St. James Palace, urged that libraries throughout the land be opened to all and that the Librarian of Bodley actively "trade" with scholars in England and abroad to exchange and publish their knowledge; however, once a year university professors would select from the rest the works worthy to be catalogued as additions to the common store of knowledge. This was a version of

Hartlib's pet project (which he went some distance toward embodying in his own person)—a state-sponsored Office of Address for Communication to facilitate exchange of information about scientific experiments, inventions, scholarship in all subjects, religious knowledge, and "intellectual rarities." Though Hartlib envisioned few explicit controls, he did charge the Warden of this Office to report on his negotiations once a year to the University Professors, who will then decide which works ought to be preserved.[25]

Early to late, Milton distanced himself from these positions on several vital points. Though he urged the use of public funds to establish schools nationwide, he did not project a comprehensive, articulated system, but rather, two models of schools for boys. Also, despite his own A.M. from Cambridge, he scornfully repudiated university education for arts students and ministers. From his university academic exercises (the Prolusions), to his antiprelatical tracts of 1641–42, to his demand for a disestablished church in 1659, he denounced the Aristotelian-scholastic university curriculum as a "Lernian bog" of fallacies, apparently finding reformist efforts to expand humanistic and scientific studies in the universities woefully inadequate.[26] He castigates the universities for their petty disputations and "scragged and thorny lectures of monkish and miserable sophistry" that only make the student "a more finished fool," and leave him "almost completely unskilled and unlearned in Philology and Philosophy."[27] Milton's educational ideas were formed by his own (essentially humanist) education at St. Paul's School; by his experience (c. 1640–46) in running a school in his home for his nephews and a few other boys; and especially by the highly disciplined five-year reading program he undertook after university at his father's charge—in history, theology, philosophy, all the natural sciences, classical and modern literature in Greek, Latin, Hebrew, French, Italian, and English.[28] Milton's deepest conviction, founded on this experience, is that genuine education (and especially higher education) must be largely self-motivated and self-directed. He has no faith in perfect methods or systems, nor in epitomes and encyclopedias.

Milton's *Of Education* proclaims both a religious and a civic humanist purpose for education: "The end then of learning is to repair the ruins of our first parents by regaining to know God aright . . . as we may the neerest by possessing our souls of true vertue" (*YP* 2.316–17); "I call therefore a compleate and generous Education that which fits a man to perform justly, skilfully and magnanimously all the offices both private and publike of peace and war" (377–79). Probably alluding to the Commons Act of 15 June 1641 that calls for use of the confiscated property of Bishops, Deans and Chapters for the advancement of learning, Milton proposes that "edifices [be] converted to this use . . . in every City throughout this land, which would tend much to the encrease of learning and civility every where" (380–81). But unlike Hartlib and Dury, he makes no provision for state oversight and regulation of these essentially private academies, and he explicitly declines to work out a Comenian articulated system of schools "from the cradle" (414). Like Dury's Noble Schools Milton's academies are aristocratic, each designed for about 150 of "our noble and gentle youth" (406) between the ages of twelve and twenty-one. They assume literacy in English and some preparation from the entering boys, and promise them a complete education to the level of Master of Arts.

Milton's tract incorporates several Comenian principles (common also to Bacon and some Renaissance humanists): that education should proceed from "sensible things" to those more abstract and founded in reason; that the process, while rigorous, should also be delightful; that languages should be studied, not for the "words or lexicons" (360) but to make available the "experience and . . . wisdom" of others; and that present methods of learning Latin and Greek are prodigiously wasteful of time and ineffective. Instead of *Januas,* however, Milton would begin with the grammar now used [Lily] "or any better"[29]—and proceed quickly to practice in pronunciation and the reading of good authors. After the basics of arithmetic and geometry the boys would turn to subjects founded on the senses—agriculture and geography, then Greek, then Greek and Latin texts on natural science, astronomy, meteorology, architecture, physics. They would then proceed to the "instrumental" sciences of trigonometry, fortification, architecture, military engineering, meteors, zoology, anatomy, medicine. Throughout, Milton proposes to use classical (and presumably some modern) books rather than Comenian epitomes. Dury proposes a similar progression of subjects and books in *The Reformed School* (1650), apparently adopting these features from Milton's treatise in a gesture of accommodation. Also, Milton's students would conjoin scientific and literary tests. Concomitant with the natural sciences they would read the poetry of nature—pastoral, georgic, Lucretius and other "scientific" poems. After the sense-based sciences, they are ready for subjects grounded in reason: moral philosophy, economics, politics and law, history, epic, tragedy, and classical rhetoric. Their moral philosophy—Plato, Xenophon, Cicero, Plutarch and the like—is to be "reduc't in their nightward studies" by the "determinate sentence" of scripture (396–97). Their studies in economics (household management) are to be leavened with choice Greek, Latin, and Italian domestic comedies and tragedies (the boys will by now have learned "at any odde hour the *Italian* tongue" [397]). They then study politics, law, and history, together with the great classical epics and tragedies, and the orations of Cicero and Demosthenes. Milton's course, like that of Comenius, ends with logic and rhetoric. But Milton also adds poetics, and Dury follows suit in *The Reformed School*, apparently his most direct appropriation from Milton. Compositions in all these kinds, Milton argues forcefully, are not for the "empty wits" of children but should be the product of mature and independent reflection, based on "long reading, and observing" (372).

Sundays are for theology and church history; in the final years of the course the students (some of them prospective ministers) will have learned "the Hebrew Tongue at a set hour," along with the Chaldian and Syriac dialects, so they can read the scriptures in the original (400). After meals and exercise they hear or perform music for voice, organ, or lute, to compose their spirits and passions, as Plato recommended. Given the Civil War milieu, Milton makes place also for military training—not only gentleman's swordplay (and wrestling) but also "embattailing, marching, encamping, fortifying, beseiging, battering" and tactics, to make the students "perfect Commanders in the service of their country" (411–12).

To this essentially humanistic program, Milton added something of the practical and experiential learning Hartlib and Dury located in the Vulgar or Mechanical schools. To supplement their readings in agriculture and in the natural and instrumental sciences, Milton's students would gain "a reall tincture of natural knowledge" from presentations and demonstrations by "Hunters, fowlers, Fishermen, Shepherds, Gardeners, *Apothecaries* . . . Architects, Engineers, Mariners, *Anatomists*" (393–94), as well as by springtime travels throughout the land, observing agriculture, trade, military encampments, ships and seafights. At age twenty-four or so (but not earlier, lest they be corrupted) they might travel to foreign lands "to enlarge experience and make wise observation" (414).

Like the Hartlib Circle Milton also undertook a broader educational mission—in his case, to teach statesmen and the nation at large. In *The Reason of Church Government* (1642) he declared himself "Church-outed by the Prelats" (*YP* 1.823)—that is, prevented by the Laudian takeover in the English Church from exercising a minister's teaching office. In its place he formally assumed the role of prophet-teacher, both in his polemic and in his poetry. His deepest concern was to form the virtuous man and the good commonwealthsman—one whose inner liberty assures his devotion to political liberty and to the common good. *Areopagitica*, published in November, 1644, six months after *Of Education*, spells out Milton's fundamental conviction that such formation requires the practice of liberty on an individual basis, not grand cooperative encyclopedias, or Pansophias, or the resolution of dissent into unity. Indeed, his argument for the removal of prior censorship and publication of all kinds of books intends to foster a constant clash of opinions, and thereby promote arduous intellectual struggle and individual choice. In the moral realm this will produce virtue and inner liberty: "He that can apprehend and consider vice with all her baits and seeming pleasures, and yet abstain, and yet distinguish, and yet prefer that which is truly better, he is the true warfaring Christian" (*YP* 2.514–15). In the intellectual realm it will promote knowledge, which "thrives by exercise" (543), and will advance truth: "The light which we have gain'd, was given us, not to be ever staring on, but by it to discover onward things more remote from our knowledge" (550). Milton describes an England shaken by God and becoming a nation of prophets: many "by their studious lamps, [are] musing, searching, revolving new notions and ideas" while others are "reading, trying all things, assenting to the force of reason and convincement" (554).

The soaring optimism of *Areopagitica* dissipated as the nation of prophets found itself unable to settle church or state, and as popular nostalgia for the old monarchical "tyranny" increased. But Milton continued to hope that the kind of learning proposed in *Of Education* and *Areopagitica* would form a better citizenry. In the "Digression" to his *History of Britain* (perhaps written around 1648) he complains that the English by temperament lack political wisdom and "civic virtues," and urges that these "bee imported into our mindes from forren writings & examples of best ages" (*YP* 5.1, 451)—presumably ancient Greece, republican Rome, and continental republican theory. In the *Defensio Secunda* (1654), echoing Plato and Aristotle, he exhorts his countrymen to understand the link between inner freedom grounded upon virtue, and political liberty: "a nation which cannot rule and govern itself, but has delivered itself into slavery to its own lusts, is enslaved also to other masters whom it does not choose . . . You, therefore, who wish to remain free . . . learn to obey right reason, to master yourselves" (*YP* 4.684). In the same work he urges Cromwell (then Protector) to give more support to education, but pointedly steers him away from the comprehensive schemes of Comenius, Dury, and Hartlib:

> [Do not] feel it right for the teachable and the unteachable, the diligent and the slothful to be instructed side by side

at public expense. Rather should you keep the rewards of the learned for those who have already acquired learning, those who already deserve the reward (679).

This individualistic, meritocratic precept evidently points back to *Of Education*, referred to elsewhere in this tract as a brief but "sufficient" treatise on the role of education "in moulding the minds of men to virtue (whence arises true and internal liberty), in governing the state effectively, and preserving it for the longest possible space of time" (625). Milton also presses upon Cromwell the argument of *Areopagitica*, that free inquiry and publication without prior censorship is the best means to make Truth flourish.

In *Considerations Touching the Likeliest Means to Remove Hirelings out of the Church* (August, 1659) Milton proposed free state-financed schools for lower class boys. Unlike Hartlib and Dury, however, Milton's basic concern was to provide for ministers' education in such schools; and his proposal runs directly counter to the Dury-Hartlib plan for special colleges or university courses to produce a learned ministry. With Cromwell dead and the republican Rump Parliament restored, Milton urged complete disestablishment of the church, deriding the argument that tithes are an appropriate compensation for the ministers' university education. In an unlikely fusion of radical sectarian principles and elitist impulse, Milton here moves beyond his earlier denunciations of ministers' university education to claim (with the radicals) that the ministers' only *essential* knowledge is "from above" (*YP* 7.316)—that is, from scripture and the Spirit's illumination. He does, however, recognize certain studies as directly relevant to that calling:

> To speak freely, it were much better, there were not one divine in the universitie; no schoole-divinitie known, the idle sophistrie of monks, the canker of religion; and that they who intended to be ministers, were traind up in the church only, by the scripture and in the original languages therof at schoole; without fetching the compas of other arts and sciences, more then what they can well learn at secondary leasure and at home (317–18).

Undergirding Milton's position is a radical spiritual egalitarianism that obliterates any real distinction in status or function between clergy and laity. As "a holy and a royal priesthood" all Christians have "equally access to any ministerial function whenever calld by thir own abilities and the church"; and ministers may be "elected out of all sorts and orders of men ... from the magistrate himself to the meanest artificer" (319–20).

Specifically, Milton proposes that revenues from glebes and augmentations, normally used to supplement ministers' income, be used instead to "erect in greater number all over the land schooles and competent libraries to those schooles, where languages and arts may be taught free together" (305). These free schools are something like Dury's Vernacular and Mechanical schools in that they would teach prospective ministers a trade to live by (as the apostles did) should their congregations be unable to support them; and in gratitude for their free education these ministers would remain to serve in their own locales, "without soaring above the meannes wherin they were born" (305). The elitist note here is intensified as Milton heaps scorn on poor scholarship boys educated at others' expense, who make the ministry a route to social advancement. But in Milton's free schools the curriculum—"languages and arts," scripture and its original languages—seems closer to *Of Education* than to the Mechanical schools of Dury. Presumably, ministerial aspirants of higher rank would continue to be educated in academies like those in *Of Education*, and would support their ministry without a trade. To address the need for well educated theologians and controversialists, Milton takes a leaf directly out of Dury's *Reformed Librarie-Keeper*: if the state will but "erect in publick good store of libraries," some "of thir own inclinations" and by their own independent study will fit themselves for these roles—as Milton himself did (317).

As the revolution teetered on the brink of collapse in March and April, 1660, Milton published in two versions a jerry-built utopia, *The Readie and Easie Way to Establish a Free Commonwealth*, whose true intent was, against all odds, to try to stave off the Restoration. It sets forth a federal scheme with a national supreme council (perpetual so as to avoid elections certain to return royalists) and with the several counties exercising large legislative and judicial powers, rather like subordinate commonwealths. Vital to this proposal is an extensive system of schools, probably meant to be state supported. These would "mend our corrupt and faulty education" so as to "make the people fittest to chuse, and the chosen fittest to govern" (*YP* 7:443). Unlike the schools described in *The Likeliest Means*, these schools, located in each largely self-governing county, are explicitly designed for the propertied classes able to vote and hold office—nobles, gentry, wealthier citizens—and the course of study seems to resemble that in *Of Education*:

> They should have heer also schools and academies at thir own choice, wherin thir children may be bred up in thir own sight to all learning and noble education not in grammar only, but in all liberal arts and exercises. This would soon spread much more knowledge and civilitie, yea religion through all parts of the land, by communicating the natural heat of government and culture more distributively to all extreme parts, which now lie numm and neglected, would soon make the whole nation more industrious, more ingenuous at home, more potent, more honorable abroad (460).

Still more important to Milton's concept of education is his sense of himself as prophet-poet, and of poetry as a powerful educative force "to imbreed and cherish in a great people the seeds of vertu, and publick civility" (*YP* 1.816). In this he is very far indeed from the scientific emphasis of the Comenius and the Hartlib Circle. In *The Reason of Church Government* Milton suggests that the state might sponsor "wise and artfull recitations" in theaters and solemn assemblies, so as to "win the people to receiv at once both recreation, & instruction" (*YP* 1.819–20). His great epics written after the Restoration, *Paradise Lost* and *Paradise Regained*, also make education and learning central, representing them in quintessentially Miltonic terms as individual, self-generated, arduous, dialogic processes. Going beyond the received view of the Homeric and Virgilian epics as *paideia*, fundamental education in all knowledge, Milton sought to engage his readers actively with the *uses* of knowledge, exercising them in making the difficult intellectual and moral discriminations that he saw as fundamental to producing good men and women, and free citizens.

Paradise Lost is unique among the great epics in that a good half of it presents formal scenes of education—pre- and post-lapsarian, and divine. In books 5 to 8, the archangel Raphael, termed "Divine/ Historian" (*PL* 8.6–7), provides unfallen Adam and Eve with warnings, knowledge, vicarious experience, and above all exercise in making intellectual and moral judgments, to prepare them for Satan's temptations.[30] Raphael's several discourses—on the nature of the universe, the War in Heaven, the Creation, the cosmos—are all prompted by questions from Adam, formulated in erroneous or even near-blasphemous terms; Raphael's responses are designed to help Adam clarify first principles, so he can learn to learn by trial and error but yet without sin. The best example is the astronomy sequence, prompted by Adam's startling question about the cosmos that implies the ineptitude of God in designing an apparently irrational and inefficient Ptolemaic universe. Raphael responds with two cogent arguments, first for the Ptolemaic, then for the Copernican systems—echoing the strategy and arguments in Galileo's *Dialogue of the Two World Systems*. But he pointedly refuses to decide between them, though his own Copernican perspective is evident in the advanced scientific speculations to which he introduces Adam. By thus declining to provide a definitive answer on his angelic authority, he removes astronomy from the province of revelation and the usual contemporary appeals to Genesis, placing it squarely in the realm of human speculation. At the same time, by letting Adam discover the limitations of human perspective he underscores the humility and the humanistic emphases that ought to govern scientific inquiry.

The prelapsarian educational curriculum incorporated in Raphael's discourses includes ontology, physics, cosmology, metaphysics, moral philosophy, history, epic poetry, and astronomy. Eve sits (silently) through the whole course, except for the astronomy lesson, and she will learn that from Adam later. Also, her dialogic experience is with Adam, not the angel. This is Milton's representation of what he presumably saw as an ideal female education: its remarkable inclusiveness in content goes well beyond what Comenius or Dury proposed, though it is clearly designed to reinforce gender hierarchy.

Divine teaching in *Paradise Lost* is through a species of Socratic dialogue. In the Council in Heaven in book 3, God deliberately refrains from revealing his providential plan for humankind's salvation, challenging his Son (whom Milton's antitrinitarian theology makes neither equal to the Father nor omniscient)[31] to discover that plan and his own part in it, through dialogue with him. In another such scene (8.354–451) God responds to Adam's request for a mate with apparent opposition, leading Adam, though dialogue with him, to attain self-knowledge and define the human need for completion, help, and solace in human companionship and love.

In books 9 to 12, the archangel Michael, apostrophized as "Seer blest" (*PL* 12.553), provides Adam with the education needed for life in the fallen world. Now the essential subject is revealed biblical history from his own time to the apocalypse, presented as a series of visions and narratives which Adam must interpret. Through trial and error and sometimes harsh correction Adam must learn by stages to read events as moral exempla and in typological terms, as providential history. From the cases of Nimrod and other tyrants Adam also learns the tragic politics of the postlapsarian world, and the inevitable Miltonic link between moral degeneracy and loss of liberty. To Eve, the essence of revelation history is conveyed through dreams, and her interpretative dialogues about it will again be with Adam.

The whole of *Paradise Regained* portrays an educative experience, the temptation of Jesus in the wilderness by Satan. God proclaims that this is the means whereby Jesus will define "the rudiments/ Of his great warfare" (PR 1.157–58). The process is almost entirely dialogue and debate. This hero (who no longer remembers his heavenly identity as Son of God, nor yet fully understands what his mission on earth will involve) is tempted continuously to accept worldly, or inferior, or literal constructions of his prophesied roles, and he must make difficult and complex intellectual discriminations and moral choices.[32] The subject of the debates is human history, and how Jesus ought to relate himself to it in seeking to liberate his people. How far should past models—Old Testament prophets like Moses and Elijah, martial kings like Caesar or Alexander or David, wise philosophers like Plato or the Stoics—determine his self-definition, and wherein should he redefine those norms so as to become himself a model for the future? Satan's temptations constantly invite Jesus to accept the classical notion of history as cyclical repetition—what has been will be again. But Jesus must learn to read history as linear and typological, involving spiritual progress, redefinition, and recreation.

The climactic temptation offered to Jesus, in wonderfully evocative and moving terms, is Athens—classical learning. He rejects it categorically, and in terms whose harshness makes problems for many readers. It helps to recognize that Milton is again forcing discriminations—that Satan offers classical learning for power, for dominion, for fame, as essential for Jesus's teaching mission, as embodying truth, and as equivalent to wisdom—and that Jesus must refuse it on those perverse terms. Though his answers show that he knows these things, he insists that, like the ministers of *The Likeliest Means*, he receives his only necessary knowledge from above. But he goes further, articulating the Miltonic precept that learning is not simply to be received but is to be engaged with, judged, and made one's own— that (like the Sabbath, marriage, and all things else) books were made for man, not man for books:

> who reads
> Incessantly, and to his reading brings not
> A reading and judgment equal or superior
> (And what he brings, what needs he elsewhere seek)
> Uncertain and unsettl'd still remains,
> Deep verst in books and shallow in himself,

Crude or intoxicate, collecting toys,
And trifles for choice matters, worth a sponge;
As Children gathering pebbles on the shore.

(*PR* 4.322–30)[33]

In *Paradise Regained* the Miltonic *paideia* invites the reader to engage with the difficult discriminations, not always fully explained, by which Jesus refuses the Satanic temptations involving distrust, sensual pleasure, wealth, kingship, fame, misguided zeal, military might, the kingdoms of the world, and learning. In *Paradise Lost* the Miltonic *paideia* invites readers to reevaluate genres and topics from the whole panoply of literature—epic, pastoral, tragic drama, petrarchan lyric, ovidian myth, political rhetoric, and more—probing and refining the values and assumptions long associated with those forms, about man and woman, nature, language, heroism, virtue, pleasure, work, love. In the Restoration ethos, Milton cannot hope that his poems will teach the nation as a whole: he addresses them explicitly to a "fit audience . . . though few" (*PL* 7.31). Yet these poems undertake directly what his educational projects and anti-censorship arguments could only propose: that is, to develop the moral and political consciousness of a now self-selected "fit audience," through a literary regimen at once intellectually arduous and delightful.

Notes

Notes to Introduction

1. *Intentionality and the New Traditionalism: Some Liminal Means to Literary Revisionism* (University Park: The Pennsylvania State University Press, 1991), 1.

2. *The Complete Poetry of John Milton* (2nd ed. rev.; Garden City: Doubleday, 1971); *Achievements of the Left Hand* (Amherst: University of Massachusetts Press, 1974).

3. *With Mortal Voice: The Creation of* Paradise Lost (Lexington: University Press of Kentucky, 1982) and Paradise Regain'd: 'Worthy T'Have Not Remain'd So Long Unsung' (Pittsburgh: Duquesne University Press, 1988).

4. *John Milton and Influence: Presence in Literature, History and Culture* (Pittsburgh: Duquesne University Press, 1991).

5. *John Milton: The Self and the World* (Lexington: University Press of Kentucky, 1993).

6. *Milton: A Bibliography For the Years 1624–1700* (Binghamton: Medieval and Renaissance Texts and Studies, 1984) and *Milton: A Bibliography For the Years 1624–1700: Addenda and Corrigenda* (Binghamton: Medieval and Renaissance Texts and Studies, 1990).

7. *Milton: The Critical Heritage* [1624–1731] (London: Routledge & Kegan Paul, 1970; New York: Barnes and Noble, 1970) and *Milton: The Critical Heritage, 1732–1809* (London: Routledge & Kegan Paul, 1972).

Notes to Chapter 1/Schwartz

1. *The Imitation of Christ,* generally attributed to Thomas á Kempis, was written in the fifteenth century and enjoyed enormous popularity even before the invention of the printing press, with more than seven hundred manuscripts surviving. Its public included not only the secular clergy but also pious laymen.

2. Thomas á Kempis, *The Imitation of Christ,* trans. Leo Sherley-Price (London: Penguin, 1952), 27.

3. All quotations of Milton are from *John Milton: Complete Poems and Major Prose,* ed. Merritt Y. Hughes (New York: Odyssey Press, 1957).

4. A veritable literature on "seeming" in *Paradise Lost* has been produced. Concerning the relation of "seeming" to predestination and free will, see Julia Walker, "For each seem'd either": Free Will and Predestination in *Paradise Lost,*" *Milton Quarterly* 20 (1986): 13–16; the reply by Stephen Fallon, "The Uses of "Seems" and the Spectre of Predestination" *Milton Quarterly* 21 (1987): 99–101 and response by Walker *Milton Quarterly,* 101–02. More fruitful is Michael Lieb's discussion of "seeming" in relation to Milton's poetics of contradiction, "'Two of Far Nobler Shape': Reading the Paradisal Text," in this volume.

5. I deem this nostalgia because the notion of a world that is substantially linked, rather than metaphorically so is not only neoplatonic but also medieval, informed as it is by the understanding of transubstantion that the Reformers rejected.

6. See especially C. A. Patrides, *Milton and the Christian Tradition* (Oxford: Clarendon Press, 1966), William Empson, *Milton's God* (London: Chatto and Windus, 1961).

7. *Standard Edition of the Complete Psychological Works of Sigmund Freud* (hereafter *SE*), ed. James Strachey (London: Hogarth Press, 1959), 7:116.

8. *Remembering and Repeating: On Milton's Theology and Poetics* (Cambridge: Cambridge University Press, 1988, reprint Chicago: University of Chicago Press, 1992), 91–110.

9. Mikkel Borsch-Jacobsen, "Hypnosis in Psychoanalysis," *Representations* 27 (Summer 1989): 96.

10. *Studies in Hysteria* 2:6.

11. Borsch-Jacobsen, 97.

12. I maintain that this relation between religion and psychoanalysis obtains even in Freud's work, bursting through in *Moses and Monotheism,* despite Freud's explicit rejection of religion and his disparaging dismissal of it as a mass neurosis. Cf. Schwartz, "Moses and Polytheism," in *Beyond Secular Philosophy* ed. Philip Blond, London: Routledge, forthcoming.

13. The literature on the "Dora" case history is extensive; see the collection of essays, *In Dora's Case: Freud-Hysteria-Feminism*, ed. Charles Bernheimer and Claire Kahane (New York: Columbia University Press, 1985).

14. Freud, "Two Encyclopaedia Articles," *SE* 18:247.

15. Freud, "Beyond the Pleasure Principle," *SE* 18:18.

16. Freud, *SE* 18:19.

17. Jane Gallop, "Lacan and Literature," *Poetics* 13 (1984): 306. See Jacques Lacan, *Four Fundamental Principles of Psychoanalysis*, ed. Jacques-Alain Miller, trans. Alan Sheridan (New York: W.W. Norton and Co., 1978), 123–87.

18. Michel Foucault, *The History of Sexuality: Volume I*. trans. Robert Hurley (New York: Vintage, 1980), 66–67.

19. Arminius, *The Writings of Jacobus Arminius*, trans. James Nichols and W.R. Bagnall (1853, reprint Grand Rapids: Baker Book House, 1956), 2:472. The best discussion of Milton's Arminianism is Dennis Danielson's *Milton's Good God* (Cambridge; Cambridge University Press, 1982).

20. Shoshana Felman, "To Open the Question" in *Psychoanalysis and Literature* (Baltimore: Johns Hopkins University Press, 1982, originally 1977, *Yale French Studies*): 7.

21. Gallop, 307.

22. John T. Shawcross, *Intentionality and the New Traditionalism* (University Park, PA: Pennsylvania State University Press, 1991), 1.

23. A similar dynamic in the "Nativity Ode" in which "the story of Christ . . . is Milton's story as well" has been pursued by Richard Halpern in "The Great Instauration: imaginary narratives in Milton's 'Nativity Ode'" in *Re-membering Milton*, edited by Margaret Ferguson and Mary Nyquist (New York: Methuen, 1987), 3–24. "Christ's mission strongly resembles that of the epic poet: his kenotic descent into a natural body parallels the epicist's within the body of the eclogue, for in both cases, imagination, whether divine or poetic, assumes the limitations of nature as part of an ascetic preparation to regain the supernatural" (8).

24. Felman, 6.

Notes to Chapter 2/Patterson

1. Anna Nardo, *Milton's Sonnets and the Ideal Community* (Lincoln: University of Nebraska Press, 1979), 127; citing Joan Webber, The *Eloquent "I": Style and Self in Seventeenth-Century Prose* (Madison: University of Wisconsin Press, 1968), 202.

2. Jean-Paul Sartre, *What is Literature? and Other Essays* (Cambridge, MA: Harvard University Press, 1988). "Quest-ce que la litté-

rature?" was first published in *Situations II* (Paris: Gallimard, 1948).

3. Nardo, 18.

4. Mary Ann Radzinowicz, *Toward* Samson Agonistes (Princeton: Princeton University Press, 1978), 129.

5. Radzinowicz, 131–42.

6. A similar case can be made for Ben Jonson's *Under-wood*, also a collection of occasional poems, whose roughly chronological (yet sometimes achronological) arrangement can also be seen as telling the story of Jonson's career from 1614 through the early 1630s. See my *Censorship and Interpretation* (Madison: University of Wisconsin Press, 1984), 134–52.

7. This is surely the place to acknowledge my own belatedness, and the necessary dependence of this argument on generations of scrupulous scholarship. If in what follows I make capital out of the disagreements between Miltonists on the sonnets, disagreements now conveniently summarized in the *Milton Variorum*, it is certainly not in a spirit of ridicule. It is thanks to the work of David Masson, William Riley Parker, J. S. Smart and many others that modern readers have the benefit of well-annotated editions of the sonnets. Hindsight, however, must make us wonder why so much annotation is necessary for such small poems; and especially why they permit such a range of disagreement about their chronology. My proposal, that Milton was deliberately elusive or even misleading about the relation of his sequence to historical time, bears a superficial similarity to the reader-response arguments of Stanley Fish, in "What It's Like to Read *L'Allegro* and *Il Penseroso*," *Milton Studies*, 7 (1974): 77ff; or "Interpreting the *Variorum*," *Critical Inquiry*, 2 (1976): 465–85. It bears a less superficial resemblance to the deconstructive arguments of Jonathan Goldberg, "Dating Milton," in *Soliciting Interpretation*, eds. Elizabeth Harvey and Katharine Maus (University of Chicago Press, 1990), 199–220. Both Goldberg and I use the difficulties in dating sonnets 19 and 23 as evidence against a naive account of the autonomous author evolving over time. But Goldberg is correct in stating that his notion of dating "would be anathema to the New Historicism, whose great strength in showing the imbeddedness of artistic production within its cultural situation nonetheless rests upon the same empiricist ground as traditional historical accounts" (205). While I decline the label of New Historicism, I believe that a contemporary theory of authorship can reject neither the empiricist ground (past writers had "real" lives which can be partially or provisionally reconstructed using traditional scholarly tools), nor the commonsense view that past writers, like present ones, struggled to discern what might constitute a continuous self amid circumstances that frequently required self-contradiction or self-correction.

8. E. A. J. Honigmann, ed., *Milton's Sonnets* (New York: St. Martin's Press, 1966), 102–03.

9. All quotations of Milton are from *The Sonnets of Milton* (Glasgow: Maclehose, 1921; repr. Oxford: Clarendon Press, 1966).

10. A. S. P. Woodhouse and Douglas Bush, *A Variorum Commentary on The Poems of John Milton*, 2 vols. (New York: Columbia University Press, 1972): 2.374–75.

11. Woodhouse and Bush, 391–92.

12. This was first pointed out by H. Schultz, "A book was writ of late," *Modern Language Notes*, 69 (1954) 495–97. Schultz remarked that it "may too easily be taken for granted that the poet intended compliments where he intended none," a warning that I would extend to Cheke's political afterlife rather than, as did Schultz, merely to the question of whether his educational program was benign.

13. See Nardo, *Milton's Sonnets and the Ideal Community*, 57.

14. W. R. Parker argued for the latter by analogy with Milton's use of the Latin phrase *anno aetatis*. See "Some Problems in the Chronology of Milton's Early Poems," *Review of English Studies*, 11 (1935): 276–83; but compare Ernest Sirluck, "Milton's Idle Right Hand," *Journal of English and Germanic Philology* 60 (1961): 781–84.

15. Nardo's statement, that "Sonnet I was almost certainly written while Milton was at Cambridge from 1625 to 1632" (183) is based (like all such assumptions) on nothing except the poem's subject matter and its placement.

16. William B. Hunter, "The Date of Milton's Sonnet 7," *English Language Notes* 13 (1975): 10–14.

17. Goldberg, "Dating Milton," 201.

18. Milton, *Pro Se Defensio*, in *Complete Prose Works*, ed. Don M. Wolfe et al., 8 vols., (New Haven: Yale University Press, 1953–80), 4:2:796; italics added. For an analysis of the place of the *Pro se defensio* in the larger narrative of Milton's self-construction in the prose, see my "The Civic Hero in Milton's Prose," *Milton Studies*, 8 (1975):94–98.

19. That Milton saw vocational anxiety as his own special sin might perhaps be inferred from Christ's rejection of that temptation in *Paradise Regained* 1.355: "Why dost thou then suggest to me distrust . . . ?"

20. For the conjectures, see *Milton Variorum*, 481–83. If read in the light of *Pro Se Defensio*, sonnet 22, which may very well have been written in 1655, seems less resonant with "heroic confidence" than Woodhouse and Bush assumed.

21. As they may, by reading an annotated edition of the sonnets, be too easily won.

22. Sir Symonds D'Ewes, *Autobiography*, 1:160.

23. Buckingham himself was 29 in 1621 when the marriage took place; his niece would therefore have been still in her teens.

24. On the scramble for Buckingham's patronage during the summer of 1624, as it became apparent that the favorite's star was still rising and would carry him over into the next reign, see Thomas Cogswell, *The Blessed Revolution: English Politics and the Coming of War, 1621–1624* (Cambridge University Press, 1989), 271–74. On Ley's eagerness "to try his hand at finance," Cogswell cites John Chamberlain's letters to Dudley Carleton, *The Letters of John Chamberlain*, ed. N. E. McLure, 2 vols. (Philadelphia: American Philosophical Society, 1939), 2:568, 572, 576.

25. Henry Hyde, earl of Clarendon, *History of the Rebellion and Civil Wars in England*, ed. W. Dunn Macray, 6 vols. (1888; reprint, Oxford: Clarendon Press, 1969), 1:59.

26. In fact Whitelocke made this remark in 1627, close to the time of Ley's death, adding that though "wont" to be called Volpone "I think he as well deservethe it now as ever."

27. Woodhouse and Bush, 386.

28. Woodhouse and Bush, 386.

29. In fact, Milton's own punctuation, with only a comma at the octave, permits the momentary false assumption that we are still dealing with that "old man eloquent."

30. *The Early Lives of Milton*, ed. Helen Darbishire (London: Constable, 1932), 64.

31. W. R. Parker, "The Dates of Milton's Sonnets on Blindness," *PMLA* 73 (1958): 200.

32. Honigmann, ed., *Milton's Sonnets*, 110–11.

33. Louis Martz, *Poet of Exile: A Study of Milton's Poetry* (New Haven; Yale University Press, 1980), 31–59.

Notes to Chapter 3/Radzinowicz

1. That list includes:
    Doeg slandering Sam 1.22
    the Sheepshearers in Carmel a Pastoral.1 Sam 25
    Saul in Gilboa 1 Sam 28.31
    David revolted 1 Sam from the 27c to the 31
Milton's prose is quoted from The *Complete Prose Works of John Milton*, ed. Don M. Wolfe (New Haven: Yale University Press, 1982), identified in the essay as *YP*. His poetry is quoted from *The Works of John Milton*, ed. Frank Allen Patterson, (New York: Columbia University Press, 1934), identified as *CM*. Bible quotations are taken from the Authorized (King James) Version. See Trinity MS entries on 1 Samuel in *YP* 8.556; *CM* 18.236–37.

2. 1 Samuel 16.10 reads "Jesse made seven of his sons to pass

before Samuel. And Samuel said unto Jesse, The Lord hath not chosen these." 1 Chronicles 2: 13–15 reads: " And Jesse begat his first-born Eliab, and Abinadab the second, and Shimma the third, Nethaneel the fourth, Raddai the fifth, Ozem the sixth, David the seventh." David is either the eighth or seventh son. Cowley follows the second source.

3. See Richard Coggins, *Introducing the Old Testament* (Oxford: Oxford University Press, 1990), 24–26; Joel Rosenberg, *King and Kin: Political Allegory in the Hebrew Bible* (Bloomington: Indiana University Press, 1986), 125; and J. Alberto Soggin, "The Davidic-Solomonic Kingdom," in *Israelite and Judean History*, ed. John H. Hayes and J. Maxwell Miller (Philadelphia: Trinity Press, 1977), 332–61.

4. See Robert Alter, *The Art of Biblical Narrative* (New York: Basic Books, 1981), 33–35.

5. Its muddled chronology favors David. David and Solomon are said to have reigned a generation or forty years (2 Samuel 5.4, 1 Kings 2.11, 11.42), Saul is assigned a reign of two years. (1 Samuel 13.1 translated literally reads: "Saul was one year old when he began to reign and he reigned two years over Israel.")

Cowley in *Davideis*, notes: "There is nothing in the whole Scripture that admits of more several Opinions than the time of *Saul's* and *Samuel's* Reign", and concludes: "To determine punctually how long he reigned, is impossible; but I should guess about *ten Years*." Footnote 13, Book 4, *Davideis*.

Cowley will be quoted from *Davideis, a Sacred Poem of the Troubles of David* (London: Henry Herringman, 1677); *The Works of Mr. Abraham Cowley; In Two Volumes*, eleventh ed. (London: J. Tonson, 1710); from *Abraham Cowley: Poetry and Prose*, ed. L. C. Martin (Oxford: Clarendon Press, 1949), identified in the text by dates. I am grateful to Cedric Brown of the University of Reading and Patricia O'Connell of University College Galway for making the first two texts available to me.

6. Royalist identification of Charles with David was so common that William Marshall, who engraved the frontispiece of *Eikon Basilike*, gave current point to a book entitled *David Persecuted* by using the face of Charles for his frontispiece David. Lois Potter notes, "a number of paintings based on the *Eikon* frontispiece were sent to local authorities for display in prominent places. The inscription under the one at Cambridge was `Lord, remember David and all his troubles.' " S*ecret Rites and Secret Writing: Royalist Literature 1641–1660* (Cambridge: Cambridge University Press, 1989), 160–61.

7. Cowley published the uncompleted *Davideis* in 1656. Frank Kermode's suggestion that the poem was written between 1651–54 is generally accepted. See "The Date of Cowley's *Davideis*,"

Review of English Studies 25 (1949): 154–58.

8. *Hobbes Leviathan*, edited by C. B. Macpherson, (Harmondsworth: Penguin Books, 1968), 409. All quotations are from this edition.

9. See Samuel I. Mintz, *The Hunting of Leviathan* (Cambridge: Cambridge University Press, 1970) and Willis B. Glover, "God and Thomas Hobbes," *Hobbes Studies*, ed. Keith Thomas, (Oxford: Basil Blackwell, 1968).

10. Hobbes evidences from post-dated comments in 1 Samuel 5.5; 7.13, 15; 27.6; 30.25 and 2 Samuel 6.4.

11. "The Books of *Joshua, Judges, Ruth,* and *Samuel,* to the time of *Saul,* describe the acts of Gods people, till the time they cast off Gods yoke, and called for a King, after the manner of their neighbour nations: The rest of the History of the Old Testament, derives the succession of the line of *David,* to the Captivity, out of which line was to spring the restorer of the Kingdome of God, even our blessed Saviour *God the Son* ... " (424).

12. He writes of David's ritual fasting, for example, so as to give a rational explanation of David's faith in the supernatural (651–52). Hobbes does not look at faith as a source of power, but at power as a guarantor of a particular faith.

13. Hobbes's rationalism finds a certain parallel in both Milton and Cowley. Milton holds that "miracles ... cannot produce [faith]"; they were "worked" by "imposters ... and ... the false church" (*YP* 6.564–65).

Cowley describes the dubious in Samuel as "a Subtlety that I cannot for my life comprehend" (1711, 382), "humanly most hard to believe" (1711, 385) or "more than wonderful" (1711, 386). When he shows an angel "make up a Vision [of the future] in David's Head," he explains that the Fates are "according to the Christian Poetical manner of speaking, the Angels" (1711, 386); both, metaphors.

14. Conventionally, David walks through a princely hall where tapestries tell the history of Lot and the cities of the plains; a lieutenant tells their royal host the story of David's winning Michal with the help of Jonathan as chivalric go-between; David chooses between Saul's two daughters, Merob and Michal, drawn as much from Sidney's Pamela and Philoclea as from Scripture. Cowley is a serious reader of the Old Testament, however, and does harmonize the two accounts of Saul's offering a daughter's hand in 1 Samuel 17.17–20 and 1 Samuel 18.17–19.

15. When Cowley writes against the grain of his own sense of biblical truth, he says so. For example, he writes: "I confess I ... believe, that it was not so much *Saul's* Invasion of the *Priestly* Office, by offering up the Sacrifice himself (for in some Cases ...

it is probable he might have done that) as his Disobedience to God's Command by *Samuel*, that he should stay *seven Days*, which was the Sin so severely punish'd in him. Yet I follow here the more common Opinion, as more proper for my purpose" (1711, 496).

16. See David Trotter, *The Poetry of Abraham Cowley* (London: Macmillan, 1979), 85–108.

17. For Milton's gloss, see my essay "'In those days there was no king in Israel': Milton's Politics and Biblical Narrative," *The Yearbook of English Studies* 21 (1991): 242–52.

18. Anne Krook suggests that Cowley may think of Charles, Prince of Wales abroad as like David at Moab's court. I owe her thanks for reading this essay.

19. Cowley calls his choice of a biblical theme a baptism of poetry in the Jordan, opening up a plenitude of true stories, adding: "There is not so great a *Lye* to be found in any *Poet*, as the vulgar conceit of men, that *Lying* is *Essential* to good *Poetry*." (1949, 71) His privileging of biblical over classical tales is conventional: Noah over Deucalion, Samson over Hercules, Jephthah's Daughter over Iphigenia, the friendship of David and Jonathan over that of Theseus and Perithous, the travels of Moses over those of Ulysses or Aeneas. He questions if "*Thebes* and *Troy* [be] half so stored with great, heroical and supernatural actions (since *Verse* will needs *find* or *make* such) as the wars of *Joshua* . . . *Judges*, [or] *David* . . . " (1949, 72).

20. Cowley makes a conventionally poor fist of it, as in the following:

> Still did the Prince midst all this Storm appear,
> Still scatter'd *Deaths* and *Terrors* every where.
> Still did he break, still blunt his wearied Swords;
> Still Slaughter new Supplies to'his Hands affords.
> Where Troops yet stood, there still he hotly flew,
> And'till at last all fled, scorn'd to *pursue*.
> All fled at last, but many in vain; for still
> Th'insatiate *Conqu'ror* was more swift to kill
> Than they to save their lives (1711, 471).

21. In *Eikonoklastes*, Milton explains that David took the hallowed bread not in sacrilege but from necessity and defines Parlament's taking action against the king similarly, not from sacrilege but the necessities of "his own civil Warr" (YP 3.557–58). He also converts the charity of giving David the shewbread into an argument for divorce, Jesus having turned away Pharisee objections to his picking corn on the Sabbath with the same citation. (He also suggests that David sent Michal away because of religious differences.) (YP 2.301, 263).

22. YP 6.751, 765, 766, 800. Cowley broke off *Davideis* having

dramatized the first half of this episode: David's flight to Nob, and his continued flight to the Cave of Adullah and the court of Moab. Hobbes does not take it up in Le*viathan*. Milton contrasts Saul's slaves, who refuse to attack the priests, with Doeg.

23. What is certain is that Milton liked the way it was written. He defended his own strong words in *Apology against a Pamphlet* by citing David's vow not to leave "of all that pertain to him by the morning light any that pisseth against the wall." (1 Samuel 22; *YP* 1.902) He appropriated Abigail's prophecy, "thine enemies . . . he shall sling out, as out of the middle of a sling," for God's prophecy of the Sons finishing "*Sin* and *Death* and yawning *Grave*" "at one sling / Of thy victorious Arm, well-pleasing Son." *Paradise Lost* 10.633–35.

24. See Lana Cable, "Milton's Iconoclastic Truth," *Politics, Poetics and Hermeneutics in Milton's Prose.* ed. David Loewenstein and James Grantham Turner (Cambridge: Cambridge University Press, 1990), 151.

25. Milton explains the discrepancy between the Amalekite's story and the direct report as the witness lying for his own advantage. That has become the received but not unanimous reading. See P. Kyle McCarter, Jr., II *Samuel* (New York: The Anchor Bible, Doubleday, 1985), 62–65.

26. Milton rebukes Salmasius: "Think not then to wrong God so cruelly, and make him appear to teach that the perverse and wicked deeds of kings are their royal rights, when he specifically shows his abhorrence of the society of wicked kings for their bringing upon their people every trial and tribulation under the claim of royal rights." Referring to the Witch of Endor, he continues ironically: "Do not bring a false change against the prophet of God; for in thinking that . . . he is an advocate of the rights of kings[,] you present us with no true Samuel, but like the witch, summon an insubstantial ghost, though . . . not even her hell-sprung Samuel was such a liar as to name what you call royal rights anything but unbridled tyranny" (*YP* 4.352).

27. Conscious of the dangers of kingship "*Aristotle* and the best of Political writers have defin'd a King, him who governs to the good and profit of his People, and not for his own ends, it follows from necessary causes, that the Titles of Sov'ran Lord, natural Lord, and the like, are either arrogancies, or flatteries, not admitted by Emperours and Kings of best note, and dislikt by the Church both of Jews . . . and ancient Christians . . ." Milton concludes: "Although generally the people of Asia, and with them the Jews also, especially since the time they chose a King against the advice and counsel of God, are noted by wise Authors much inclinable to slavery" (*YP* 3.203).

28. Milton refers only to the second, politically realistic, version of David's sparing Saul.

29. John Shawcross, *Intentionality and the New Traditionalism: Some Liminal Means to Literary Revisionism* (University Park, Pennsylvania: Pennsylvania State University Press, 1991), 5, 12.

30. See Adele Berlin's distinction among the agent, the type, and the character in *Poetics and Interpretation of Biblical Narrative* (Sheffield: Almond Press, 1983), 23–34.

31. "The Histories of David," *"Not in Heaven": Coherence and Complexity in Biblical Narrative,* ed. Jason P. Rosenblatt and Joseph C. Sitterson, Jr. (Bloomington: Indiana University Press, 1991), 200.

32. "The Legitimacy of Solomon," *Genesis as Myth and Other Essays* (London: Jonathan Cape, 1969), 81. See Robert L. Cohn, The *Shape of Sacred Space: Four Biblical Studies* (Chico, California: Scholars Press, 1981) for adaptations of the anthropological theories of Victor Turner and Mircea Eliade to Old Testament scriptural exegesis.

Notes to Chapter 4/McColley

1. John Shawcross discusses deconstructive illogicality in *Intentionality and the New Traditionalism: Some Liminal means to Literary Revisionis*—(University Park: Pennsylvania State University Press, 1991), 7–8.

2. Shawcross, *Intentionality*: "Such artistic planning—the writer writing—has been the burden of this book," 201.

3. I allude to Gerard Manley Hopkins, "As Kingfishers Catch Fire."

4. *John Milton: Paradise Lost: A Poem in Twelve Books,* ed. Merritt Y. Hughes (New York: Odyssey Press, 1962). All quotations from the epic are from this edition.

5. Greene, *The Descent from Heaven: A Study in Epic Continuity* (New Haven: Yale University Press, 1963), 383–84.

6. Michael Lieb reproduces some pictorial theophanies in *Poetics of the Holy: A Reading of* Paradise Lost (Chapel Hill: University of North Carolina Press, 1981), figs. 6–7 and 14–16. Sanford Budick shows ways Milton "sets visual analogies into motion with an eye to their imminent depletion" (7) in *The Dividing Muse: Images of Sacred Disjunction in Milton's Poetry* (New Haven: Yale University Press, 1985).

7. "Hid" of course does not conceal Milton's opinion of the danger that elaborate liturgy can obscure truth when practiced by and for fallible human beings; and even "fuming" and, by its sound, "Censers" might be thought cautionary.

8. Margaret Byard reconstructs Milton's musical experience in Rome in "'Adventrous Song': Milton and the Music of Rome," in *Milton in Italy,* ed. Mario A. Di Cesare (Binghamton: Medieval

and Renaissance Texts and Studies, 1991), 305–28, and, in the same collection, M. N. K. Mander reads *L'Allegro* and *Il Penseroso* in the context of Italian Renaissance music theory: "The Music of *L'Allegro* and *Il Penseroso*," 281–91. Claudio Monteverdi's psalm settings in "Selva morale et spirituale" (Venice, 1640) are a good introduction to the music Milton describes in *Paradise Lost*; performed by Emma Kirkby, Rogers Covey-Crump, Nigel Rogers, David Thomas, and The Taverner Consort, Choir, and Players, directed by Andrew Parrott on EMI/Angel LP S-38030.

9. Verse anthems alternate solo or reduced voice parts with larger vocal ensembles.

10. *Book of Common Prayer, 1559: The Elizabethan Prayer Book*, edited by John E. Booty (Washington: The Folger Shakespeare Library, 1976), 53. Quotations from the *Te Deum Laudamus* are from this edition. The *Benedicite*, on which Milton models the hymn of Adam and Eve in 5.153–208, was used alternatively. The *Te Deum* used to be attributed to Saints Ambrose and Augustine.

11. My descriptions derive from *Thomas Tallis: English Sacred Music: II, Service Music*, edited by Leonard Ellwood, in *Early English Church Music* 13 (London: Stainer and Bell, 1971): 10–21; William Byrd, "The Great Service," ed. Craig Monson in *The Byrd Edition*, gen. ed. Philip Brett, vol. 10 (London: Stainer and Bell, 1982), performed by the Choir of King's College, Cambridge, dir. Stephen Cleobury, on EME CDC 7 47771 2; Robert Ramsey, "Service of Four Parts," in *Robert Ramsey: I*, transcribed and edited by Edward Thompson, in *Early English Church Music* 7 (London: Stainer and Bell, n. d.): 1–16; Thomas Tomkins, "Third" or "Great Service," in *Thomas Tomkins, Tudor Church Music* 8 (London: Oxford University Press, 1928): 82–129, performed on *Thomas Tomkins: The Great Service* by the Tallis Scholars, directed by Peter Phillips on Gimell CDGIM 02; and Orlando Gibbons, "Second Service," in *Tudor Church Music*, vol. 4, eds. P. C. Buck, E. H. Fellows, A. Ramsbotham, and S. Townsend Warner (London: Oxford University Press, 1925), performed by the Choir of New College, Oxford, directed by Edward Higginbottom, on CRD Records CD CRD3451, 1988. Of course, not all of the features I mention are used by all of these composers.

12. Leonard, *Naming in Paradise: Milton and the Language of Adam and Eve* (Oxford: Clarendon Press, 1990), 240–42; Alistair Fowler and John Carey, eds., *The Poems of John Milton* (London: Longmans, 1968), 585; Lewalski, *Paradise Lost and the Rhetoric of Literary Forms* (Princeton: Princeton University Press, 1985), 166. Lewalski also points out resemblances between the structure of the anthem and the classical ode, 165, and Francis Blessington compares it with Virgil's hymn to Hercules in "'That Undisturbed Song of Pure Concent': *Paradise Lost* and the Epic-Hymn," in

Renaissance Genres: Essays on Theory, History, and Interpretation, ed. Barbara Kiefer Lewalski (Cambridge, Mass., and London: Harvard University Press, 1986), 468–95.

13. Lieb illuminates the names of God in Hebrew tradition and *Paradise Lost* in *Poetics of the Holy*, 171–84.

14. Taverner, "Mater Christi sanctissima," bars 9–10, 17–18, 23 and 30, in *Taverner: II, Tudor Church Music*, vol. 3 (London: Humphrey Milford, 1924): 92–98. Performed on *Missa Mater Christi* by the Christ Church Cathedral Choir, dir. Stephen Darlington. Nimbus NI 5218, 1987.

15. *Christian Doctrine* 1.7: "Since all things come not only from God, but out of God, no created thing can be utterly annihilated. . . . All entity is good: nonentity, not good. It is not consistent, then, with the goodness or wisdom of God, to make out of entity, which is good, something which is not good, or nothing. . . . Our glorification will be accompanied by the renovation of, and our possessing of, heaven and earth and all those creatures in both which may be useful or delightful to us." In *The Complete Prose Works of John Milton*, general editor Don M. Wolfe, vol. 6 edited by Maurice Kelley and translated by John Carey (New Haven and London: Yale University Press, 1973), 310–11 and 632. My thanks to Annabel Patterson for producing this reference just when I needed it.

16. Entzminger, *Divine Word: Milton and the Redemption of Language* (Pittsburgh: Duquesne University Press, 1985), 133; Radzinowicz, *Milton's Epics and the Book of Psalms* (Princeton: Princeton University Press, 1989), 192; Lieb, *Poetics of the Holy*, 180.

17. George Wesley Whiting provides background for the golden compasses and a fourteenth century illustration in *Milton and This Pendant World* (Austin: University of Texas Press, 1958), 104–10.

18. T. Lucretius Carus, *De Rerum Natura*, with an English translation by W. H. D. Rouse (Cambridge, Mass.: Harvard University Press, and London: William Heinemann, 1947), 5.783–800.

19. Sandys, George, and Henry Lawes, *A Paraphrase vpon the Psalms of David. And vpon the Hymnes Dispersed throughout the Old and New Testaments* (London, 1638), 126; tune on 87. In *Pseudodoxia Epidemica* Browne remarks on the error of thinking dolphins "bent" in shape because we see them that way when they leap from the water, in *Works*, ed. Geoffrey Keynes (Chicago: University of Chicago Press, 1964) 4:340–41. Sandys "crooked" seems to share this error, while Milton's "bended" may suggest action rather than nature. On "monstrous whales" compare Du Bartas, below.

20. I have discussed the polysemousness of animal emblems

in *A Gust for Paradise: Milton's Eden and the Visual Arts* (Urbana and Chicago: University of Illinois Press, 1993), 77–84.

21. *Virgil: The Georgics*, translated by L. P. Wilkinson (Harmondsworth and New York: Penguin Books, Ltd., 1982), 1.130.

22. Du Bartas, Guillaume de Sallust, Seigneur, *Du Bartas his Deuine Weekes and Workes*, translated by Josuah Sylvester (London, 1613), 115. This text, though it describes species in great detail, lacks Milton's mimetic empathy. For further discussion of Leviathan see Leonard, *Naming in Paradise*, 267–70, and Regina Schwartz, *Remembering and Repeating: Biblical Creation in Paradise Lost*, (Cambridge: Cambridge University Press, 1988), 28–31.

23. Robert Alter discusses these passages in *The Art of Biblical Poetry* (New York: Basic Books, 1985), chapter 5, and shows how the Voice from the Whirlwind "confronts Job with the limits of his moral imagination" (106).

24. Blessington traces this image to Virgil's simile for Mercury's flight in *Aeneid* 4, "auis similis," in Paradise Lost *and the Classical Epic* (Boston, London, and Henley: Routledge and Kegan Paul, 1979), 29. Du Bartas has an extended passage on the phoenix in *Deuine Weekes*, 130–31.

25. Blith, *The English Improver Improved* (London, 1653), 3–4.

26. Topsell, *The Historie of Fovre-Footed Beastes* (London, 1607), sig. A4.

27. "Lycidas," line 164. Du Bartas narrates Arion's rescue in *Deuine Weekes*, 126–29.

28. Caxton, *Mirrour of the World*, edited by Oliver H. Prior. *Early English Text Society* no.101–02 (London, 1913), 77–78.

29. Du Bartas, *Deuine Weekes and Workes*, 145-47; cf. Topsell, 190–200.

30. Browne, *Hydrotaphia*, in *Works* 1:140.

31. Freely translated from Cotton Vesp. Aiii, lines 679–80, in *Cursor Mundi: Four Versions*, ed. Richard Morris. *Early English Text Society* 57 (London: Oxford University Press, reprint 1961).

32. *The Towneley Plays*, I: *The Creation*, ed. George England in *Early English Text Society* Extra Series no. 70–71 (London: Kegan Paul, Trench, Trubner, 1897), 166–73.

33. Du Bartas, *Deuine Weekes*, 170.

34. Pordage, *Mundorum Explicatio* (London, 1661), 58–59.

35. Milton's consideration is rare but not unique. In a fifteenth century *Histoires de la Bible par figures*, the Creator (as Christ-logos) stands by a lake and holds a fish in his hand under water, alongside two other fish, blessing them. Rheims, Bibliblioteque Municipale, MS. 61, folio 1.

36. These examples assume that only Adam is monarch over the animals, in spite of the fact that Genesis 1.26–28 is plural.

The gloss in the Latin Bible translated from the Hebrew by Immanuel Tremellius and Francis Junius (London, 1580) notes that *"qui dominentur"* includes the man and his wife and their posterity.

37. Davenant, *Gondibert: An Heroick Poem* (London, 1651), 2.6.57–64.

38. Cowley, "The Garden" ("Essay" to John Evelyn), in *The Complete Works in Verse and Prose of Abraham Cowley*, ed. Alexander B. Grosart (New York: AMS Press, 1967), 117.

39. Cavendish, "The Hunting of the Hare, " in *Kissing the Rod: An Anthology of Seventeenth-Century Women's Verse*, ed. Germaine Greer (New York: Farrar Strauss Giroux, 1989), 170.

40. Traherne, *Centuries of Meditations* 3.74, in *Thomas Traherne: Centuries, Poems, and Thanksgivings*, ed. H. M. Margoliouth (Oxford: At the Clarendon Press, 1958).

Notes to Chapter 5/Benet

1. John T. Shawcross, *Intentionality and the New Traditionalism: Some Liminal Means to Literary Revisionism* (University Park: Pennsylvania State University Press, 1991), 197.

2. Irene Samuel, "The Dialogue in Heaven: A Reconsideration of *Paradise Lost* 3.1–417." *PMLA* 72 (1957): 601-11. Reprint in *Milton: Modern Essays in Criticism*, ed. Arthur E. Barker (London: Oxford, 1965), 234, 237.

3. On the drama of the exchange between the Father and the Son in book 3, see Albert C. Labriola, "'God Speaks': Milton's Dialogue in Heaven, and the Tradition of Divine Deliberation," *Cithara* 25 (May 1986), 5-30; and Michael Lieb, "The Dialogic Imagination" in *The Sinews of Ulysses: Form and Convention in Milton's Works* (Pittsburgh: Duquesne University Press, 1989).

4. Quotations from *Paradise Lost* are taken from *John Milton. Complete Poems and Major Prose*, ed. Merritt Y. Hughes (New York: Macmillan Publishing Co., 1957).

5. Watson Kirkconnell, *The Celestial Cycle. The Theme of Paradise Lost in World Literature with Translations of the Major Analogues* (New York: Gordian Press, 1967), 625.

6. See Gary D. Hamilton, "Milton and the Anti-Rump Tracts: On Revising *The Readie and Easie Way*," *Renaissance Papers* 1989: 101–17.

7. *A Phanatique Prayer, by Sir H. V. Divinity-Professor of Raby Castle,* (N.p. 1660); *A Phanatique League and Covenant, Solemnly enter'd into by the Assertors of the Good Old Cause* (N.p., "Printed for G. H.," 1660).

8. *The Devil in his Dumps or a sad Complaint of Malignant Spirits, at the Settling of Peace and Truth in a late Conventicle* (N.p. 1647).

9. [James Howell] *A Trance or, Newes from Hell, Brought fresh to Towne by Mercurius Acheronticus* (London, 1648), 5.

10. See *The Devil in his Dumps, The Parliaments Petition to the Divell* (N.p. 1648), and *A Declaration of Great Lucifer, Prince of the Ayre, and of Divells, and of all the damned crew in Hell* ("Hell neere Westminster," 1648).

11. Roy Flannagan, "Introduction," in *John Milton. Paradise Lost*, ed. Roy Flannagan (New York: Macmillan, 1993), 43. Christopher Hill suggested some time ago that "The Satanic Parliament gave Milton the chance to stress what was most lacking in 1658–60—unity among the defenders of the Good Old Cause." See *Milton and the English Revolution* (New York: Viking, 1978), 369.

12. Kirkconnell, *The Celestial Cycle*, 625.

13. "For the Renaissance poets who write wars in Heaven, Lucifer is primarily a kind of 'pagan' general or prince. To give him proper ceremony, many poets create 'council' scenes before the war in which he can demonstrate his princely qualities. . . . these prelapsarian councils often have as direct analogues or sources 'hellish' councils, which some poets of the Renaissance had granted to the fallen Lucifer." See Stella P. Revard, *The War in Heaven*: Paradise Lost *and the Tradition of Satan's Rebellion* (Ithaca: Cornell University Press, 1980), 213.

14. *The Devil in his Dumps*, 2, 6.

15. *Hells Triennial Parliament, Summoned Five Yeeres Since by King Lucifer* ([London] 1647), 5.

16. *The Devill and the Parliament: or, The Paliament and the Devill. A Contestation between them for the precedencie* (London, 1648), 5.

17. Arnold Stein, *Answerable Style: Essays on* Paradise Lost (Minneapolis: University of Minnesota Press, 1953), 41. Robert Thomas Fallon, *Captain or Colonel: The Soldier in Milton's Life and Art* (Columbia: University of Missouri Press, 1984), 157. See Fallon's discussion (157–61) of the Council as an example of fallen government.

18. M. Christopher Pecheux, "The Council Scenes in *Paradise Lost*," in *Milton and Scriptural Tradition: The Bible into Poetry*, ed. James H. Sims and Leland Ryken (Columbia: University of Missouri Press, 1984), 89.

19. Michael Wilding, *Dragons Teeth: Literature in the English Revolution*. (Oxford: Clarendon Press, 1987), 215–16. Mary Ann Radzinowicz, "The Politics of *Paradise Lost*," in *Politics of Discourse. The Literature and History of Seventeenth-Century*

England, eds. Kevin Sharpe and Steven N. Zwicker (Berkeley: University of California Press, 1987), 212.

20. Flannagan, *John Milton. Paradise Lost,* 157n, 172–73n.

Notes to Chapter 6/Lieb

1. *The Muse's Method: An Introduction to* Paradise Lost (Cambridge, Mass.: Harvard University Press, 1962), 95–96.

2. For corresponding analysis, see, among other studies, Isabel Gamble MacCaffrey, Paradise Lost *as 'Myth'* (Cambridge: Harvard University Press, 1967), 97–98. According to MacCaffrey, the depiction of first man and woman in this passage reflects the Miltonic attempt to portray forms in their "essence," an act tantamount to the poetic manifestation of Platonic "form." For MacCaffrey there is almost an iconic or "painterly" quality about the depiction, one in which the poet strives "to combine physical and abstract qualities into single, luminous shapes." In his study of Milton's visual imagination, Roland Mushat Frye, *Milton's Imagery and the Visual Arts: Iconographic Tradition in the Epic Poems* (Princeton: Princeton University Press, 1978) explores the passage as a reflection of the idealization of beauty. Frye associates the depiction with the Renaissance pictorial tradition, as well as with portraits of Milton himself (262–75). Approaching the passage from the perspective of genre, Barbara K. Lewalski, Paradise Lost *and the Rhetoric of Literary Forms* (Princeton: Princeton University Press, 1985), explores the description as a "blason, the French epigram-like poem describing and celebrating a single object—usually, some part or parts of the female anatomy" (181–83).

3. References to Milton's poetry in my text are taken from *The Complete Poetry of John Milton,* ed. John T. Shawcross (Garden City, New York: Doubleday, 1971).

4. *The Muse's Method,* 95. Summers is actually concerned with lines 288–318. My own concern is centered on the somewhat briefer passage. This encounter with the unfallen pair is not, of course, entirely unprecedented in the events leading up to the fourth book of Milton's epic: providing a divine perspective in the third book, God Himself beholds "our two first Parents" in "the happie Garden plac't,/ Reaping immortal fruits of joy and love" (3.64–69). Defined by the immediate circumstances surrounding God's all-embracing perception, this thumbnail description of the unfallen couple, we might suggest, is essentially proleptic. Along with the correspondingly brief survey of Satan's journey from Hell to the upper reaches (3.69–76), the account of "our two first Parents" in the third book establishes a local context

for the drama that is to follow in the celestial sphere and an anticipatory and prospective formulation of the drama that is to occur within the terrestrial sphere in the later books.

5. So highly charged is that climate that it is a full-time enterprise keeping up with the amount of lively scholarship being produced. Among the most provocative studies are those of Mary Nyquist, including "Gynesis, Genesis, Exegesis, and the Formation of Milton's Eve," *Cannibals, Witches, and Divorce: Estranging the Renaissance*, Selected Papers from the English Institute, 1985, New Series, no. 11 (Baltimore: The Johns Hopkins University Press, 1987), 147–207, among others.

6. *Feminist Milton* (Ithaca: Cornell University Press, 1987), 85–86. For further discussion, see Wittreich's essay "'Inspir'd with Contradiction: Mapping Gender Discourses in *Paradise Lost*" in this volume.

7. This paper has since been published in *Hellas* 2 (1991), 195–220.

8. See John T. Shawcross's discussion of "limina" in *Intentionality and the New Traditionalism: Some Liminal Means to Literary Revisionism* (University Park: The Pennsylvania State University Press, 1991), *passim*.

9. *Feminist Milton*, 86. In this context, Wittreich is responding to J. Hillis Miller's analysis of the deconstructive dimensions of certain aspects of the passage. See Miller's note "How Deconstruction Works," *New York Times Magazine*, 9 February 1986: 25.

10. As Diane Kelsey McColley, *Milton's Eve* (Urbana: University of Illinois Press, 1983), wisely observes, "the narrative voice is at this point telling us what Satan saw. Satan, with his 'fixt mind,' is observing and defining Adam and Eve for his own purposes. The passage is by no means Satanic, but the narrator tells us only what even Satan, with his vestiges of heavenly percipience limited by his lost sense of process and response, is able to discern" (40–42). It is Satan's act of "defining" what he sees that is germane here. To some extent, Satan himself has complicity in what is beheld. Compare James Turner, *One Flesh: Paradisal Marriage and Sexual Relations in the Age of Milton* (Oxford: Clarendon Press, 1987): "Both 'fallen' and 'unfallen' responses are included when Milton comes to constitute the fit reader of *Paradise Lost*. The narrative design ensures that at first the former predominates: the epic of Satan is launched with such overwhelming power that by the fourth Book the reader is invaded or possessed by the Satanic viewpoint, and travels with him to encounter Paradise" (256).

11. This idea is certainly not new. Stanley Fish's seminal *Surprised by Sin: The Reader in* Paradise Lost (1967; paperback

version: Berkeley: University of California Press, 1971) has revolutionized our understanding of the nature of the postlapsarian response to Milton's epic. (This version also contains related material, including his important essay "Discovery as Form in *Paradise Lost*," 340–56).

12. For a full discussion of the distinction between prelapsarian and postlapsarian perspectives in *Paradise Lost*, see Kathleen M. Swaim *Before and After the Fall: Contrasting Modes in "Paradise Lost"* (Amherst: University of Massachusetts Press, 1986), *passim*.

13. For an interesting discussion of the Miltonic use of the word "seems," see Julia M. Walker, "'For each seem'd either': Free Will and Predestination in *Paradise Lost*," *MQ*, 20 (1986): 13–16. According to Walker, forms of the word "seems" appear 114 times in Milton's epic. Walker distinguishes three different ways in which the word is used: first, to mean a false appearance, "a seeming not an actual reality"; second, to suggest that which appears to be so, but without a clear sense of what is really so; third, to indicate that which really is. In the description of first man and first woman, the lines "Not equal, as thir sex not equal seem'd" are an example of the third use, to indicate that which really is. Obviously, I very much disagree with this reading. Stephen M. Fallon is also in disagreement. See his "The Uses of `Seems' and the Spectre of Predestination," *MQ*, 21 (1987): 99–101, as well as Walker's rebuttal of Fallon in the same issue, 101–02.

14. For the importance of the act of naming in the prelapsarian world of Milton's epic, see John Leonard, *Naming in Paradise: Milton and the Language of Adam and Eve* (Oxford: Clarendon Press, 1990), *passim*. For a discussion of the significance of naming as a divine act, see my *Poetics of the Holy: A Reading of* Paradise Lost (Chapel Hill: University of North Carolina Press, 1981), 171–84.

15. *Intentionality and the New Traditionalism, passim*.

16. See my discussion of the generative dimensions of this passage in *The Dialectics of Creation: Patterns of Birth and Regeneration in* Paradise Lost (Amherst: University of Massachusetts Press, 1970), 71–72.

17. Compare the comments in Edward Le Comte's *Milton and Sex* (New York: Columbia University Press, 1978), 89. In the reference to Hyacinth (beloved of Apollo but slain accidentally by his discus [Ovid, *Metamorphoses* 10.162–63]), "a note of appropriate foreboding about Adam is struck. Hyacinth, turned into the purple 'flower inscribed with woe' ('Lycidas,' 106) had been a favorite reference of this author." For the Ovidian basis of the depiction in general, see Richard J. Du Rocher, *Milton and Ovid* (Ithaca: Cornell University Press, 1985), 183–84.

18. A close study of the Pauline texts will reveal that these

strictures must be qualified considerably. I adopt the extreme view in order to drive home my point.

19. In this regard, see Timothy J. O'Keeffe's full and informative *Milton and the Pauline Tradition: A Study of Theme and Symbolism* (Lanham, Md.: University Press of America, 1982), *passim*.

20. References to Milton's prose by volume and page number in my text are to *The Complete Prose Works of John Milton*, 8 vols. in 10, gen. ed. Don M. Wolfe et al. (New Haven: Yale University Press, 1953-82), hereafter designated *YP*. Corresponding references to the original Latin (and on occasion to the English translations) are to *The Works of John Milton*, 18 vols. in 21, ed. Frank Allen Patterson et al. (New York: Columbia University Press, 1931–38), hereafter designated *CM*.

21. The most informative study of the whole concept of the *imago Dei* in Milton's thought is Anthony C. Yu, "Life in the Garden: Freedom and the Image of God in *Paradise Lost*," *Journal of Religion*, 60 (1980): 247–71.

22. "The Book of M: Milton's *Paradise Lost* as Revisionary Text," *Cithara: Essays in the Judaeo-Christian Tradition*, 31 (1991), 28–35. This study approaches Milton's appropriation of "help meet" from the perspective of *The Book of J*, translated by David Rosenberg and interpreted by Harold Bloom (New York: Grove Weidenfeld, 1990). For additional and superb commentary on the biblical text from a literary perspective, see Phyllis Trible, *God and the Rhetoric of Sexuality* (Philadelphia: Fortress Press, 1978), *passim*, and Carol Meyers, *Discovering Eve: Ancient Israelite Women in Context* (New York: Oxford University Press, 1988), *passim*. For enlightened and informative discussions of "help meet" in *Paradise Lost*, see, among other studies, McColley, *Milton's Eve*, esp. 43–48; F. Peczenik, "Fit Help: The Egalitarian Marriage in *Paradise Lost*," *Mosaic*, 17 (1984): 29–48; and Philip J. Gallagher, *Milton, the Bible, and Misogyny*, ed. Eugene R. Cunnar and Gail L. Mortimer (Columbia: University of Missouri Press, 1990), esp. 26–44. In his *One Flesh*, Turner elaborates the complex relationships between the divorce tracts and *Paradise Lost*.

23. In the text "meet for him" is bracketed as the phrase in question, but the full phrase "help meet for him" is involved. Elaborating upon the the phrase in *The Doctrine and Discipline of Divorce*, Milton views "help meet" as a condition in which the minds of man and woman "are fitly dispos'd, and enabl'd to maintain a cherfull conversation, to the solace and love of each other" (*YP* 2.328). Compare Milton's discussion of "help meet" in *Christian Doctrine* (I.x). This phrase implies that "goodwill, love, help, solace and fidelity are firm on both sides, which, as all admit, is the essential form of marriage [*si benevolentia, si*

amor, ausilium, solatium fides utrobique constet, quae, ut omnes fatentur, forma ipsa matrimonii est]" (*YP* 6.371; *CM* 15.156).

24. I refer here, of course, to the basic assumptions of Dennis H. Burden's book *The Logical Epic: A Study of the Argument of Paradise Lost* (London: Routgledge and Kegan Paul, 1967).

25. The idea is fundamental to the outlook of *Areopagitica*: "Where there is much desire to learn, there of necessity will be much arguing, much writing, many opinions; for opinion in good men is but knowledge in the making" (*YP* 2.554).

Notes to Chapter 7/Wittreich

1. This essay was completed with generous assistance from the PSC-CUNY Research Foundation. Its preliminary epigraphs derive from Shawcross's *Intentionality and the New Traditionalism: Some Liminal Means to Literary Revisionism* (University Park: Pennsylvania State University Press, 1991), 4, and from the concluding chapter of Morrison's *Playing in the Dark: Whiteness and the Literary Imagination* (Cambridge, Mass. and London: Harvard University Press, 1992), 66. As their respective subtitles imply, this essay is a companion piece to my own "'John, John, I Blush for Thee!': Mapping Gender Discourses in *Paradise Lost*," in *Out of Bounds: Male Writers and Gender(ed) Criticism*, eds. Laura Claridge and Elizabeth Langland (Amherst: University of Massachusetts Press, 1990), 22–54.

2. Newton quoting Thyer in *Paradise Lost*, 9th ed., ed. Thomas Newton (2 vols., London, 1790) 2:190; but see also *Paradise Regain'd ... To which is added Samson Agonistes and Poems upon Several Occasions*, new ed., ed. Thomas Newton (2 vols.; London 1785) 1:276–77. The Milton of Newton's edition is reinscribed in *The Poetical Works of John Milton*, ed. Henry John Todd, 7 vols. (London, 1801), see esp. 3:203; 4:437. Thyer and Newton, whose comments first appeared in the editions of 1749 and 1752 respectively, apparently have in mind Richard Bentley's annotation to *Paradise Lost*, 4.634 ["*Eve* with perfect *beauty* adorn'd"]. Says Bentley: "*Our Author, through his whole Poem, had certainly that in his View, to make the Female Sex favour it.* But here he seems to incline needlessly too much to *Eve's* outside, even with straining of his Verse. I would have it, to comprehend both her outward and inward Endowments, *To whom thus* Eve *with perfect* GIFTS *adorn'd*" (see *Milton's "Paradise Lost". A New Edition* [London, 1732], 129–30; my emphasis in the first sentence). On the leaf opposite the half-title page of the British Library copy of this edition, there is a note in Bentley's hand emending 8.221 in such a way as to render even more

emphatically the point that generic Man is "God's Image fair." The shelf mark for this copy is 11626.h.6.

3. Dunton, *The Challenge Sent by a Young Lady to Sir Thomas &c. Or, The Female War* (London, 1697), 233–34 (see also 210); and Hopkins, *Milton's* Paradise Lost *Imitated in Rhyme. In the Fourth Sixth and Ninth Books* (London, 1699), preface. Hopkins revises Milton's identification of *both* Adam and Eve with Samson (9.1059–066) so that Adam alone is identified with Samson, while Eve is now likened to Delilah (see 54).

4. Hayley, *A Philosophical, Historical, and Moral Essay on Old Maids*, 3 vols. (London, 1785) 2:10–11.

5. For elucidation, see the fine study by Keith W. F. Stavely, *Puritan Legacies:* Paradise Lost *and the New England Tradition, 1630–1690* (Ithaca and London: Cornell University Press, 1987), 57–58 and *passim*.

6. Jordan, *Renaissance Feminism: Literary Texts and Political Models* (Ithaca and London: Cornell University Press, 1990), 10.

7. See the brilliant exposition by Bal, *Lethal Love: Feminist Literary Readings of Biblical Love Stories* (Bloomington and Indianapolis: Indiana University Press, 1987), 104–30. Nyquist dismisses such a reading, along with that by Phyllis Trible, as "revisionary and profoundly ahistorical," although this is precisely the kind of reading one would expect from a poet, particularly an epic poet, whose obligation is to delineate the evolution of human consciousness; see Nyquist, "The Genesis of Gendered Subjectivity in the Divorce Tracts and in *Paradise Lost*," in *Remembering Milton*, ed. Mary Nyquist and Margaret W. Ferguson (New York and London: Methuen, 1987), 101.

8. See *Complete Prose Works of John Milton*, ed. Don M. Wolfe et al., 8 vols. (New Haven: Yale University Press, and London: Oxford University Press, 1953–83), 2:594, 588–92.

9. Cardinal Pierre de Berulle as quoted by Colleen McDannell and Bernhard Lang, *Heaven: A History* (New Haven and London: Yale University Press, 1988), 157. Walter Clyde Curry approaches such a perception in his chapter, "The Lordship of Milton's Sun," in *Milton's Ontology, Cosmogony and Physics* (Lexington: University of Kentucky Press, 1966), 143.

10. Morrison, *Playing in the Dark*, 43.

11. "Women in the Beehive: A Seminar with Jacques Derrida," in *Men in Feminism*, ed. Alice Jardine and Paul Smith (New York and London: Methuen, 1987), 203.

12. *Explanatory Notes and Remarks on Milton's* Paradise Lost (London, 1734), 376.

13. Corum, "In White Ink: *Paradise Lost* and Milton's Ideas of Women," in *Milton and the Idea of Woman*, ed. Julia M.

Walker (Urbana and Chicago: University of Illinois Press, 1988), 128. On Milton's narrative strategies, see also Catherine Belsey, *John Milton: Language, Gender, Power* (Oxford and New York: Basil Blackwell, 1988), 83–105, and especially the following pages in John Mulder's "'Ambiguous Words and Jealousies': A Secular Reading of *Paradise Lost*," *Milton Studies*, 13 (1979):163–76.

14. Rosen, *Hermeneutics as Politics* (New York and Oxford: Oxford University Press, 1987), 23, 24, 35.

15. See Margaret Patterson Hannay, "Lady Wroth: Mary Sidney," in *Women Writers of the Renaissance and Reformation*, ed. Katharina M. Wilson (Athens and London: University of Georgia Press, 1987), esp. 551–52. It is possible to see in this triad of figures (Copernicus, Galileo, Urania) what John Guillory sees in one of them, "a cryptic self-portrait," as well as a return of contemporary history; that is, a return of what is suppressed, or supposedly so, in the poem; see Guillory's *Poetic Authority: Spenser, Milton, and Literary History* (New York: Columbia University Press, 1983), 161.

16. Hume, *Annotations on Milton's* Paradise Lost (London, 1695), 231.

17. Richardson, *Explanatory Notes and Remarks*, 291, 293, 294, 327.

18. For a brilliant discussion of Galileo's presence in Milton's poem, see Judith Scherer Herz, "'For whom this glorious sight?': Dante, Milton, and the Galileo Question." Herz asks intriguingly: "Does the optic glass baffle or enable the poem's visionary enterprise?"—a question to which she eventually responds: "the answer must be that it enables it precisely because it baffles it" (149, 156). And for an equally revealing discussion of the same topic as it must have included a knowledge of Copernicus and Brahe, esp. the latter, see Donald Friedman, "Galileo and the Art of Seeing" (159–74), both essays in *Milton in Italy: Contexts, Images, Contradictions*, ed. Mario A. Di Cesare (Binghamton, N. Y.: Medieval and Renaissance Texts and Studies, 1991).

19. Ibid., 293. The best recent discussion of the cosmological debate in *Paradise Lost* is provided by Barbara K. Lewalski, "The Genres of *Paradise Lost*: Literary Genre as a Means of Accommodation," in *"Composite Orders": The Genres of Milton's Last Poems*, ed. Richard S. Ide and Joseph Wittreich (Pittsburgh: University of Pittsburgh Press, 1983), 75–103 (a special issue of *Milton Studies*, vol. 17). Lewalski does not interrelate the cosmological and creation narratives (as I have done), but she does elucidate the disposition of voices therein and the wily manner in which such disputes are resolved: "Galileo's dialogue has as interlocutors three friends . . . [meeting] . . . in a spirit of friendly inquiry. Salviati, who undertakes to 'act the part of Copernicus . . .

' . . . Simplicio . . . [who] grounds his arguments chiefly upon ancient authority and piety. Sangredo . . . an urbane, open-minded, intelligent layman who desires to be informed about the two systems so that he might decide rationally which to credit. Galileo's dialogue leaves no question whatsoever that Salviati's arguments carry the day: the inconclusiveness of the ending and Simplicio's final appeal to the unsearchable way of God . . . were a transparent, and in the event futile, attempt to satisfy the censors" (89). The cosmological and creation debates in *Paradise Lost* run parallel courses, although the Creation debate, in which the stakes are higher, introduces what, by Lewalski's account, is missing from the cosmological debate: "appeals to authority" and "to the need for higher illumination" (90). If the function of the latter is to establish appropriate terms and attitudes for cosmological inquiry, the function of the former is to array discrepant attitudes while advancing the terms by which one attitude may be approved over another.

20. Eagleton, *Criticism and Ideology: A Study in Marxist Literary Theory* (London: Verso, 1976), 127.

21. Richardson, *Explanatory Notes and Remarks*, 365. Zachary Pearce thinks otherwise: "No doubt he [Raphael] learned this story . . . from other Angels which were present" (see *A Review of the Text of Milton's* Paradise Lost [London, 1732], 237). Alongside 8.229, Bentley adds the question: "How then could he relate the Creation" (250 in the British Library copy of *Milton's* Paradise Lost cited in note 2 above).

22. Homans, *Bearing the Word: Language and Female Experience in Nineteenth-Century Women's Writing* (Chicago and London: University of Chicago Press, 1986), 160.

23. Philip J. Gallagher remarks upon Milton's "habitual tendency to prefer the protocols of chapter 1 [of Genesis]," though contrary to my own argument he also concludes that "Milton's unchanging mind" opts for reconciliation, not contradiction, as it seeks "always to accommodate the details of the received narrative to a pious interpretation"; see Gallagher, *Milton, the Bible, and Misogyny*, ed. Eugene R. Cunnar and Gail L. Mortimer (Columbia and London: University of Missouri Press, 1990), 2, 32, 133.

24. Bal, *Murder and Difference: Gender, Genre, and Scholarship on Sisera's Death*, tr. Matthew Gumpart (Bloomington and Indianapolis: Indiana University Press, 1988), 96.

25. Nyquist, "The Genesis of Gendered Subjectivity," in *Remembering Milton*, ed. Nyquist and Ferguson, 115, 116.

26. Newton, ed., *Paradise Lost* 2:53.

27. Nyquist, "The Genesis of Gendered Subjectivity," in *Remembering Milton*, ed. Nyquist and Ferguson, 117.

28. Jacob Boehme, *Mysterium Magnum. Or, An Exposition of the First Book of Moses called Genésis* (London, 1654), 80–81. This commentary was written in 1623.

29. McColley, "Beneficient Hierarchies: Reading Milton Greenly," in *Spokesperson Milton*, ed. Charles W. Durham and Kristin P. McColgan (Selinsgrove, Pa.: Susquehanna University Press, 1994), forthcoming.

30. One cannot ignore the problematical character of Raphael's words here, "worthy well / Thy cherishing, thy honouring, and thy love, / Not thy subjection" (8.568–70), nor the alternating currents of the speech as a whole. Raphael's words submit to contrary interpretations; and in a poem of vacillating perspectives, no single current in a speech, indeed no single speech in a poem, is definitive in its observations and conclusions. The first half of this speech is slippery in the extreme. Its last half, on the other hand, conspires with Adam's earlier valuations of Eve as if to remind us of what Lorenzo tells Misogenos: that woman's "iust fame / Merits an Angels Pen to register" (see *Swetnam the Woman-hater: The Controversy and the Play*, ed. Coryl Crandall [Lafayette, Ind.: Purdue University Studies, 1969], 3.2.57–58). Further, the last half of this speech dwells emphatically on the *shared* humanity of Adam and Eve.

31. Perkins, "The Gnostic Eve," in *Old Testament Women in Western Literature*, ed. Raymond-Jean Frontain and Jan Wojcik (Conway, Arkansas: UCA Press, 1991), 46.

32. See Sowernam, *Ester hath hang'd Haman*, in *The Woman's Sharp Revenge: Five Women's Pamphlets from the Renaissance*, ed. Simon Shepherd (London: Fourth Estate, 1985), 99.

33. The phrase is borrowed from Guillory's *Poetic Authority*, ix.

34. See Poole, *Annotations upon the Holy Bible* (2 vols.; London, 1683), esp. the annotation to Genesis 3.1 and, in that annotation, the reference to "A late ingenious and learned Writer," as well as the comment by John T. Shawcross, *Milton: A Bibliography for the Years 1624–1700* (Binghamton, N. Y.: Medieval and Renaissance Texts and Studies, 1984), 274.

35. "Harold Bloom," in *A Recent Imagining: Interviews*, ed. Robert Moynihan (Hamden, Conn.: Archon Books, 1986), 21.

36. See, e. g., Jane Lead, *A Fountain of Gardens Watered by the Rivers of Divine Pleasure* 3 vols. (London, 1696–1701), esp. the poem at the beginning of the first volume where Lead pleads with Milton to join his voice to hers in singing in the millennium (sig. [F4v]): "Now Mighty Bard . . . / Come thou and joyn / Thy loud Prophetick Voice with mine." Cf. Sir Allen Apsley, *Order and Disorder: Or, The World Made and Undone. Being Meditations Upon the Creation and the Fall; As it is recorded in the beginning of GENESIS* (London, 1679), preface and *passim*. Apsley's

poem is written as a fortification against "the pernicious and perplexed . . . inventions," especially of "inspired Poets and divine Philosophers" who, in their scriptural supplements, have "walk'd in the dim light of corrupted nature and defective Traditions," in the process "turning Scripture into a Romance" (see unpaginated Preface).

37. Kelly, *Women, History, and Theory* (1984; rpt. Chicago and London: University of Chicago Press, 1986), 75.

38. Kelly, *Women, History, and Theory*, xviii.

39. See the fine essay by John Rumrich, "Uninventing Milton," *Modern Philology*, 87 (1990): 249–65.

40. H. J. C. Grierson, *Cross Currents in English Literature of the XVIIth Century* (London: Chatto and Windus, 1929), 161. Here Milton figures prominently in a series of lectures on "The Evolution of Civilization" (see the title page).

41. Figes, *The Tree of Knowledge* (New York: Pantheon Books, 1990), 3, 116, 143. A tradition of Milton-bashing is already in place by the eighteenth century. Of that tradition, Figes's novel is a modern-day continuation. Her novel is also an interesting deviation from its apparent prototype; see Anne Manning, *The Maiden and Married Life of Mary Powell . . . And the Sequel Thereto Deborah's Diary* (1849–50, 1860; Reprint [with an Introduction by W. H. Hutton] London, 1898). Unlike Figes's book, this one makes clear, in the words of Hutton, that "the faults were not all on one side" (xxi) and, further, as proposed in *Deborah's Diary*, that men and women are *equally* able to stand and fall: "This is what Man has done, and Man may do,—and Woman too" (358).

42. Hurston, *Moses: Man of the Mountain* (1939; Reprint Urbana and Chicago: University of Illinois Press, 1984), 303.

43. Armstrong and Tennenhouse, *The Imaginary Puritan: Literature, Intellectual Labor, and the Origins of Personal Life* (Berkeley, Los Angeles, and Oxford: University of California Press, 1992), 47, 149. Better than any other of Milton's critics, Armstrong and Tennenhouse show that the disjunctions and contradictions in Milton's poetry, often said to mirror the divisions and discontinuities of Milton's mind, are instead revelations of the culture producing the poems, of a culture Milton's poetry would create anew.

Notes to Chapter 8/Fallon

1. Here and elsewhere, I quote Milton's poetry from Merritt Hughes's edition, *John Milton: Complete Poems and Major Prose* (New York: Macmillan, 1957).

2. A useful introduction to the appearances of Bellerophon in

classical literature and the appropriation of Bellerophon in the Renaissance can be found in Marianne Shapiro's "Perseus and Bellerophon in *Orlando Furioso,*" *Modern Philology* 81 (1983): 109–30.

3. Hesiod, *Theogony,* 319–25; Pindar, *Olympia* 13; Apollodorus, *Library* II.iii.1–2; Pausanias, *Description of Greece* II.iv.1.

4. *Concerning the Virtues of Women,* 9, *Plutarch's Morals,* trans. by several hands, ed. William W. Goodwin (London: Atheneum, 1870), 351.

5. *Odes* III.vii.15, in *The Third Book of Horace's Odes,* ed. Gordon Williams (Oxford: Clarendon, 1969): 68.

6. *The Odes of Pindar,* 2nd ed., trans. Richmond Lattimore (Chicago: University of Chicago Press, 1976), 153–54.

7. See, for example, the version familiar to Milton in Charles Estienne (Carolus Stephanus), *Dictionarum Historicum, Geographicum, Poeticum* (Paris, 1596; facsimile reprint, New York: Garland, 1976), 98ᵛ. For Milton's knowledge of this work, see DeWitt T. Starnes and Ernest William Talbert, *Classical Myth and Legend in Renaissance Dictionaries* (Chapel Hill: University of North Carolina Press, 1955), 226–27.

8. Shapiro, "Perseus and Bellerophon in *Orlando Furioso,*" 116–17.

9. *The Complete Prose Works of John Milton,* ed. Don M. Wolfe, et al., 8 vols. (New Haven: Yale University Press, 1953–82), 1:802. Further references to Milton's prose in English and in translation are taken from this edition.

10. Paul Fry has elucidated the tensions in this work, tensions epitomized in the paradoxical phrase "humble ode" and in that phrase's juxtaposition with the title of 'Hymn' inserted four lines later; the ode presupposes a single and assertive speaker, the hymn a choir of humble voices. See "Milton's Light-Harnessed Ode," in *The Poet's Calling in the English Ode* (New Haven: Yale University Press, 1980), 37–48.

11. Stanley Fish, "A Poem Finally Anonymous," in *Milton's Lycidas: The Tradition and the Poem,* rev. ed., ed. C. A. Patrides (Columbia: University of Missouri Press, 1983), 319–40.

12. Later in the same work, Milton suggests that the "pious and just honoring of ourselves" will "globe itself upward from the mixture of any ungenerous and unbeseeming motion or any soil wherewith it may peril to stain itself" (*CP* 1.841–42). Referring in the same passage to the "fire sent from heaven to be ever kept alive upon the altar of our hearts," Milton domesticates and generalizes the singular and anointing fire of Isaiah. In conversation years ago William Fuller pointed out to me the contrast between the globes and squares of angels in *Paradise Lost* and Satan's "Pyramid of fire" (2.1013).

13. At least by the time of writing the *Apology* shortly before his marriage, he had concluded that "mariage must not be call'd a defilement" (*CP* 1.893).

14. "'No meer amatorious novel'?" in David Loewenstein and James Turner, eds., *Politics, Poetics, and Hermeneutics in Milton's Prose* (Cambridge: Cambridge University Press, 1990), 85–101.

15. As part of a book in progress on Milton's self-representations, I will trace in detail the destabilizing of Milton's claims of prophetic vocation in the divorce tracts, examine the effect of this destabilizing on the language of the tracts, and plot the afterlife of this moment in Milton's subsequent writings.

16. Hughes, 696.

17. *Milton: Poet of Exile*, 2nd ed. (New Haven: Yale University Press, 1986), 97.

18. In what follows I will assume that the narrator, while a literary construct, speaks authentically for the author.

19. Christine Hogan pointed out to me the overtones of the Bellerophon myth in Milton's expansion of Matthew 4.5 and Luke 4.9 when he writes of Satan's flight with the Son to the pinnacle in *Paradise Regained*, "without wing / Of *Hippogrif*" (4.541–42).

20. Michael Lieb, *Milton and the Culture of Violence* (Ithaca: Cornell University Press, 1994), ch. 3, "The Dismemberment of Orpheus."

21. *Milton and Ovid* (Ithaca: Cornell University Press, 1985), 73.

22. Orpheus had foresworn the love of women after losing Eurydice for the second time. The Jonathan Richardsons, father and son, eighteenth century editors of *Paradise Lost*, stress Orpheus's chastity; their paratactic account suggests but does not confirm that chastity was the cause of his death: "Orpheus . . . lost his Beloved Wife *Eurydice* and was very Chaste, the *Ciconian* Women, mad Worshipers of *Bacchus*, tore him to pieces on the Mountain *Rhodope*" (*Explanatory Notes and Remarks on Milton's Paradise Lost* [London, 1734], 292).

23. *Metamorphoses*, Book 10; I owe this observation to John Rumrich.

24. Ernest Sirluck argued that, after a failure of chastity (which Sirluck reads as a breaking of a vow of celibacy), Milton adopts blindness as the "new symbol of poetic inspiration" ("Milton's Idle Right Hand," *Journal of English and Germanic Philology* 60 [1961]: 771). While suggesting that a vow of celibacy would be out of character for Milton, E. R. Gregory has recently added his voice to those who see blindness at the heart of the inspiration of the late poems (*Milton and the Muses* [Tuscaloosa: University of Alabama Press, 1989], 84–89). William Kerrigan has argued cogently that blindness is the punishment that precedes and

authorizes the transgression of writing the epic (*The Sacred Complex: On the Psychogenesis of Paradise Lost* [Cambridge: Harvard University Press, 1983], 190). My reading shares with Kerrigan's a reluctance to dismiss the relation of blindness and transgression.

25. *Intentionality and the New Traditionalism: Some Liminal Means to Literary Revisionism* (University Park: Pennsylvania State University Press, 1991), 4.

26. I have used Hughes's translation here (614). The Yale translation loses "rapt" for the less Miltonic "drive." The Latin appears in *The Works of John Milton*, ed. F. A. Patterson et al., 20 vols. (New York: Columbia University Press, 1931–40), 12:212.

27. "On Mr. Milton's Paradise Lost," ll. 7–8, in *The Poems and Letters of Andrew Marvell*, ed. H. M. Margoliouth, 2nd ed., 2 vols. (Oxford: Clarendon, 1952), 1:131–32.

28. In Kenneth Gross's "'Pardon Me, Mighty Poet': Versions of the Bard in Marvell's 'On Mr. Milton's Paradise Lost'" (*Milton Studies* 16 [1982] 77–96), there is a hint of the connection between Marvell's and Milton's fields. Gross writes that the next line, "Lest he perplext the things he would explain," "deploys the opposed words 'perplext' and 'explain' so that their etymological meanings ('tangle together' and 'smooth out') reinforce the figurative representation of thought and faith in terms of travel and topography, as in Milton's 'on th'*Aleian* Field I fall / *Erroneous* there to wander and forlorne'" (86; emphasis Gross').

29. On this strategy, see Gross's subtle analysis (87).

30. My terms are relative here; I do not question the manner in which form fits theme in Milton's poem, a fit in the case of prosody expressed in Milton's characterization of his avoidance of rhyme as a recovery of "ancient liberty" from "troublesom and modern bondage" in his note on the verse of *Paradise Lost*.

31. Reading for this essay was supported by a summer research grant from Notre Dame's Institute for Scholarship in the Liberal Arts. For advice and responses, I am indebted to Christine Hogan, John Rumrich, and Henry Weinfield.

Notes to Chapter 9/Rosenblatt

1. *John Milton: Complete Poems and Major Prose*, ed. Merritt Y. Hughes (New York: Odyssey, 1957), 424. All further references to *Paradise Lost* will be to this edition and will be included in parentheses in the text. Part of this essay appears in my book, *Torah and Law in "Paradise Lost,"* and I am grateful to Princeton University Press for permission to reprint it.

2. *Christian Doctrine,* in *Complete Prose Works of John Milton,*

gen. ed. Don M. Wolfe (New Haven: Yale University Press, 1953–1982), 6.384. This edition will be cited hereafter as *YP*.

3. On the Pauline theme of faith and law, see Alan F. Segal, *Paul the Convert: The Apostolate and Apostasy of Saul the Pharisee* (New Haven and London: Yale University Press, 1990), 181.

4. Gulielmus Bucanus, *Institutions of Christian Religion*, tr. Robert Hill (London: George Snowdon, 1606), 210–11.

5. *Christian Doctrine*, in *The Works of John Milton*, gen. ed. Frank Allen Patterson (New York: Columbia University Press, 1931–1938), 16.133. This edition, hereafter cited as *CM*, though stiffer in translation than *YP*, offers fuller scriptural quotation.

6. Tertullian, "An Answer to the Jews," in *The Writings of Quintus Sept. Flor. Tertullianus*, tr. S. Thelwall, *Ante-Nicene Christian Library* (Edinburgh: T. & T. Clark, 1870), 203–04.

7. Bucanus, *Institutions*, 191.

8. John Wollebius, *The Abridgment of Christian Divinity*, tr. Alexander Ross (1650; reprint London: John Saywell, 1656), 86.

9. Wollebius, 87.

10. Jeremy Cohen skillfully and patiently traces the proliferation of interpretations generated by this verse in *"Be Fertile and Increase, Fill the Earth and Master It": The Ancient and Medieval Career of a Biblical Text* (Ithaca, N.Y. and London: Cornell University Press, 1989).

11. Bucanus, *Institutions*, 194.

12. Bucanus, 193. See also James Ussher, *A Body of Divinity* (London, 1649), 145: *"But doth not God wrong to man, to require of him that he is not able to perform? No: for God made man so that he might have performed it: but he by his sin spoiled himself and his posterity of those good gifts."*

13. See Hans von Campenhausen, *The Formation of the Christian Bible*, tr. John Austin Baker (London: A. and C. Black, 1972), 46.

14. See *Milton: Poetical Works*, ed. Douglas Bush (London: Oxford University Press, 1966), 417n.

15. Bucanus, *Institutions*, 193.

16. John Marbeck, *A Booke of Notes and Common Places* (London, 1581), 615.

17. Peter Bulkeley, *The Gospel-Covenant* (London, 1615), Sig. 13ᵛ.

18. John Calvin, *Sermons upon . . . Deuteronomie*, tr. Arthur Golding (London: Henry Middleton, 1583), 946.

19. Frank Kermode, "Adam Unparadised," in his edition of *The Living Milton: Essays by Various Hands* (London: Routledge & Kegan Paul, 1960), 117–18. In this essential article, Kermode regards Adam, "[d]eprived of Original Justice," as "merely natural" (118).

20. David Pareus, *A Commentary Upon the Divine Revelation of the Apostle and Evangelist John*, tr. Elias Arnold (Amsterdam, 1644), 269. And see Martin Luther, *Lectures on Genesis 1–5*, in *Works*, ed. Jaroslav Pelikan (St. Louis: Concordia, 1958), 240, on the "despair and blasphemy" begotten by Adam's "transgression of the command. . . . Man cannot do otherwise when no hope of forgiveness and promise of grace is available."

21. John Milton, *Poems Reproduced in Facsimile from the Manuscript in Trinity College, Cambridge* (Menston: Scolar Press, 1972), 35, 40.

22. William Pemble, *Vindiciae Fidei* (Oxford, 1629), 2.

23. Bucanus, *Institutions*, 362.

24. This entire paragraph relies on E. P. Sanders's discussion of dualism in *Paul* (Oxford and New York: Oxford University Press, 1991), 93.

25. Philo Judaeus, *On Rewards and Punishments*, in *Philo*, tr. F. H. Colson and G. H. Whitaker, Loeb Classical Library (London: Heinemann; New York: Putnam's, 1929–1962), 8.395. Milton might well have known the 1561 Latin translation: "*quales ferútur epulae máctatis Thyestae filiis, redeuntibus calamitatú priscarum tempo ribus.*"

26. On thinness as the recognition of only a narrow range of historical experience, see Mary Douglas, *Natural Symbols* (Harmondsworth: Penguin, 1970), 40–41; cited by Gabriel Josipovici, *The Book of God: A Response to the Bible* (New Haven and London: Yale University Press, 1988), 270.

27. A. J. A. Waldock, Paradise Lost *and Its Critics* (Cambridge, England: Cambridge University Press, 1947), 82.

28. John Marbeck, *Notes and Common places*, 615, under the heading "How the lawe maketh us to hate God."

29. Compare Joseph Beaumont's *Psyche, or Love's Mystery* (London, 1648), 6.266, which explicitly excludes the Sinai of Hebrews from the voice in the garden:

> Had he in Thunder and in Lightning spake,
> And of fierce Veng'ance breath'd a flaming stream,
> Just had the Dialect been: But He did make
> A soft enquiry of the Fault, and seem
> To beg Confession, and to wait whil'st they
> Did with their Crime their Penitence display.

30. Herbert Marks demonstrates convincingly Paul's "drastic evacuation of the past into the present" in "Pauline Typology and Revisionary Criticism," *Journal of the American Academy of Religion* 52 (1984): 79.

31. "Bereshith," *Zohar* [thirteenth century] (Vilna, 1894), 1.57b.

Notes to Chapter 10/Lewalski

1. John Milton, *Complete Prose Works,* ed. Don M. Wolfe et al., 8 vols. (New Haven: Yale University Press, 1953–82), 2.362–63. Milton's prose is cited in text and notes from this edition (*YP*). Milton's poetry is cited from *Complete Poems and Major Prose,* ed. Merritt Y. Hughes (New York: Odyssey, 1957).

2. G. H. Turnbull, *Hartlib, Dury, and Comenius: Gleanings from Hartlib's Papers* (London: University Press of Liverpool, 1947). Charles Webster, ed., *Samuel Hartlib and the Advancement of Learning* (Cambridge: Cambridge University Press, 1970). This work reprints several tracts by Comenius, Hartlib, and Dury, with a very useful brief introduction, 11–41. Cf. Webster, The *Great Instauration: Science, Medicine, and Reform, 1626–1660* (London, 1970); and Michael Leslie's description of the ongoing retrival and publication of materials by and relating to Hartlib and his circle, "The Hartlib Papers Project: Text Retrival with Large Datasets," *Literary and Linguistic Computing,* 5: 58–69.

3. Turnbull identifies the first mention of Milton in Hartlib's papers, the *Ephemerides,* between April and September, 1643: "Mr Milton of Aldersgate Street has written many good books a great traveller and full of projects and inventions" (*Gleanings,* 40); an edition of Hartlib's "Ephemerides," ed. Michael Leslie et al., is in progress from the Hartlib Papers Project. In *Of Education* Milton himself refers to their "private friendship" (*YP* 2.363). For Comenius' visit see R. F. Young, *Comenius in England* (London: Oxford University Press, 1932). Cf. David Masson, *The Life of John Milton: Narrated in Connexion with the Political, Ecclesiastical, and Literary History of his Time,* 7 vols. (London, 1881–1894; reprint Gloucester, Mass.: Peter Smith, 1965), 3:232.

4. Ernest Sirluck, "Introduction" to *Of Education* (*YP* 2.184–16).

5. Turnbull, *Gleanings,* 39.

6. Turnbull, *Gleanings,* 40; Masson, 4:229.

7. Turnbull, *Gleanings,* 40.

8. The Letters are dated: Stockholm, 5 June 1652; The Hague, 14 April 1654; Amsterdam, 19 April 1654; Basle, 3 October 1654; Zurich, 18 November 1654; Zurich, 9 December 1654.

9. Turnbull, *Gleanings,* 41-44. The tract Milton attributed to More, *Regii Sanguinis clamor ad Coelum Adversus Parricidas Anglicanos* (The Hague, 1652) was written by an Englishman, Peter de Moulin.

10. John Dury (with Samuel Hartlib), *Considerations Tending to the Happy Accomplishment of Englands Reformation* (London, 1647; reprint in part in Webster, *Samuel Hartlib*), 123. For an

overview of educational practices in pre-Restoration England, see Foster Watson, T*he English Grammar Schools to 1660: Their Curriculum and Practice* (Cambridge: Cambridge University Press, 1908).

11. Jan Amos Comenius, *Janua linguarum reserata* (Leszno, 1631); *Porta linguarum trilinguis reserata* [Latin-English-French], ed. John Anchoran (London, 1631); *Janua linguarum reserata* [Latin-English], ed. Thomas Horne (London, 1636). Anchoran published the first English version; Horne's Latin-English edition was often reprinted.

12. Comenius, *Didactica Magna* (Amsterdam, 1657). It was summarized in Comenius's *Conatuum Comenianorum Praeludia* (Oxford, 1637), his *Pansophiae Prodromus* (Oxford, 1639), and his *A Reformation of Schools*, ed. and trans. Samuel Hartlib (London, 1642).

13. Comenius, *The Great Didactic*, ed. and trans. M. W. Keatinge (London, 1896), 221. My citations are to this edition.

14. Comenius, 410.

15. Comenius, 219–20.

16. Samuel Hartlib, *The Parliament's Reformation Or a Worke for the Presbyters, Elders, and Deacons, to Engage themselves, for the Education of all poore Children, and imployment of all sorts of poore* (London, 1646); Hartlib, *Londons Charitie stilling the Poore Orphans Cry* (London, 1649); *Londons Charitie Enlarged, stilling the Orphans Cry* (London, 1650).

17. E. G. Dury (with Samuel Hartlib), *Considerations . . . of Englands Reformation*, and *The Reformed School* (London, 1650); Dury, *Some Proposalls Towards the Advancement of Learning* ([London, 1653], reprint from MS in Webster, *Samuel Hartlib*), 179.

18. *The Reformed School*, 163–64. Cf. Dury and Hartlib, *Considerations*, 123, and Dury, *The Reformed Librarie Keeper. With a Supplement to the Reformed-School* (London, 1650). These texts were printed together as *The Reformed-School: and the Reformed Librarie-Keeper* (London, 1651).

19. *The Reformed School*, 57–61.

20. *The Reformed School*, 20.

21. Dury, *Reformed Librarie-Keeper*, 7.

22. For a sketch of Pansophia and the encyclopedia, see Comenius's *Conatuum Comenianorum praeludia, Pansophiae Prodromus*, and *A Reformation of Schooles*; his scheme for achieving unity of religious knowledge is outlined in Comenius, *Via Lucis* (Amsterdam, 1668), written and circulated in 1642. Cf. Turnbull, *Gleanings*, 367.

23. *Great Didactic*, 383–400; he recants this position formally in *A Reformation of Schools*, 32–33.

24. Samuel Hartlib, *A Description of the Famous Kingdome of Macaria* (London, 1641, reprint in Webster, *Samuel Hartlib*), 79–90.

25. Hartlib, *A Further Discoverie of the Office of Publick Address for Accommodations* (London, 1648); Dury and Hartlib, *Considerations*, 131–36.

26. *Reason of Church Government*, (*YP*, 2.854). For an overview of mid-seventeenth century education and the reformist efforts, see Richard L. Greaves, T*he Puritan Revolution and Educational Thought*, (New Brunswick: Rutgers University Press, 1969); Anthony Grafton and Lisa Jardine, *From Humanism to the Humanities: Education and the Liberal Arts in Fifteenth-and Sixteenth-Century Europe* (Cambridge, MA: Harvard University Press, 1986); and Charles G. Nauert, Jr., "Humanist Infiltration into the Academic World: Some Studies of Northern Universities," *Renaissance Quarterly* 43 (1990), 799–812. See also the Bibliography on Education in the Renaissance in Hauert's article, 818–19.

27. "Prolusion III," (*YP*, 1.241, 245); "Prolusion VII," (*YP*, 1.301); "Letter to Alexander Gill" (1628), (*YP*, 1.314).

28. Milton gave some account of his reading program in *Ad Patrem* and in *Apology against a Pamphlet*, (*YP*, 1.889–92). For notes on some of his reading, see his *Commonplace Book*, (*YP*, 1.362–508). For overviews, see Donald L. Clark, *John Milton at St. Paul's School* (New York: Columbia University Press, 1948); and J. Holly Hanford, "The Chronology of Milton's Private Studies," *PMLA* 36 (1921), reprinted in *John Milton Poet and Humanist* (Cleveland: Press of Western Reserve University, 1966), 75–125.

29. At St. Paul's School Milton used a revised edition of William Lily's *A Shorte Introduction of Grammar Generally to be used*. Bound with *Brevissima Institutio seu Ratio Grammatices cognoscendae ad omnium puerorum utilitatem praescripta* (London, 1574). The earliest edition of Lily, prepared for use at St. Paul's, was published in 1513; the revision of 1540 was mandated by royal authority as a required textbook and it remained so through several revisions during Milton's life and beyond (Clark, *Milton at St. Pauls*, 132–33). The comment "or any better" may suggest that Milton had already written or planned his own *Accidence Commenc't Grammar*, published in 1669.

30. For a more complete discussion of the educative discourses of Raphael and Michael and the genres they employ, see Barbara K. Lewalski, Paradise Lost *and the Rhetoric of Literary Forms* (Princeton: Princeton University Press, 1985), 25–54, 208–10.

31. See Milton, *De Doctrina Christiana* (*YP* 6.133–35). Also see Maurice Kelley, T*his Great Argument: A Study of Milton's*

De doctrina Christiana *as a gloss upon* Paradise Lost (Princeton: Princeton University Press, 1941); Kelley, "Milton's Arianism Again Considered." Harvard Theological Review 54 (1961), 195–205; and Lewalski, *Milton's Brief Epic: The Genre, Meaning and Art of* Paradise Regained (Providence: Brown University Press and London: Methuen, 1966), 133–63.

32. For a more complete discussion, see Lewalski, *Milton's Brief Epic*, 164–321.

33. See Irene Samuel, "Milton on Learning and Wisdom," *PMLA* 64 (1949), 708–23; and Lewalski, *Milton's Brief Epic*, 281–302.

Publications of John T. Shawcross on John Milton

"Milton's Fairfax Sonnet," *Notes & Queries*, n. s. 2 (1955): 195–96.

"*Epitaphium Damonis*: Lines 9–13 and the Date of Composition," *Modern Language Notes* 71 (1956): 322–24.

"Milton's Sonnet 23," *Notes & Queries*, n. s. 3 (1956): 202–04.

"Milton's Sonnet 19: Its Date of Authorship and Its Interpretation," *Notes & Queries*, n. s. 4 (1957): 442–46.

"Notes on Milton's Amanuenses," *Journal of English and Germanic Philology* 58 (1959): 29–38.

"The Date of Milton's 'Ad Patrem'," *Notes & Queries*, n. s. 6 (1959): 358–59.

"The Manuscript of 'Arcades'," *Notes & Queries*, n. s. 6 (1959): 360–64.

"Speculations on the Dating of the Trinity MS of Milton's Poems," *Modern Language Notes* 75 (1960): 11–17.

"Certain Relationships of the Manuscripts of *Comus*," *Papers of the Bibliographical Society of America* 54 (1960): 38–56.

"Anne Milton and the Milton Residences," with Rose Clavering, *Journal of English and Germanic Philology* 59 (1960): 680–90.

"The Manuscripts of *Comus*: An Addendum," *Papers of the Bibliographical Society of America* 54 (1960): 293–94.

"Two Milton Notes: 'Clio' and Sonnet 11," *Notes & Queries* n. s. 8 (1961): 178–80.

"Division of Labor in *Justa Edovardo King Naufrago*," *Library Chronicle* 27 (1961): 176–79.

"The Chronology of Milton's Major Poems," *PMLA* 76 (1961): 345–58.

Review-Article, Calvin Huckabay's *John Milton: A Bibliographical Supplement* in *Seventeenth-Century News* 19 (Autumn 1961): 29–34.

"Establishment of the Text of Milton's Poems Through a Study of *Lycidas*," *Papers of the Bibliographical Society of America* 56 (1962): 317–31.

"Milton's Decision to Become a Poet," *Modern Language Quarterly* 24 (1963): 21–30.

The Complete English Poetry of John Milton, editor. Garden City: Doubleday, Anchor Books, 1963; reprinted 1964, 1965, 1968; New York: New York University Press, 1963. Revised edition: *The Complete Poetry of John Milton*. Garden City: Doubleday, Anchor Books, 1971; reprinted 1978, 1982, 1987, 1991.

"One Aspect of Milton's Spelling: Idle Final 'E'," *PMLA* 78 (1963): 501–10.

"Of Chronology and the Dates of Milton's Translation from Horace and the *New Forcers of Conscience*," *Studies in English Literature* 3 (1963): 77–84.

"What We Can Learn From Milton's Spelling," *Huntington Library Quarterly* 26 (1963): 351–61.

"Henry Lawes's Settings of Songs from Milton's *Comus*," *Journal of Rutgers University Library* 28 (1964): 22–28.

"The Date of the Separate Edition of Milton's *Epitaphium Damonis*," *Studies in Bibliography* 18 (1965): 262–65.

"Milton's European Itinerary," with Rose Clavering, *Studies in English Literature* 5 (1965): 49–59.

"The Dating of Certain Prolusions, Letters, and Poems by Milton," *English Language Notes* 2 (1965): 350–55.

"Milton's *Nectar*: Symbol of Immortality," *English Miscellany* 16 (1965): 131–41.

"The Balanced Structure of *Paradise Lost*," *Studies in Philology* 62 (1965): 696–718.

"Milton's 'Tenure of Kings and Magistrates': Date of Composition, Editions, and Issues," *Papers of the Bibliographical Society of America* 60 (1966): 1–8.

"The Son in His Ascendance: A Reading of *Paradise Lost*," *Modern Language Quarterly* 27 (1966): 388–401.

"The Authorship of 'A Postscript'," *Notes & Queries* 13 (1966): 378–79.

Paradise Lost. Philadelphia: Educational Research Associates, 1966.

"A Metaphoric Approach to Reading Milton," *Ball State University Forum* 8 (1967) : 17–22.

"Milton's Italian Sonnets" An Interpretation," *University of Windsor Review* 3 (1967): 27–33.

"A Note on Milton's Hobson Poems," *Review of English Studies* 18 (1967): 433–37.

Review, C. A. Patrides's *Milton and the Christian Tradition* in *Renaissance Quarterly* 20 (1967): 515–17.

"The Metaphor of Inspiration," pp. 75–85, in *Th'Upright Heart and Pure*, ed. Amadeus Fiore. Pittsburgh: Duquesne University Press, 1967.

Language and Style in Milton. Co-editor with Ronald David Emma. New York: Frederick Ungar, 1967. Includes "Orthography and the Text of *Paradise Lost*," 120–53.

The Prose of John Milton, ed. J. Max Patrick. Garden City: Doubleday, Anchor Books, 1967. New York: New York University Press, 1968. London: University of London Press, 1968. Includes editions of *The Tenure of Kings and Magistrates*, 335–81, and "Selected Familiar Letters," with translations, 591–626.

"The Prosody of Milton's Fifth Ode of Horace," *Tennessee Studies in Literature* 13 (1968): 81–89.

"Some Literary Uses of Numerology," *Hartford Studies in Literature* 1 (1969): 25–31.

The Critical Temper, 1660–1800, editor. New York: Frederick Ungar, 1969. Updated, New York: Frederick Ungar, 1978. Updated, New York: Continuum Publishing Co., 1989.

"The Style and Genre of *Paradise Lost*," pp. 15–33, in *New Essays on* Paradise Lost, ed. Thomas Kranidas. Berkeley: University of California Press, 1969. Reprinted, 1971.

Milton: The Critical Heritage [1624–1731]. London: Routledge & Kegan Paul, 1970; New York: Barnes and Noble, 1970. *Milton: The Critical Heritage, 1732–1809* [Vol. II]. London: Routledge & Kegan Paul, 1972.

"Form and Content in Milton's Latin Elegies," *Huntington*

Library Quarterly 33 (1970): 331–50.

"*Paradise Lost* and the Theme of Exodus," *Milton Studies* 2 (1970): 3–26.

"An Early Echo of Milton's *Comus*," *Milton Quarterly* 4 (1970): 19–20.

Reviews of Scolar Press editions of "Lycidas" and of "The Trinity MS," *Seventeenth-Century News* 28 (1970): 61, 61–62.

"Irony as Tragic Effect: *Samson Agonistes* and the Tragedy of Hope," pp. 289–305, in *Calm of Mind*, ed. Joseph A. Wittreich. Cleveland: The Press of Case Western Reserve University, 1971.

Review, *Variorum Commentary of Milton's Poems*, Volume I, in *Seventeenth-Century News* 29 (1971): 1–4.

Addenda to Huckabay's Bibliography of Milton, 1929–1968, in *Milton Quarterly* 5 (1971): 64–65.

Review, Mindele Treip's *Milton's Punctuation* in *English Language Notes* 8 (1971): 326–31.

"The Simile of Satan as a Comet, *PL* II, 706–11," *Milton Quarterly* 6 (1972): 5.

"A Note on the Piedmont Massacre," *Milton Quarterly* 6 (1972): 36.

"Two Comments," *Milton Quarterly* 7 (1973): 97–98.

Achievements of the Left Hand: Essays on Milton's Prose, edited with Michael Lieb. Amherst: University of Massachusetts Press, 1974. Reprinted, 1976. Includes "The Higher Wisdom of *The Tenure of Kings and Magistrates*," 142–59, and "A Survey of Milton's Prose Works," 291–391.

"*Paradise Lost* and 'Novelistic' Technique," *The Journal of Narrative Technique* 5 (1975): 1–15.

"The First Illustrators for *Paradise Lost*," *Milton Quarterly* 9 (1975): 43–46.

"The Etymological Significance of Biblical Names in *Paradise Regain'd*," *Literary Onomastics Studies* 2 (1975): 34–57.

"Milton and Diodati: An Essay in Psychodynamic Meaning," pp. 127–63, in *Eyes Fast Fixt*, ed. Albert C. Labriola and Michael Lieb. *Milton Studies* 7 (1975).

"The Rhetor as Creator in *Paradise Lost*," *Milton Studies* 8 (1975): 209–19.

A Milton Encyclopedia, gen. ed. William B. Hunter. Vols. 1–9.

Lewisburg: Bucknell University Press and Associated Presses (London), 1979–81. Coeditor and contributor.

"A Note on 'Grogam: Light after Light,'" *Factotum* No. 4 (1978): 6.

"Stasis, and John Milton and the Myths of Time," *Cithara* 18 (1978): 3–17.

"The Hero of *Paradise Lost* One More Time," pp. 137–47, in *Milton and the Art of Sacred Song*, ed. J. Max Patrick and Roger H. Sundell. Madison: University of Wisconsin Press, 1979.

"The Bee-Simile Once More," *Milton Quarterly* 15 (1981): 44–47.

"Some Inferences about Literary History from the John Milton Collection in the Margaret I. King Library," *Kentucky Review* 2 (1981): 85–99.

"A Contemporary Letter Concerning Milton's State Papers," *Milton Quarterly* 15 (1981): 119–20.

With Mortal Voice: The Creation of Paradise Lost. Lexington: University Press of Kentucky, 1982.

"Pictorialism and the Poetry of John Milton," *University of Hartford Studies in Literature* 13 (1982): 143–64.

"*Paradise Lost*: 'Erased'," *Milton Quarterly* 16 (1982): 80–81.

Response to "Milton and Early America," pp. 85–90, in *Ringing the Bell Backward; The Proceedings of the First International Milton Symposium*, ed. Ronald G. Shafer. Indiana, PA: Indiana University of Pennsylvania Press, 1982.

"The Structure and Myth of *Paradise Regain'd*," pp. 1–14B, in *The Laurel Bough*, ed. G. Nageswara Rao (Dehli: Blackie and Son, 1982).

"Research and the State of Milton Studies," *Literary Research Newsletter* 7 (1982): 143–53.

"The Genres of *Paradise Regain'd* and *Samson Agonistes*: The Wisdom of Their Joint Publication," pp. 225–48, in *Composite Orders: The Genres of Milton's Last Poems*, ed. Richard S. Ide and Joseph A. Wittreich. *Milton Studies* 17 (1983).

"Influence for the Worse?: Hart Crane Rethinks Milton," *The Visionary Company* 1 and 2 (1983): 71–89.

Review, A. N. Wilson's *The Life of John Milton* in *Renaissance Quarterly* 37 (1984): 148–52.

Review, Volume 8 of *Complete Prose of John Milton* (Yale University Press) in *Milton Quarterly* 18 (1984): 27–32.

Milton: A Bibliography For the Years 1624–1700. Binghamton: Medieval and Renaissance Texts and Studies, 1984.

"Milton and Covenant: The Christian View of Old Testament Theology," pp. 160–91, in *Milton and Scriptural Tradition, The Bible into Poetry*, ed. James H. Sims and Leland Ryken (Columbia: University of Missouri Press, 1984).

"Early Milton Bibliography: Its Nature and Implications," *TEXT* 2 (1985): 173–80.

The Collection of the Works of John Milton and Miltoniana in the Margaret I. King Library, University of Kentucky. Occasional papers, No. 8. Lexington: University of Kentucky Library, 1985.

Milton's English Poetry, Being Entries from A Milton Encyclopedia, edited with William B. Hunter. Lewisburg: Bucknell University Press, 1986.

Foreword, pp. ix–xii, to Shahla Anand, *Magnificent Quest: Isa Charan Sada, Urdu Poet and Milton Scholar*. Dehli: I. S. P. C. K., 1986.

"The Poet in the Poem: John Milton's Presence in *Paradise Lost*," *The CEA Critic* 48/49 (Summer/Fall 1986): 32–55.

"Further Remarks on Milton's Influence: Shelley and Shaw," *Milton Quarterly* 20 (1986): 85–92.

Review-Article, Leo Miller's *John Milton & the Oldenburg Safeguard* (New York: Lowenthal, 1985), in *Milton Quarterly* 20 (1986): 106–10.

"A Note on Milton's Latin Translator, M. B.," *Milton Quarterly* 21 (1987): 65–66.

"A Note on T. P.'s Latin Translation of *Paradise Lost*," *Milton Quarterly* 21 (1987): 66–68.

Paradise Regain'd: "Worthy T'Have Not Remain'd So Long Unsung". Pittsburgh: Duquesne University Press, 1988.

" 'They that dwell under his shadow shall return': Joyce's *Chamber Music* and Milton," pp. 200–09, in *New Alliances in Joyce Studies: 'When it's Aped to Foul a Delfian'*, ed. Bonnie Kime Scott. Newark; University of Delaware Press, 1988.

"An Eighteenth-Century Epigram on Milton," *ANQ* 1.4 n.s. (1988): 130–32.

"Scholarly Editions: Composite Editorial Principles of Single Copy-Texts, Multiple Copy-Texts, Edited Copy-Texts," *TEXT* 4 (1988): 297–317.

"The Life of Milton," pp. 1–19, in *The Cambridge Companion to Milton*, ed. Dennis Danielson. Cambridge: Cambridge University Press, 1989.

"Some Aspects of John Milton's Eighteenth-Century Influence: Aesthetic Theory," *Studies on Voltaire and the Eighteenth Century* No. 264 (1989): 1061–63.

Edition of Harris F. Fletcher's *John Milton's Copy of Lycophron in the Library of the University of Illinois*. Binghamton: Medieval and Renaissance Texts and Studies, as *Milton Quarterly* 23 (December 1989).

Milton: A Bibliography For the Years 1624–1700: Addenda and Corrigenda. Binghamton: Medieval and Renaissance Texts and Studies, 1990.

"Contributions to a Milton Bibliography," *Kentucky Review* 10 (1990): 45–54.

"Milton and Blank Verse Precedents," *ANQ* 3 (1990): 160–63.

"Milton and Jung's Concepts of the Apocalyptic," *LIT Literature Interpretation Theory* 2 (1991): 275–87.

Review, Paul J. Klemp's *The Essential Milton: An Annotated Bibliography of Major Modern Studies* in *Analytical & Enumerative Bibliography* 3 (1989): 180–84.

John Milton and Influence: Presence in Literature, History, and Culture. Pittsburgh: Duquesne University Press, 1991.

Intentionality and the New Traditionalism: Some Liminal Means to Literary Revisionism. University Park: Pennsylvania State University Press, 1991. Chapter 11, pp. 141–56: "Milton's Shorter Poems."

Remarks on William B. Hunter's "The Provenance of the *Christian Doctrine*," *Studies in English Literature* 32 (1992): 155–62.

John Milton: The Self and the World. Lexington: University Press of Kentucky, 1993.

"Allegory, Typology, and Didacticism: *Paradise Lost* in the Eighteenth Century," pp. 41–74, in *Enlightening Allegory*, ed. Kevin I. Cope. New York: AMS Inc., 1993.

"The Political and Liturgical Subtext of Milton's 'On the Death of a Fair Infant Dying of a Cough,'" *ANQ* 7 (1994): 18–21.

"Milton and Epic Revisionism," pp. 186–207, in *Epic and Epoch: Essays on the Interpretation and History of the Genre*, ed. Steven M. Oberhelman, Van Kelly, and Richard J. Golsan. Lubbock: Texas Tech University Press, 1994.

FORTHCOMING

" 'Connivers and the Worst of Superstitions': Milton on Popery and Toleration" to be published in a Festschrift for J. Max Patrick in 1994.

"John Milton Spokesperson" to be published in *John Milton Spokesperson: Essays from the First Southeastern Conference on Milton* , ed. Kristin McColgan and Charles Durham. Selingsgrove, PA: Susquehanna University Press, 1993.

The Uncertain World of Samson Agonistes to be published in 1994.

About the Contributors

REGINA M. SCHWARTZ is associate professor of English and religious studies at Duke University. Her publications on theology, psychoanalysis and religious poetry include *Remembering and Repeating: On Milton's Theology and Poetics* (Cambridge: Cambridge University Press, 1988), which received the James Holly Hanford Award of the Milton Society for the most distinguished book on Milton in 1988; *The Book and the Text, The Bible and Literary Theory*, editor (Oxford: Basil Blackwell, 1990); *Desire in the Renaissance: Literature and Psychoanalysis*, coeditor (Princeton: Princeton University Press, 1994); and *The Postmodern Bible*, coeditor (New Haven: Yale University Press, forthcoming).

ANNABEL PATTERSON is currently Andrew W. Mellon Professor of the Humanities at Duke University, and will be moving to Yale University in 1994. Her most recent books are *Censorship and Interpretation* (Madison: University of Wisconsin Press, 1984); *Shakespeare and the Popular Voice* (Oxford: Basil Blackwell, 1989); *Fables of Power* (Durham: Duke University Press, 1991); and *Reading Between the Lines* (Madison: University of Wisconsin Press, 1993), the last (which features three essays on Milton) on the relations between literature, history, high culture, popular culture and academic mediations of these categories. Forthcoming is a revisionary account of "Holinshed's" *Chronicles*, a further extension of these interests into the territory of historiography, law and politics.

MARY ANN RADZINOWICZ is Jacob Gould Schurman Professor of English emeritus at Cornell University. Her publications include *Toward Samson Agonistes: The Growth of Milton's Mind* (Princeton: Princeton University Press, 1978) , which received the James Holly Hanford Award of the Milton Society for the most distinguished book on Milton in 1978; and *Milton's Epics and the Book of Psalms* (Princeton: Princeton University Press, 1989). She is currently working on a new book, *"Tendentious Purposes": Milton's Old Testament Reading*. She was made Honored Scholar of the Milton Society of America in 1987.

DIANE KELSEY MCCOLLEY is professor of English at Rutgers, the State University of New Jersey, Camden College of Arts and Sciences. She is the author of *Milton's Eve* (Urbana: University of Illinois Press, 1983) and *A Gust for Paradise: Milton's Eden and the Visual Arts* (Urbana: University of Illinois Press, 1993).

DIANA TREVIÑO BENET is Director of Great Books at the Gallatin Division of New York University. In addition to essays on Milton and other seventeenth century authors, she is the author of *Secretary of Praise: The Poetic Vocation of George Herbert* (Columbia: University of Missouri Press, 1984) and *Something to Love: The Novels of Barbara Pym* (Columbia: University of Missouri Press, 1986).

MICHAEL LIEB is professor of English and research professor of humanities at the University of Illinois at Chicago. His books on Milton include *Milton and the Culture of Violence* (Ithaca: Cornell University Press, 1994); *The Sinews of Ulysses: Form and Convention in Milton's Works* (Pittsburgh: Duquesne University Press, 1989); *Poetics of the Holy: A Reading of* Paradise Lost (Chapel Hill: University of North Carolina Press, 1981), which received the James Holly Hanford Award of the Milton Society of America for the most distinguished book on Milton in 1981; and *The Dialectics of Creation: Patterns of Birth and Regeneration in* Paradise Lost (Amherst: University of Massachusetts Press, 1970), as well as coedited collections of essays on Milton. In the area of Bible, he has published *The Visionary Mode: Biblical Prophecy, Hermeneutics, and Cultural Change* (Ithaca: Cornell University Press, 1991). Dr. Lieb was made Honored Scholar of the Milton Society of America in 1992.

JOSEPH WITTREICH is Executive Officer of The Ph.D. Program and Distinguished Professor of English at The Graduate School and University Center of The City University of New York. His recent books are *Interpreting* Samson Agonistes (Princeton: Princeton University Press, 1986) and *Feminist Milton* (Ithaca: Cornell University Press, 1987). Currently, he is at work on a study entitled *Wars of Truths: Milton and the New Criticisms.* He was the Honored Scholar of the Milton Society of America in 1993.

STEPHEN M. FALLON is associate professor of liberal studies and English at the University of Notre Dame. He has published articles on Milton and the Renaissance in *English Literary Renaissance,* the *Journal of the History of Ideas, PMLA* and in multicontributor volumes. His *Milton among the Philosophers: Poetry and Materialism in Seventeenth-Century England* (Ithaca: Cornell University Press, 1991) received the James Holly Hanford Award of the Milton Society of America for the most distinguished book on Milton in 1991.

JASON P. ROSENBLATT, professor of English at Georgetown University, has published two dozen essays on Milton and the seventeenth century. He is coeditor of *"Not in Heaven": Coherence and Complexity in Biblical Narrative* (Bloomington: Indiana University Press, 1991) and author of *Torah and Law in* Paradise Lost (Princeton: Princeton University Press, 1994).

BARBARA K. LEWALSKI is William R. Kenan Professor of English Literature and of History and Literature at Harvard University. Her publications include: *Writing Women in Jacobean England* (Cambridge: Harvard University Press, 1993); *Paradise Lost and the Rhetoric of Literary Forms* (Princeton: Princeton University Press, 1985), which received the James Holly Hanford Award of the Milton Society of America for the most distinguished book on Milton in 1985; *Protestant Poetics and the Seventeenth-Century Religious Lyric* (Princeton: Princeton University Press, 1979), winner of the James Russell Lowell Prize of the MLA in 1979; *Donne's Anniversaries and the Poetry of Praise: The Creation of a Symbolic Mode* (Princeton: Princeton University Press, 1973); and *Milton's Brief Epic: The Genre, Meaning, and Art of Paradise Regained* (Providence: Brown University Press, 1966). She was the Honored Scholar of the Milton Society of America in 1977.

For his technological assistance with this project, the editors are grateful to J. Peter Benet.

Index

Abbey, Edward, 80
Abdiel, 99–100, 111
Abigail, 57
Abraham, 82
Achievements of the Left Hand, xx
Achish, King, 58
Adam, 19, 46, 85, 87, 104, 134, 137–50, 152–55, 216–17: Eve's identification with, 20; hypnosis and, 14–15; identification of, 18; identity of, 6, 8; law soliloquy of, 180–201; as Man, xvi–xvii, 114–32, 140–41, 151; and monarchy, 89; musical aspects of, 72; postlapsarian soliloquy of, xviii; Raphael to, 79; repentance of, 11, 12; snake and, 4–5; submission to God, 17; transference, 15
Addison, Joseph, 75
Ahab, 103
Ahimelech, 56–57
Alchemist, 7–8
Aleian Field, 161–63, 173
Alexander, 27–28, 218
Alienation, 93–97
Allusion, xv, xvii–xviii, 45–66, 173–75: forced, 45–66; scriptual, 46
Amalec beasts, 58
Amalekites, 57, 58–60
Anteia, 162, 164
Anti-Cavalierisme, 49
Aonian Mount, 169
Apology for Smectymnuus, An, 166
Appolodorus, 163, 164
Areopagitica, 39, 44, 211–13
Arion, 87
Aristarchus, 145
Aristotle, 208, 212
Arminius, 17–18, 20–21
Armstrong, Nancy, 160

Athena, 163
Athenian Walls, 28
Athens, 39–40, 218
Augustine, 87
Autobiography, 26, 31–36
Ayres and Dialogues, 30

Bacchae, 174
Bacchus, 173–74
Bacon, Sir Francis, 39, 40, 204–05, 209
Bathsheba, 64
Beelzebub, 93–95, 98, 104–09, 173
Belial, 3–4, 13, 99, 104, 107–08
Bellerophon, xvii–xviii, 161–79
Benet, Diana Treviño, xvi
Bentley, Richard, 75
Blake, William, 91, 176
Blindness, 34, 35, 162, 170
Blith, Walter, 87
Bloom, Harold, 157
Borsch-Jacobsen, Mikkel, 13
Boyle, Robert, 203
Brahe, Tycho, 145–46
Browne, Sir Thomas, 63, 87–88
Bucanus, Gulielmus, 181, 187–88, 191
Buckingham, Duke, 39, 59
Bulkeley, Peter, 191–92
Bush, Douglas, 28
Butler, Jane, 39
Byrd, William, 77

Calvin, John, 192, 200
Cambridge manuscript, 27, 28, 30–31
Carson, Rachel, 80
Cavendish, Margaret, 89
Caxton, 87
Chaeronea, 37, 38–39, 40
Charles I, 37–61 *passim*, 112
Charles II, 112

269

Chastity, 167–68, 171
Cheke, Sir John, 29, 30
Chimaera, 161, 163
Christ-like, 2–3
Christian Doctrine, xiv, 56, 57
Chronology, 26–27, 31
Cicero, 164, 210
Circe, 89
Clarendon, 39
Colossians, 124, 125
Comenius, J. A., 203–17 passim
Committee for the Propagation of the Gospel, 31
Commons Act, 209
Commonwealth sonnets, 30–31
Complete Poetry of John Milton, The, xx
Comus, 166
Considerations Touching the Likeliest Means to Remove Hirelings out of the Church, 213, 215, 218
Context, xii, xiii
Copernicus, 142, 145–46, 149, 216
Copia, 67–69
Corinthians, 124, 197
Corum, Richard, 143
Cowley, Abraham, xv, 45–49, 53–56, 62, 65, 89
Creation, 88
Cromwell, Oliver, 31, 45, 47, 53, 212–13
Culpepper, Sir Cheney, 203–04
Cursor Mundi, 88
Cyriack, 35

Dalila, 134
Danielson, Dennis, 11
Dante, 166
Darwin, Charles, 80
D'Avenant, Sir William, 89
David, xv, 45–66, 218
Davideis, 49, 53
Death, portrait of, xvii
de Bruyn, Nicholaes, 85–86
De Doctrina Christiana, 125–26, 147–48, 155–56, 180–85, 190, 193
Defenses, 204
Defensio Secunda, 204, 212
Demosthenes, 40, 210
Derridean temporality, 35
Deuteronomy, 196
Devil in his Dumps, The, 98, 102

de Vos, Maerten, 85–86
D'Ewes, Sir Symonds, 39
Dialogue of the Two World Systems, 216
Dictionary of National Biography, The, 39–40, 42
Didactica Magna, 205
Dionysius, 174
Discourse, gender, 133–60
Dissembly, 4–5, 10, 20
Doctrine and Discipline of Divorce, 33, 44, 167–69
Doeg, 56–57
Downame, John, 78
Du Bartas, Sylvester, 84–85, 87, 88
Dunbar, William, 31, 142
Dunton, John, 134
DuRocher, Richard, 173
Dury, John, 203–17 passim

Eagleton, Terry, 148
Ecolographic, 68
Education, 202–19
Educational theories, xviii–xix
Edward VI, 29, 39
Eikon Basilike, 49, 57, 58
Eikonoklastes, 49, 57, 58
Eiseley, Loren, 80
Electra, 28
Elegy 5, 32
Eleven Years' Tyranny, 37
Elijah, 165, 218
Emathian Conqueror, 27
Emmanuel, as name of the Son, 77
Entzminger, Robert L., 78
Ephesians, 124, 125
Epic narrator, 19–20
Epistle of Barnabas, 186
Euripedes, 157, 174
Eve, 85, 87, 104, 137, 140–43, 150, 152–56, 159–60, 189, 195, 216–17: hypnotic trance of, 13–14, 15; identification of, 6–9, 18; identification with Satan by, 20; musical aspects of, 72; Raphael to, 79; repentance of, 11; suicide suggestion of, 197; temptation of, 4–5; as Woman, xvi–xvii, 6, 8–9, 89, 114–32, 134
Ezekiel, 169

Fairfax, Lord General, 31
Fallon, Robert, 103

Fallon, Stephen M., xvii–xviii
Fanatics (political group), 98
Felman, Shoshana, 18, 21
Felton, Nicholas, 165
Feminine Monarchie, 152
Feminist Milton, 116
Figes, Eve, 159
Finch, Sir John, 37
First Defence of the English People, The, 49, 59, 60
Fish, Stanley, 165
Flannagan, Roy, 104
Florentine Camarata, 72
Foucault, Michel, 17
Fowler, Alistair, 75
Free will, 9–11
Freud, Sigmund, 11–13, 15–16, 63: Dora case, 16

Gabriel, 77
Galatians, 181, 189
Galileo, 144, 216
Gardiner, Bishop, 29
Gauden, John, 49, 58
Gender contradictions, xvii, 133–60
Genesis, 80–88 *passim*, 125–51 *passim*, 186, 197
Georgicon, 88
Georgics, 84
God's image, 127–31
Goldberg, Jonathan, 33–34, 35
Goliath, 63
Goodwin, John, 49
Grace, 11, 17
Grand Encyclopedia, 207
Greene, Thomas, 70

Haak, Theodore, 203–04
Hagar, 189–90
Hall, John, 203–04
Hall, Joseph, 166
Hartlib, Samuel, xix, 202–19
Hartlib Circle, 202–19
Hayley, William, 135
Hell, 91–113
Hell's Council, xvi, 92–97
Hesiod, 163
Historicity poetics, 36–44
History of Britain, The, 134, 204, 212
History of Muscovia, 204
Hobbes, Thomas, xv, 45–55, 62, 65

Hobson, Captain John, 42, 43
Homans, Margaret, 149
Homer, 162–63, 164, 216
Honigmann, E. A. J., 27, 28, 34, 41, 43
Hopkins, John, 134
Hubner, Joachim, 203
Hughes, Merritt, 169
Hume, Patrick, 145
Hunter, William, 33
Hurston, Zora Neale, 160
Hurt of Sedicion, The, 29–30
Hutton, Katharine, 30
Hypnosis, 12–13

Icarus, 162, 171
Identification: definition of, 3; dissembling and, 1–9; reading and, 18–21
Identity, 3, 10
Iliad, 162
Imitatio Christi, 2–3, 16
Imitation, definition of, 3
In obtium praesulis Eliensis," 165
Intention, limits of, 161–79
Intentionality, xi, xii–xiii
Intentionality and the New Traditionalism, xviii, 61–62, 122
Interpretation, xii, 9–18
Iobates of Lycia, 162–63, 164
Isaac, 189
Isaiah, 166
Ishmael, 189
Isocrates, 39, 40
Italian sonnets, 31–32, 33–34

James Holly Hanford award, xxi
James I, 38, 39, 42
Janua linguarum reserata, 203, 205–09
Jehovah, 76–77
Jeremiah, 66
Jerome, 187
Jerusalem, 189
Jesus, 51, 77–78, 142, 186, 199, 217–18
Job, 79, 82, 85, 88
John Milton: The Self and the World, xx
John Milton and Influence: Presence in Literature, History and Culture, xx
Jonathan, 56
Jordan, Constance, 136
Joshua, 54

Kant, Immanuel, 195
Kelly, Joan, 157
Kerrigan, William, 116
Kett, Robert, 29–30
King's Bench, 39

Lacan, Jacques, 16–17
Langbaine, Gerard, 30
Language: ontologically anchored,
    5–6; untrustworthiness of, 5
Latin Schools, 205–06
Lawes, Henry, 30, 82
Leach, Edmund, 64
Leonard, John, 75, 76
Leviathan, 49, 53, 65, 84, 85
Leviticus, 182–83
Lewalski, Barbara K., xviii–xix, 75
Lex, Rex, 49
Ley, James, 37, 39–40, 42
Ley, Lady Margaret, 36–37, 41–44
Lieb, Michael, xvi–xvii, 76–78, 172
Limina, xi–xii, xv–xvi, 62, 117, 123
Literature, xii, 22–26, 69, 117
Loyola, Ignatius, 102
Lucifer, 92, 98, 99, 101–02
Lucretius, 80, 210
Luke, 188
Lycia, 162
Lycidas, 31, 87, 165

Macaria, 207
McColley, Diane, xv–xvi, 154
Machiavelli, 99
Maeonides, 170
Mammon, 93, 97, 104, 107–08
Manichees, 87
Marbeck, John, 191
Marcion dualism, 196
Marriage, 167–68
Martz, Louis, 44, 170
Marvell, Andrew, 177–79
Mary, 77
Mask at Ludlow, 82
Mater Christi, 78
Matthew, 164
Mechanical Schools, 206, 211, 214
Metamorphoseon, 88
Micaiah, 103
Michael, Archangel, 134, 187
Military training, 210–11
Milton, Deborah, 159

Milton, Katherine Woodcock, 36
Milton, Mary Powell, 33, 36, 42, 43,
    167
Milton Society of America, xx, xxi
Milton Variorum, 28, 29, 30, 40–41
*Milton: A Bibliography For the Years
    1624–1700*, xx–xxi
*Milton: A Bibliography For the Years
    1624–1700: Addenda and
    Corrigenda*, xxi
*Milton: The Critical Heritage, 1624–
    1731*, xxi
*Milton: The Critical Heritage, 1732–
    1809*, xxi
Misogyny, 135, 136, 157, 159–60
Moab, 55–56
Modern Language Association, xxi
Moloch, 93, 96, 97, 104, 107
Monteverdi, 72
Moralia, 163
More, Alexander, 204
Morrison, Toni, 133, 142
*Mortal Voice: The Creation of Paradise
    Lost*, xx
Mosaic law, xviii, 181–201
Moses, 50, 62, 76–77, 160, 194, 218
Mount Gilboa, 57
Mount Zion, 199
Muir, John, 80
Muse's Method, The, 114
Musical Milton, 73–78

Nabal, 57
Nardo, Anna, 22–24, 25–26, 30
"Nativity Ode," 165, 166
New Criticism, 22–26
New Testament, xviii, 181, 198–99, 200
Newton, Sir Isaac, 145
Newton, Thomas, 134, 152
Nicene Creed, 6, 72
Nimrod, 99, 217
Nisroch, 101
Nob, 56
Noble Schools, 206–07, 209

Occasionality, 26–31
Oedipus, 63
Of Education, xiv, xviii–xix, 202–03,
    209, 214–15
Of Reformation, 166
Old Testament, 200, 218

Olympus, 163, 164, 171
"O Nightingale," 32
Onomastic music, 69–78
Ontology, 5–6
Orphean Lyre, 170
Orpheus, 161–62, 173–74
Other, 3, 15–16
Ovid, 174
Ovide moralisé, 164
Oxford Companion to Classical Literature, 40, 42

Paideia, 202, 216–19
Pansophia, 207, 211
Paradise Lost, xiii: 74–79, 84–88, 215: Adam's law soliloquy in, 180–201; allusive phrase, 62; Bellephoron in, 169–79; contradictions in, 135–36; copia, 68–69; David in, 46; gender discourse in, 133–60; liminality of, xv–xix, perfect man and woman in, 114–32; psychoanalysis of, 1–21; Satan in, 91–113; transference in, xiv
Paradise Regained, xix, 71, 144, 215–19: David in, 46–47; "Sion's songs," 68
Paradise Regain'd: "Worthy T'Have Not Remain'd So Long Unsung, xx
Pareus, David, 193
Parker, William Riley, 34, 43
Patterson, Annabel, xiv–xv, 167
Paul, St., 124–31, 137, 180–201
Pausanias, 163
Pecheux, M. Christopher, 103–04
Pegasus, 163, 171
Pell, John, 203
Pentheus, 174
Perkins, Pheme, 155
Petrarch, 166
Petty, William, 203
Phaedrus, 175
Phaeton, 162, 171
Philip of Macedon, 38–39, 40–41
Philippians, 200
Philippus, 40
Philistines, 48–50, 57, 60
Phillips, Edward, 42–43
Philo, 196
Pindar, 163
Pindarus, 28
Plato, 175, 210, 212, 218
Plutarch, 59, 163, 210

Pluto, 98–99
Poems of Mr. John Milton, 36, 44
Poetics, 22–26: of historicity, 36–44; of sequentiality, xiv–xv
Politics, fallen and unfallen, 97–101
Poole, Matthew, 156
Pordage, Samuel, 88
Poseidon, 163
Prelude, 20
Presbyter, Sir John, 102
Pretext, xii–xiii
Pro Se Defensio, 35
Proetus of Argos, 162
Psalms, 79, 82, 85, 88
Psychoanalysis, 13
Ptolemy, 142, 146, 153, 216
Pythagoras, 145

Radzinowicz, Mary Ann, xv, 24–25, 35, 78, 104
Raphael, 69, 7–8, 69, 75–90, 134, 143–54 passim, 181, 189, 195, 216
Readie and Easie Way to Establish a Free Commonwealth, The, 97–98, 214–15
Reason of Church Government, The, 34, 164–66, 168, 211, 215
Recollection, 12–13
Reformed Librarie Keeper, 207, 214
Reformed School, The, 210
Regii Sanguinis Clamor ad Coelum, 49, 60, 204
Revelation, 169
Richardson, Jonathan, 143, 145, 148
Romans, 198
Rosen, Stanley, 144
Rosenblatt, Jason P., xviii
Rump Parliament, 98, 213
Rutherford, Samuel, 49

St. James Palace, 207
St. John's College, 29
St. Paul's School, 208
Salmasius, 49, 59, 60–61, 66, 204
Samson, 46
Samson Agonistes, xx, 62–63, 134
Samuel, xv, 45–66
Samuel, Irene, 91–92
Sanders, E. P., 196
Sandler, John, 203
Sandys, George, 82
Sarah, 189–90

Satan, 173, 192, 198: on Adam and Eve, 117–21; in Council, 101–13; Eve's identification with, 20; Fall of, 11–12; false identity of, 4; as hypnotist, 13–14; identification of, 18; and learning for power, 218; in *Paradise Lost*, 91–113; portrait of, xvi
Saul, 48, 49, 50–60
Saumaise, Claude, 49, 59–61, 66
Schwartz, Regina, xiv, 12, 63–64
Second Defense, 34, 35, 170
Self, 3: defining of, 15–16
Sexuality, 114–32
Shawcross, John T., xi–xiii, xviii, 61–62, 91, 116, 122, 123, 133, 175–76: authorial intent, 19; on textual experience, 1; works of, xix–xxi, 257–64
Sidney, Sir Philip, 90
Sin, xvii, 173
Sinai, 189–90, 193, 198
Sirluck, Ernest, 203
Solomon, 64
Sonnet, xiv–xv, 24–26
Sonnet 1, 31–32
Sonnet 7, 31–32
Sonnet 8, 29
Sonnet 10, 36–44
Sonnet 12, 38
Sonnet 13, 30
Sonnet 14, 30
Sonnet 15, 30–31
Sonnet 16, 30–31
Sowerman, Esther, 156
Stein, Arnold, 103
Stile concertante, 73
Stile concertato, 73
Studies in Hysteria, 12–13
Summers, Joseph H., 114–15
Swetnam, Joseph, 157

Taverner, John, 78
Te Deum Laudamus, 69–78
Tennenhouse, Leonard, 160
Tenure of Kings and Magistrates, The, 49, 60
Tertullian, 183
Tetrachordon, 28–29, 127, 130, 141, 182–83
Thomason, George, 30

Thomason, Catharine, 30
Thomason Tracts, 30
Thracian Bard, 173
Thresholds, xi–xii
Thyer, Dr. Robert, 134
Timothy epistle, 124
Toad, 14–15
Topsell, Edward, 87
Torah, xviii, 181–201
Towneley, *Creation*, 88
Traherne, Thomas, 89
Transference, xiv, 11–19
Transubstantiation, 6–8
Trinity Manuscript, 46, 56
Trotter, David, 53
True Subject to the Rebell, The, 30
Turnbull, G. H., 203
Tusculan Disputations, 164

Universal College, 207
Universities, 205–08
Urania, 145, 162, 171
Uriel, 4, 141, 143, 145
Ussher, James, 166

"Vacation Exercise," 165
Vernacular Schools, 205–06, 214
Virgil, 84, 88, 216
Vulgar Schools, 206, 211

Waldock, A. J. A., 198
Webber, Joan, 22–23, 25
Webster, Charles, 203
Weston, Sir Richard, 39
Whitelocke, Sir James, 40
Wilding, Michael, 104
Witch of Endor, 51, 57
Wittreich, Joseph, xvii, 116, 118
Wollebius, John, 184
Woodhouse, A. S. P., 28
Wordsworth, William, 19–20
Worsley, Benjamin, 203
Wroth, Lady Mary, 145

Xanthian plain, 163, 164
Xenophon, 210

Yahweh, 57, 59, 138–39

Ziklag, 58, 61
Zipporah, 160
Zohar, 200